# RADIO'S BEAUTIFUL DAY

Eye Witness Account of the First Half Century of Broadcasting in America Based on the Everett Mitchell Experience

## By Richard Crabb

"It's a beautiful day in Chicago, it's a great day to be alive and I hope it is even more beautiful wherever you are..." — Mitchell

*Its a beautiful day*
*Everett Mitchell*

*Richard Crabb*

Everett Mitchell, radio and television star, looks back on his twenty-fifth anniversary in radio (November 3, 1948).

# Radio's Beautiful Day

*Dedicated to Clara and Peter*

*If any little word of mine
   can set a heart to singing*

*If any little word of mine
   can set a bell to ringing*

*God let me say that word*

*And set their heart to singing...*

> *—Chapter 19
> Radio's Beautiful Day*

# Radio's Beautiful Day

*\*\*\**

## Everett Mitchell's Memoirs
## Of The First Fifty Years
## Of Broadcasting In America

By Richard Crabb
With Special Assistance From Jean Moore

**Great People Of DuPage Book Two**

Limited Edition Commissioned by the
DuPage Heritage Gallery
Box 77, Wheaton, Illinois 60189

Published in the United States by
Crossroads Communications
P.O. Box 7, Carpentersville, Illinois 60110

Library of Congress Catalog Card No. 82-073438

Credits:
Cover design and art: Judy L. Karpus
Photographs:
  Frontispiece: National Broadcasting Company
  Radio's Beautiful Day pg. 198: *Life Magazine*
  1982 Parade Grand Marshall: *Wheaton Daily Journal*
All other photographs from the private collection of Everett Mitchell
Editing: Joan B. Crabb
Manuscript Preparation: Marlene Bennett
Historical Research: Jean Layman and Reference Staff at Wheaton
Public Library
  Several experts from across the nation in the fields of writing,
broadcasting and agriculture.

# Table Of Contents

# Preface
# A Few Words to the
# Reader at the Beginning

There are compelling reasons to record the highlights of Everett Mitchell's broadcasting career. He is perhaps the last living person who had a decision-making role in radio's formative period and who can provide an eyewitness account of the beginning.

Because Mitchell and radio were "born" and grew up together, *Radio's Beautiful Day* documents the important steps that led to today's broadcasting. The Italian inventor, Guglielmo Marconi, for example, was granted his first patent for his wireless telegraph in 1897, just eight months before Everett Mitchell was born. Scheduled daily radio broadcasting began in the United States at 6 p.m. on November 2, 1920. This was radio's coming of age date. Mitchell was 21 the year before. Chicago had its first radio station in 1922. Mitchell did his first broadcast in 1923, launching a pace-setting career that lasted until the mid-1960s.

The book also gives close attention to Mitchell's childhood and youth. In many ways, his early experiences were a preparation for his career in radio. His early years are also dramatic proof that the historic American breakthrough in living comforts has occurred within the lifetime of one man still living.

Everett Mitchell actually had two careers. The first and lesser known achievement came in the Great Station Era before network broadcasting existed. During this period, in the 1920s, he conceived and presented a long list of "firsts" in Chicago radio, some of them firsts in the nation as well. In Chicago, Mitchell, as a radio station manager, was the first to establish definite daily broadcasting periods for the entire week to come, requiring the first advance hour-by-hour program scheduling. He posted the schedules in the studio and on request sent them to Chicago newspaper radio editors.

Mitchell did Chicago's first "pickup" of a radio program outside the studio and beyond the reach of phone lines. He wrote and presented Chicago's first radio commercial, and in what was a first for Chicago and the nation, he created a daily (including Saturday) children's participation educational program that in its first six months enrolled 32,000 youngsters in twenty states.

In his "second" career with the first radio network in the United States, Mitchell served as moderator of the *National Farm and Home Hour* with such distinction that he became internationally recognized as the Voice of American Agriculture—an honor accorded to no one else. It was during his network career, in the depths of the Great Depression, that Mitchell, in defiance of network rules, introduced his Beautiful Day philosophy. The uplifting salutation made him one of the best known radio personalities in the United States and around the world.

As an aid to easier reading, *Radio's Beautiful Day* is divided into six parts. Because of the extreme diversity of periods covered from the 1890s to the 1960s, there is at the beginning of each of the six parts a short introduction. This permits placing before the reader introductory information focused specifically on the immediate chapters that follow.

A documentary of this nature can only come to be as a result of a major team effort involving a considerable number of persons.

Appreciation must first go to Everett Mitchell. All his life Mitchell seems to have had a special affinity for being touched by unusual events and persons. The first great sorrow of his life was dealt by the Iroquois Theater fire, one of the two greatest disasters in Chicago history in terms of immediate loss of life. The fire killed his beloved first grade teacher. As a young man he was present at the other, watching helplessly as victims struggled to survive in the Chicago River after the excursion boat, The Eastland, capsized and took nearly a thousand lives.

Two very different but famous men, Billy Sunday and Samuel Insull, both called him "son." In addition, Everett Mitchell is one of those rare persons who from childhood on has had a sense of history. This, and his deeply religious outlook on life—he understood the importance of prayer before he was six—has given him an unusual ability to assess the importance of the events going on around him.

Richard Crabb
Wheaton, Illinois
December 1, 1982

# Part 1
# In The Beginning

Advances in communication have from time immemorial brought with them vast changes in the pattern of civilization itself. This is true not only because of the obvious necessity to have information before it can be acted upon but because communication is a great deal more than merely the transmission of fact and comment. Perhaps no one has described communication's formidable extra dimension as well as Abba Eban when he was Israel's foreign minister. Eban said:

> Breakthrough has come at the level of communication and not by prior commitment ahead of communication. The lesson is plain. Communication itself creates a change in substantial positions . . . It is a principle of dynamic effects.

In all history there have been few sweeping changes in communication, and most of them have taken effect in the last century. For untold centuries, information could travel only as fast as a man could run. In 490 B.C. it was a human runner, the legendary Pheippides, who raced from Marathon to Athens to immortality, carrying the news of the epic Greek victory over the Persians.

The Romans were the first to substitute the horse for the human runner, a revolutionary advance that remained unchallenged for two thousand years. Until just before the American Civil War, news could travel only as fast as a horse could run. Paul Revere used a horse to warn the colonists that the British were coming in 1775.

Samuel B. Morse laid the foundation for today's communication explosion when he invented the telegraph, which came in time to be widely used by President Abraham Lincoln and the

1

Union Army during the Civil War. Soon after that war, Alexander Graham Bell invented the telephone, which transformed the social and business life of the nation by the turn of the century.

The coming of radio in the 1920s began a communications breakthrough that expanded the capabilities for the dissemination of information by greater lengths than all previous advances put together. Radio permitted instant transmission of a human voice through the air in all directions over great distances.

Everett Mitchell, who started life on a small farm northwest of Chicago, was destined to become one of radio's first important innovators. Part One, "In the Beginning," describes Mitchell's career highlights during the 1920s, in the Great Station Era before the advent of nationwide network broadcasting.

# Chapter 1
# "On Your Knees Begging"

Radio was very new on this early summer day in 1925. The nation's first radio station, KDKA in Pittsburgh, was four and a half years old. Chicago's first station, KYW, a sister station to KDKA, had been on the air three years and nine months. At this time, the entire focus of radio was on entertainment.

Chicago radio broadcasting was generally limited to afternoon, evening and nighttime, except on Mondays when all stations went off the air at 7 p.m. for the evening. This was done so the thousands of families who owned home receivers, many of them crystal sets they had built themselves, could "fish" for distant stations without interference from Chicago transmitters. Radio parties were held in homes on these evenings. This practice cut so severely into the audiences at the big Chicago theaters that they sponsored special attractions and giveaways to lure back their Monday evening customers.

Chicago radio stations were not yet giving regular attention to either weather or news reports. Neither Chicago stations nor those of the nation were yet using any advertising. There were no commercials or even sponsored programs. Radio stations were owned by organizations or individuals who maintained them as a public service.

On this June morning, Everett Mitchell had just come to work at his office on South Michigan Avenue. Mitchell, who as a boy in knickers had sung the invitation songs for Evangelist Billy Sunday, had become fascinated with the nation's latest communications rage—radio.

An accomplished baritone soloist, Mitchell was in demand for personal appearances on most of Chicago's fledgling radio stations and had been since his first appearance in 1923, when the radio fever was just beginning. At this time Mitchell was making a living for himself and his young wife, Mildred, working as a claims adjuster for the Continental Casualty Company on Michigan Avenue. He was good at his job.

The office manager, Frank Hooper, a man in his late forties, ran a tight ship with the thirty men and women on his staff. He had at first been intrigued by being able, during the evening, to tune in, originally on his crystal set and now on a battery set with the remarkable new De Forest vacuum tube,[1] and hear his man Mitchell sing the "Prisoner's Song" or a favorite hymn.

But recently two developments disturbed him. Mitchell had begun doing some announcing, not only of his own numbers, but for entire programs, especially at a new station, WENR. On one occasion Hooper had stayed up on a Saturday night until the station signed off at 2 a.m. and learned that Mitchell announced right on through the night to the finish.

At about the same time Hooper thought that he noticed Mitchell seemed to be tired at his desk and not as alert as usual, especially in the afternoon. Then just the day before the explosion, Hooper actually saw Mitchell dozing at his desk after the lunch break. Hooper was convinced that he must move decisively. After all, the thirty other members of his staff also knew of Mitchell's moonlighting activities in radio.

When Mitchell arrived the next morning, Hooper summoned him to his office and told his claims adjuster that he was aware of the extravagant amount of time Mitchell was giving to the radio stations. Matters had arrived, Hooper said, at a point where Mitchell's office work at the agency was suffering, and that could not be.

Then the ultimatum. "This has reached the point where you have to make up your mind," Hooper said with finality in his voice. "You have to give up this radio foolishness or leave the Continental Insurance Company."

Surprised, Mitchell said he would talk to Mildred that evening and meet with Hooper the next morning. Hooper seemed upset that Mitchell was so calm and that he felt it was necessary to talk to his wife before making a decision. He motioned Mitchell from his office.

When Mitchell arrived at the agency the next morning, he went directly to Hooper's office, closed the door and then announced in a low, firm voice that he would like to give notice and leave his insurance adjuster's job as soon as possible.

Frank Hooper seemed stunned by Mitchell's decision. His face

Everett Mitchell, who as a boy sang the invitation songs at Billy Sunday revivals, was a well known soloist at Chicago church and community programs for ten years before his first radio broadcast on Chicago's first radio station, KYW.

colored and the veins stood out in his neck. Mitchell feared that he might have a heart attack.

"You mean you are going to give up your job and a promising career in insurance and try to make a living at a radio station?"

"Radio is nothing but a passing fad," Hooper shouted so loudly that everyone in the agency could hear. "Within six months you will be back here on your knees begging to get your job back. Well, let me save you the trouble, because I can tell you now there won't be a job here for you ever again."

The confrontation with Hooper cost Mitchell his insurance job, but Mitchell was soon grateful that it had. Almost exactly six months later, in mid-November, the twenty-eight-year-old former claims adjuster was appointed manager of Chicago radio station WENR.

In the precedent-setting career that followed, which lasted for nearly half a century and embraced both radio and television, Everett Mitchell distinguished himself as the first of a new breed of broadcasters. They provided their listeners with service, information and inspiration to advance radio from an entertaining hobby, little more than a toy, to a new and indispensable role in American life.

### FOOTNOTE

(1) In 1906 Lee De Forest developed his magical "Audion" vacuum tube, adding a third element or "grid" to vacuum tubes experimented with by Thomas Edison and Professor John Ambrose Fleming in England. The De Forest tube not only detected radio waves more effectively but could intensify them.

# Chapter 2
# Mitchell Leads the Way

In a whirlwind of innovation following his appointment as manager of radio station WENR, Everett Mitchell introduced an impressive number of "firsts" to the young Chicago broadcasting industry. Some of them were national firsts as well. Radio was still so new when Mitchell took charge at WENR in 1925 that there were few guidelines to follow; he had to find his own solutions to broadcasting problems and create his own program formats. Many of his innovations provided the basis on which radio and television programming in the United States operates today.

When Mitchell took the station manager's job, after six months as an announcer-performer at WENR, the little Chicago station was hardly more than a year old. Its sole owner, E. N. Rauland, was a young Chicago businessman with a genius for engineering and an ability to foresee the future importance of the country's newest craze.

Rauland owned and managed a successful business, the All American Radio Company of Chicago, which in 1924 was producing battery-powered radio receivers listened to through headphones. (Rauland would soon introduce a home radio with a "loud" speaker built into the set, the kind universally used today.) The All American Radio Company factory was located at 4201 Belmont Avenue, just north and west of Chicago's Loop, and Rauland's first radio studio was in a converted office in the factory. The studio consisted of a single room.

In the beginning the radio station was hardly more than a hobby that enabled Rauland to make use of a small transmitter he had built in the basement of his home, working long hours at nights and on weekends. The transmitter had some special features that Rauland believed would give it more reach and also more signal quality, but its most dramatic feature was its size.

Rauland had a special talent for developing radio parts which were increasingly smaller and more efficient, perhaps as a result of his World War I army experience where he struggled to operate and move massive radio equipment. His basement-built transmitter is believed to be the smallest ever used to deliver a clear radio signal to a large city and beyond. Mounted on a single board thirty-six inches long and twenty inches wide, it could be moved easily by one man.[1]

The little 10-watt station went on the air in the fall of 1924, one of more than a dozen broadcasting in the Chicago area. Rauland did as many other station owners were doing and hired a small music group to provide much of the entertainment to broadcast. The group was directed by Frank Westphal, a recognized musician and entertainer in Chicago, who also doubled as announcer and station manager.

Rauland was surprised at the way business picked up immediately for the All American Radio Company. Since radio commercials had not yet come into use, the only reference made to the business was in connection with the station break announcement, "This is the All American Radio Station WENR in Chicago."

Eager to have this sales stimulus over a wider area, early in 1925 Rauland built a 100-watt transmitter that made it possible to hear WENR as far away as southern Wisconsin, northeastern Indiana and across the lake in western Michigan. At the same time he began designing a 1,000-watt transmitter which he believed could send a dependable nighttime signal one thousand miles in any direction from Chicago—from New York City to Denver. It was an electrifying idea at that time.

Rauland took his design to the Western Electric Company in Chicago, whose main business was (and still is) building equipment for the Bell Telephone System. Western Electric built the new transmitter, which was placed in service at 4201 Belmont Avenue in August, 1925.

Within weeks Rauland knew that his goal of a thousand-mile reach for the new transmitter had been accomplished. The hard evidence was coming from the post office. Letters were arriving from most states of the union. Soon the mail was coming in such volume that it was possible to reply only to the most urgent communications. By January, 1926, after Mitchell had taken charge, the geographical concentration of the mail revealed a stable listening pattern that stretched from central Pennsylvania to eastern Colorado.

E. N. Rauland,owner of Station WENR in Chicago and who appointed Everett Mitchell manager in 1925, on occasions did announcing. The station's call letters included his initials.

But it was not just the power of the station to reach out across the miles that Rauland wanted to improve. He had the technical knowledge to keep increasing WENR's capacity to reach new listeners, but he knew that radio programming, at WENR, as at all the fledgling stations, could stand great improvement. In the six months that Mitchell had been with the station as an announcer-performer Rauland had come to respect him as a person and to see that he had the kind of ideas that could take the little radio station in the direction Rauland wanted it to go.

When Mitchell took over as station manager on November 15, 1925, WENR, like most stations across the nation, did not broadcast on a fixed schedule. At this time, broadcasting schedules were often determined simply by the availability of some kind of program to put on the air. When stations signed off for the day or to take a break, the announcer would tell the listeners when the station expected to be on the air again. Listeners were in the habit of checking across the dial to find out what stations were on and what they were broadcasting.

In those days, programming was almost entirely entertainment. As was the case with WENR, stations often engaged a small studio orchestra to provide roughly half the programming, especially late evening broadcasts. The orchestra leader was often the station manager, an arrangement which seriously limited the time he could spend on programming.

Half or more of the early radio programs were provided at no cost by amateur entertainers, those who regularly performed for community and church gatherings. Seeking the thrill of "being on radio," these performers would arrive at the studios unannounced. Since there was no schedule to follow, overworked station managers had little opportunity to organize or control the quality of the performers. The station managers had radio time to fill. The amateurs came "for free." It was that elementary.

Mitchell, who had gotten his start as an amateur performer, had a first-hand understanding of the problems of the unpaid amateurs and the harried station managers. He moved quickly to work out solutions. By working seven days a week, many of them sixteen and twenty hour days, he introduced radically new procedures which quickly moved his station a long way toward the broadcasting practices of today. Mitchell was not attempting to create new concepts for all of radio; he was only trying to solve the problems he found at WENR. But the fact that many other Chicago stations soon followed his lead showed that he foresaw the direction radio programming would have to go in the future.

Mitchell realized immediately that WENR had to have a schedule, if for no other reason than to attract good amateur performers. The Belmont Avenue studios were off the beaten path; to get good performers he would have to guarantee that they could be heard on a particular day at a particular time. But what was more important, Mitchell saw, was to get and keep listeners. He wanted them to know that they could tune in to WENR at a certain hour and know that it would be broadcasting; even more, he wanted them to know what kinds of programs would be on the air at specific times.

Within three weeks Mitchell had put in place a firm broadcasting schedule for every day in the week, including Sunday, which was posted in advance in the studio. It provided the opportunity for last-minute changes but was otherwise followed. WENR would be on the air from 2 p.m. until 2 a.m. so listeners would know when to tune in to 266 on the dial. At first, he retained the station's practice of having a two-hour break at dinner time, 6 to 8 p.m., but after a few months he went to continuous broadcasting. The supper break became, instead, dinner music.

Mitchell also moved to reorganize his slender programming resources. Members of the studio orchestra had various special talents, he knew. From this group he formed an instrumental trio which could provide classical music programs and another group which could play good jazz. Now he had the flexibility of three different kinds of music: the classical trio, the jazz band and the full orchestra.

Next, he tackled the problem of the unpaid amateurs, who were indispensable if he wanted to fill out his new schedule. Amateur performers no longer stopped in unannounced. They were invited to tryouts. Those performers whose acts could be worked into the station's new format were offered specific times to perform during the week. The amateurs were delighted with the new system; now they could tell their friends in advance when they would be "on radio." Some even passed out nickels so their friends could use the nearest pay phones, call WENR and request that particular performer be on the air again soon.

As the better amateurs began coming to WENR, other Chicago stations began adopting Mitchell's procedures to protect their talent supply. Soon Mitchell was armed with a list of top amateurs with telephone numbers where they could be reached on short notice in case a program gap developed.

11

Mary M'Cormic, star of the National Opera Company of France, and Everett Mitchell, who arranged for her to do a Chicago radio "first" when she conducted a "talk show" with her fans on Station WENR following her concerts.

Mitchell's new system enabled him to create special kinds of programs, planned and announced in advance. For the first time, he could schedule a program of classical music, jazz or the great hymns and promote it ahead of time. The WENR audience mail jumped fifty percent.

Radio writers for the Chicago newspapers were not long in noticing the change at WENR. Mitchell's appointment was hailed in the November 30, 1925, editions of *The Chicago Tribune*. Radio editor Elmer Douglas wrote:

> Hurrahs and long-hoped-for congratulations to WENR. A new announcer with a very likeable voice and pleasing microphone personality—announcer Everett Mitchell.

Douglas, who had followed Mitchell's radio career as a soloist and announcer, often with favorable reports in his column, closed his announcement story with a short but pungent commentary on the general level of Chicago broadcasting that winter.

> Now, with the excellent Rauland Instrumental Trio and all else high class, the writer at least can tune to WENR with high class expectations.

Shortly after, Harry Lawrence of *The Chicago Post*, the humorous and folksy member of the Chicago radio editors' fraternity, gave his impressions of what was happening at WENR:

> Mr. Mitchell took us in hand and gave us a rubberneck tour of WENR . . . It's a businesslike little studio . . . It doesn't try to resemble an Italian villa, a Florentine garden or the Grant Park stadium, as many studios seem to be striving to do. Three or four chairs, a pair of pianos, a small switchboard desk and a microphone about finish the inventory. The businesslike air of the studio seems to have its effect on the programs, for the numbers click off in a very efficient manner.

Lawrence recognized that the new manager had for his goal the introduction of an entirely different kind of radio programming.

> He (Mitchell) is very enthusiastic about his plans for future music programs from WENR, and if his ideas as outlined to me are successful, we can look forward to something new in the way of radio programs in the near future.
>
> Says he, "Each hour of the day has its own type of audience. Therefore, each of our program hours will strive to

please the particular class which is listening at that time. For instance, we found that by advancing our classical hour of music from 6:30 to 8 p.m., we reach a larger proportion of the classical musical lovers than formerly. The young folks, who like jazz music and popular songs, keep late hours, anyhow, so our 9 to 10 dance music and our midnight frolics are especially for them."

In other words, Director Mitchell doesn't want his programs to be hodge-podge affairs, alternating between Wagner and "Red Hot Mama" all in the same hour. For them as likes musical hash, there are plenty of stations serving it. You can hear a wide variety of music, from the most profound works of the master composers down (or up according to your taste) to the most incandescent mamma who ever yodeled a flock of blues in front of the microphone. But not all in one chapter—Oh my, no. You've gotta wait for the proper hour. Then you get a full program of the kind of music you want.

That seems to be a good idea. What do you think of it, boys and girls? Write in to Director Mitchell . . . and give him a piece of your mind, one way or the other.

Scheduling programs was just the first of many innovations Everett Mitchell brought about in his years with Rauland's station. The weekend after Thanksgiving in 1925, he created an original Christmas radio feature for children, *Letters to Santa Claus.* A first in Chicago and the nation, the theme has since been widely used.

Children were invited to write to Santa with the assurance that their letters would be delivered directly to the North Pole. The delivery was made by an elf called Peter. When "Peter" came into the studio, the children would hear the door open and close, and the elf would be accompanied by the sound of bells. Peter always had a "Hello" for his listeners and sometimes a comment on the amount of mail. Then he would leave, accompanied by the sound effects, another radio first created on the spot by the performers in the studio.

Children's letters came in by the hundreds, and especially appealing ones were read on the half hour program. Mitchell and his co-workers, however, were shocked by the unexpectedly large number of letters coming from children of poor and broken homes. The gift most sought by these underprivileged children was "a puppy to love," but the second most asked for gift was a pair of shoes. WENR turned to the Salvation Army for help. The Army staff, true to its tradition, followed up to see that the children who needed shoes, at least, would not be overlooked.[2]

In 1926 Mitchell created what became the first sustained listener participation show, the kind so popular today, in which listeners calling in provide much of the program. Called *The Farmer's Exchange*, the show was broadcast at 5 p.m. each day.

Mitchell opened the program by reporting on some timely farming subject, material for which was often provided by Tommy Johnson, Purdue University's agricultural editor, one of the first in the nation to see what radio could mean to farm families. After the farm topic was given, farmers were invited to call in and give their comments. They were also asked if they had items they would like to exchange with other listeners. The program continued daily for two years, then was absorbed into a new and more inclusive farm program format.

Mitchell's acquaintance with newpaperman Harry Lawrence led to another WENR first, a late night talk show. Called *Bedtime Stories for Chorus Girls*, the program was largely by, for and about entertainers. Lawrence came to the station to do the show, usually bringing guests from the vaudeville circuit, then in its heyday. Mitchell was the announcer and producer, but Lawrence was the main attraction. The show was entirely talk.

Broadcast on Saturday nights, *Bedtime Stories for Chorus Girls* went on the air at 1 a.m. when most of the theater entertainers in Chicago were through for the evening. They would gather in the city's late night eating places, where the management or one of the entertainers would have a radio tuned in to Lawrence's program for the latest "show biz" gossip and comment. The unique format also drew a big audience among entertainers in New York City, where it came on the air at 2 a.m. When plugging the new program, *The Post* noted that Lawrence "knows more chorus girls by their first names—and last husbands—than any other authority." This show had a long run.

Another WENR first was its overseas listener club. When Mitchell and Rauland learned, via the mail what was becoming an ever-increasing indicator of listener patterns, that the program was often received across the Pacific, they invited any listener across the ocean to write describing the program, the date and the local time at which the Chicago station was heard. Each overseas listener would receive a membership in the WENR club.

Sometimes as much as two months was required for a letter from overseas to arrive at the station. Each letter was read to the WENR audience. Late in 1926, *The Chicago Daily News* commented on the overseas listener probe:

> Radio is daily becoming a bigger factor in bringing the far corners of the world closer together. In isolated places, such as mountain passes, islands of the sea, snowed-in winter camps and all sorts of out-of-the-way places, radio is coming into popular use by keeping the listeners in constant touch with the rest of the world . . .
>
> Station WENR recently conducted an interesting experiment to find out how far its programs were reaching. It was announced over the microphone that any one who would write in describing the program would receive a membership card in the "Last Minute" Listeners Club.
>
> Several weeks later letters began coming in from distant points, until over a half-dozen were received from Alaska, Hawaii and New Zealand. Another postcard from Shanghai, China, told how well WENR was received at the extreme other side of the Pacific.

Striving to make his Chicago station one of midwest and even national importance, Rauland encouraged Mitchell to develop programs of wide geographical appeal. One of the most popular was *Know and Boost Your United States*. Each program gave a kaleidoscopic view of a state, its scenic and historic features, its natural and industrial resources, its major cities and in particular its points of interest to visitors. This program immediately attracted nationwide interest.

Broadcast on Thursday evenings, each of the salutes to the states presented a message from the governor, written especially for the WENR program. The state song was used for theme music. The program proved so popular that governors of some states that had not yet been featured wrote to WENR asking when their state would be included.

But breakthroughs in the radio studio were not enough for the WENR station manager. Mitchell was already convinced that the future importance of radio would depend as much on broadcasting done from outside the studio as that done within. He believed that the radio announcer, with his microphone, must go where the action is, just as the newspaper reporter does. So in the spring of 1926, with the help of Rauland and the All American

16

Marie Tully, pianist for Station WENR in its Belmont Avenue studios in Chicago, with Everett Mitchell in 1925 when he was both manager and chief announcer for the station.

Radio Company's engineers, he did something previously un-heard-of in Chicago radio. He broadcast an event miles from the WENR studio without the use of either power line electricity or telephone lines.

Until this demonstration, radio broadcasting outside the studio had been totally dependent on a telephone line to relay the sound back to the station's transmitter. Broadcasts were often made outside of studios, particularly from hotel ballrooms where popu-lar bands were playing, but always with the microphone spliced to a telephone wire. Mitchell's broadcast demonstrated that the microphone could travel anywhere the announcer wanted to go by using what was in effect a miniature transmitter and a porta-ble source of power (a battery) to replace the telephone line.

This WENR broadcast broke new ground and opened the po-tential for almost unlimited expansion in radio's "live" coverage of events in Chicago. Mitchell had produced the prototype for the "remotes" that make up much of today's radio and television programming, presenting events as they occur.

Mitchell had been thinking of such a possibility when one of his Masonic Lodge friends asked him if he and WENR could help draw a large crowd for a family night at the LaSalle Street Ma-sonic Temple.

"Most of these people are WENR listeners," his friend said. "They feel like they know you, and I wondered if it would be pos-sible for you and your studio orchestra to come and do your 8 p.m. broadcast from the Temple."

Mitchell liked the idea. He visited the Temple and found what appeared to be an impossible situation. The stage where the broadcast would be given was so far from either electrical outlets or a telephone line that the expense of bringing these facilities to the podium would be prohibitive. Still he disliked disappointing his Masonic friends. Would there be any way to develop a small transmitter which could operate on batteries and send the Ma-sonic program back to the studio, Mitchell wondered.

The more Mitchell thought about it, the more the idea of a portable transmitter excited him. All American Radio's engineers were working hard to reduce the size of radio components, he knew. He took the matter up with Rauland, who said immedi-ately he thought it could be done. In a short time, under Rauland's careful eye, the engineers had built a mini-transmitter that weighed less than ten pounds, hardly more than the micro-phone. The transmitter's storage battery was the heaviest item.

The big night came. Mitchell appeared at the podium a few minutes before 8 p.m. and explained the unusual preparations that had been made. He told everyone in the packed Temple that they would be part of the largest "studio audience" ever to hear a regularly scheduled radio program transmitted without the aid of telephone wires. Then he stepped to the microphone.

"This is Station WENR. This evening our program comes to you from the LaSalle Street Masonic Temple before a large audience of Masons and their families. This is a very special broadcast . . . " Not only did the program go without a hitch, the applause of the big audience added to the performance, and the station engineer reported that the broadcast quality ranged from good to excellent during the entire hour.

The broadcast from the Masonic Temple was to be only the first of many "pick-ups" from out of the studio during Mitchell's long career. As equipment for remote broadcasting advanced, he took his microphone to important people and events in every state of the union and to many countries around the world.

In the spring of 1926 Mitchell brought about another Chicago radio first—he wrote and delivered the first radio commercial. The ethical restraints to permitting radio advertising were wearing away as it became obvious that to be expanded radio would have to have additional sources of revenue. Secretary of Commerce Herbert Hoover, whose office supervised non-military use of radio, had recently given radio advertising a qualified blessing. The problem now was to convince owners and managers of businesses that radio could be useful in selling goods and services.

Mitchell had found that even the mention of a new product could stimulate sales in stores. One of Rauland's engineers at All American Radio had designed and produced an impressive Christmas tree stand with colored lights, one of the first such devices on the market. One of these stands had been used for the Christmas tree in the WENR studio. On several occasions Mitchell had mentioned on the air how much the new stand added to the beauty of the studio Christmas tree. In a matter of days Chicago dealers had sold all of the lighted tree stands available, and reported that they could have sold many more.

The first advertisement in Chicago took the form of a one hour musical program with a commercial statement at the opening and again at the close. The program was called *The Bamby Bread Makers* and featured the WENR orchestra. Mitchell wrote and delivered the commercials. The impact was immediate at the grocery stores. For a time, WENR led all other Chicago stations in radio advertising.

But at least one radio first, which was copied nationwide, came about just because of Mitchell's own personal interest. Because he had always liked canaries, Mitchell brought several to the studio and by tedious experiment discovered how to get the little birds to sing along during musical programs until closing time at 2 a.m. Some listeners thought the birds were being abused, and the Anti-Cruelty Society sent an official from a neighboring city to investigate. Mitchell explained that the birds received their full schedule of rest. He demonstrated how special hoods were placed over the cages at 2 a.m. and left until three the next afternoon. The investigator left satisfied.

Mitchell's introduction of canaries led to a virtual canary craze on radio, which lasted for many years.

Chicago newpapers, of course, took note of this new fad. Evans E. Plummer, radio editor for *The Herald and Examiner*, interviewed Mitchell to learn his "secrets" for making the birds sing at the proper time. Quoting Mitchell, Plummer reported:

> "Seldom do they fail us, although when they do, I usually get near the cage of one of the birds and imitate a canary. This makes the insulted one want to tell the world how a REAL canary sounds and he begins to warble. This arouses the bird in the other cage and he chimes in to excel the first. Very simple, you see, after you know how."

Plummer ended his column with still another tribute to the increasingly popular announcer:

> So this humble scribbler suggests that we give the medal for best canaryologist and mimic to one Everett Mitchell, radio announcer and good egg.

### FOOTNOTES

(1) The small transmitter that launched WENR was later donated by Rauland to the Smithsonian Institution in Washington, D.C.

(2) This would not be the last time Mitchell was involved in a campaign to see that needy children got shoes. In 1926 he and WENR aided *The Chicago Daily Journal* and the Chicago Women's Club to raise enough money to buy almost 15,000 pairs of shoes at Christmastime.

# Chapter 3
# "Your Voice the Service Brings"

Chicago radio was changing rapidly in the mid-1920s, and no one was more closely linked to that change than Everett Mitchell. The stations whose owners were looking toward the future were quick to adopt the new and better ways to serve listeners that Mitchell had worked out at WENR. By the end of 1926 these stations were operating on stable broadcasting schedules announced to their listeners in advance. A greater variety of programs was being presented as more effective use was made of both amateur entertainers and staff performers. Also, the earlier almost total dependence on music and entertainment was giving way as more programs offering information or service to listeners were introduced.

But Mitchell's innovations continued. One of his major changes was to make the role of the announcer more important. In this he had an advantage. As chief announcer for WENR, he was handling most of the announcing duties himself. He was also station manager and he had the full confidence of station owner E. N. Rauland. As a result, he was able to experiment to an unusual degree with new responsibilities.

One of his experiments was to make the station breaks between programs more useful. In those two or three minutes, Mitchell would not only announce the time and the station but would also hold little chats with listeners, as though he had just met them on the street. He might have a humorous quip, thought for the day, or a comment on the weather or the important news. (This was long before Chicago radio stations gave regular attention to weather and news.) The WENR mail told him that listeners liked his comments during station breaks. Some even sent quips and quotes that he might use on the air.

Mitchell's use of the station break and his understanding of the

21

Dr. Ralph W. Muchow (right) with Everett Mitchell in 1980. Mitchell holds a telephone microphone, an exhibit in Muchow's Antique Radio Museum in Elgin, Illinois. Mitchell used a telephone microphone in his first years in radio.

importance of the announcer's role led to a watershed broadcasting event on May 20, 1927. The event established WENR as one of the outstanding radio stations in the nation during the climax of the Great Station Era, a year before network broadcasting began in the east and two years before it came to Chicago. Mitchell's "first" on this date has been remembered by listeners in at least half the states and in Canada.

The events which led to the unexpected broadcast began at 7:35 on the morning of May 20, as a small, single-engine, single-passenger airplane took off on a grass-covered runway in New York City. A young American pilot, twenty-seven-year-old Charles A. Lindbergh, had put his Spirit of St. Louis in the air and headed out over the ocean in an effort to become the first man to fly solo from New York to Paris.

Lindbergh's plane had a top speed of only 135 miles an hour. His take-off from New York was timed so that while there was still some daylight, he would be over Newfoundland before heading into the night over the Atlantic. His route had been carefully charted, and ships along the route had been notified to be on the lookout and report on their ship-to-shore radio when there was sight or sound of The Spirit of St. Louis. Identification should not be difficult. There would be no other plane in the air over the North Atlantic that night.

Soon after take-off the weather closed in and visibility was so poor from New York to Newfoundland that there were but two distant sightings of the plane. The weather did break over Newfoundland, and Lindbergh was there, as scheduled, at twilight. The Spirit of St. Louis was last seen, a moving sunlit speck, heading east into an ominous black cloud that hung like a curtain over the Atlantic.

As Lindbergh would later report, that black cloud proved to be more than five hundred miles long and thousands of feet high. It packed, at various points, torrential rains, hail, violent down and up-drafts and temperatures so low that at times the plane was dangerously covered with ice. For six hours Lindbergh was forced to become a flying acrobat to escape these hazards. He reported that at one time he was flying only ten feet above the water and at another up to ten thousand feet, almost too high for the little plane, which was not equipped with oxygen. The cloud cover was so dense and so low that during the entire ordeal Lindbergh did not see one ship at sea. Only one ship's crew reported hearing what they thought might have been the sound of an airplane.

Few realized how deeply concerned the American public had become about the fate of the young flier who had chosen to battle the odds over the treacherous North Atlantic. There had been newspaper stories ever since Charles Lindbergh announced he would accept the challenge of the New York hotel owner, who had posted a $25,000 prize (a small fortune in the 1920s) for the first person who could make the trans-Atlantic flight alone. The flight got more advance newpaper publicity than any other peacetime event of the century, arousing perhaps more public interest than anything since the completion of the first transcontinental railroad in 1869.[1]

While the purpose of the flight was to prove what the airplane could accomplish, it was the high risk to the young pilot that riveted the attention of the nation. Even the staid *London* (England) *Times* commented on Lindbergh's "supreme disregard for risk," and many on both sides of the Atlantic regarded the effort as just short of suicidal.

The flight turned out to be as important for the future of radio as for the airplane, revealing how impatient the public was to have the new medium fulfill its potential as a fast means of news dissemination. This was also the first time the print news media learned that in the transmission of fast-breaking news, it could not hope to compete with radio. The special newspaper editions, then so much a part of the business, were never the same again after May, 1927, and in time they disappeared.

Never before had so many people gathered to follow the news of an unfolding event. About one-third of the American families had radio receivers in 1927; these ranged from crystal sets with earphones to the newest receivers that were equipped with loudspeakers so everyone near them could hear. Many families with loudspeaker receivers opened their homes to neighbors, friends and even strangers who wanted to follow the young American's flight across the ocean. In some communities half the population stayed near radios that night, seeking to hear the latest news of the flight.[2]

This great surge of public interest took most of the more than five hundred U.S. radio stations by surprise. Not yet accustomed to broadcasting national news, most of them ignored the flight. A few stations sensed that their listeners would want to know what was happening to Lindbergh during the evening and night and made preparations. One of them was Radio Station WENR.

Everett Mitchell spent most of his commuting time that morning considering how WENR might keep listeners posted on the latest developments. He concluded that there would need to be a report at each station break from 7 p.m. until the sign-off at 2 a.m. He would do something more, something that had not been done at WENR and that he had not heard of anywhere else: he would be prepared to break into the regular programs at any time should there be decisive developments in the Lindbergh flight over the Atlantic.

Then the difficult question came to him. How would he get the up-to-the-minute reports? After the evening newspapers were printed, the only way to get late news was to call the papers, and those phone lines would likely be jammed with callers. Then Mitchell remembered that a close friend worked in the newsroom of *The Chicago Herald and Examiner* during the evening and night. He was sure he could get from his friend the latest bulletins coming over the wires of the Associated Press and the United Press.

During the daylight hours there was little news of the flight. The final editions of the newspapers reported the two sightings of the plane enroute to Newfoundland. They noted that the overcast skies had prevented further sightings but that the clouds had parted over Newfoundland and the little plane had been clearly sighted as it headed out over the ocean.

At the 7 p.m. station break, Mitchell brought the WENR listeners up to date so they were aware that Lindbergh had reached Newfoundland and had headed across the Atlantic toward Ireland. He pointed out that this news was now two hours old and there had been nothing to report since, but said as new developments came they would be reported at the station breaks during that night's broadcasting schedule.

Then the long vigil began. At 7:30 there had been no news of Lindbergh over the press wires. Nor was there any news at 8 o'clock nor at 8:30. The more time passed without news, the more the fears grew that The Spirit of St. Louis was down in the Atlantic. People gathered around their radios fell silent as the evening advanced. The strain was getting to everyone. Some cried.

Mitchell was feeling the tension, too, but he felt an added strain because he knew that thousands were tuned to WENR, hoping and expecting him to give them some evidence that Lindbergh was still flying. Now the minutes between 9 and 9:30 were slipping away. At 9:30 p.m. Mitchell again reported that there

Everett Mitchell at the time of his first radio broadcast on November 3, 1923. He was featured as a soloist on Chicago's first radio station, KYW.

was no word from The Spirit of St. Louis. But as the big hand on the studio clock moved toward the hour, he knew that he must do something more at the 10 o'clock station break. The tension was simply too great to ignore.

"But at five minutes before ten," Mitchell recalls, "I had no idea of how to meet the situation. Then I got help. When I went to the WENR microphone for the 10 p.m. break I suddenly knew what to do.

"I spoke to my radio audience as friend to friend. I explained that there had been no report of sighting the Lindbergh plane since it had been seen heading into the darkness east of Newfoundland. But, I said, we must not lose hope. We must have faith. I told my listeners that I had a conviction that this brave young American could make it, but that we must all help him.

"The one thing we can all do," I said, "is to pray for him and the success of his flight. Then I announced that Station WENR was going to be silent for a minute of prayer for Charles Lindbergh on this night of trial. 'Won't you join me in this minute of silence and each in your own way pray for this courageous young American?' I asked."

Mitchell was impressed that the members of the studio orchestra, persons not known for their devoutness, immediately bowed their heads as a single man. So did everyone else in the WENR studio that night.

Mitchell did not know it that night, but his prayer service was heard in most of the states of the union. The broadcast assumed an increasing importance as the word came the next morning from England that Lindbergh had survived the night and that his flight came to its historic close in Paris about 4 o'clock (WENR time) that afternoon.

The prayer service was not only heard, it was etched in the memories of many who heard the historic broadcast. Half a century and more later, in his *In Search of History: A Personal Adventure*, historian Theodore W. White, writing of his youth in Kansas, told how his family got its first radio in 1927 and the highlights it brought that year. "I could listen to the Yankees win the World Series, hear the Sharkey-Dempsey fight from New York and even the prayer for Lindbergh's flight to Paris."[3]

This was America's first nationwide prayer service. Mail of commendation and appreciation from WENR listeners poured in from around the country in such volume the letters were delivered by special truck.

In 1928 Everett Mitchell noted his fifth anniversary in radio, a business that had not existed eight years before. In that time, something had happened to Mitchell of which he was only vaguely aware. He had, without ever intending to, become a household name—famous—over much of the nation.

This was a new breed of fame in America, the first conferred by radio. Mitchell was acclaimed, not as a performing artist like the well-known band leaders or vaudeville performers, but as "the announcer." Announcers were the stars of radio in the Great Station Era. They did not simply introduce programs, they commented on and interpreted what was happening, talking directly to their unseen audience. They were invited into millions of homes daily and were regarded as friends of the family who could be called on the telephone, written to and even visited.

The area in which the announcer became a celebrity was limited only by the radio station's signal. For a local station the announcer's fame might extend for two hundred miles. For Everett Mitchell, supported by the powerful nighttime signal of WENR, that fame extended across the continent and all the way across the Pacific to New Zealand. Mitchell may have been known to more people in more states than any other radio announcer in the pre-network broadcasting period.

One WENR listener, Hugo Schubel of Chicago, sent a poem dedicated to his favorite announcer to *The Chicago Evening Post*. The Post published the poem, which was entitled "The Voice of Service." It was dedicated to "Everett Mitchell, announcer of Radio Station WENR." (WENR later adopted Schubel's reference, "The Voice of Service," as its motto.)

One verse read:

> You have a calm announcing way;
> Your voice does sweetly ring.
> A message, dear, it does convey;
> It's service that you bring.

The Post set the last two lines of the poem in boldface type, with capitals:

> **It chiefly does reflect on YOU--**
> **YOUR VOICE the SERVICE brings.**

The radio editor added a postscript: "Mr. Mitchell has responded very warmly and thankfully. Now, listen in, all of you. Give him a hearing."

In the spring of 1928 Everett Mitchell received an unusual letter from a most unusual man. Abner Sprague and his wife, Alberta invited Everett and Mildred Mitchell to spend their summer vacation with them in Rocky Mountain National Park. The United States Government had bought much of the land in the great national park from Sprague, who as a boy had traveled to Colorado in a covered wagon and who owned the land "by right of discovery."

The Mitchells accepted and decided to buy their first car, a Nash touring model, so they could drive rather than make the trip by train. Traveling over mainly dirt roads, they crossed Illinois to the Mississippi River, drove across Iowa to the Missouri River and up the Platte River road the length of Nebraska to Colorado. Mitchell found that he was among friends at almost every stop.

Arriving at the entrance to Rocky Mountain National Park, the Mitchells were detained by a pleasant but firm park ranger who reported that they needed to appear in court immediately. Before the judge in a matter of minutes, the Mitchells saw that a special reception had been arranged for them. The judge wanted to "sentence" them to "have the greatest vacation of their lives as guests of the Spragues and the park staff in appreciation for the years of pleasure and uplift given the people of eastern Colorado by Everett Mitchell and Station WENR." The Mitchells were given a day and night park ranger escort for their entire stay.

\* \* \*

Radio's first era, the time of the Great Stations—when WLW in Cincinnati used an astronomic 500,000 watts to blanket its signal over all of North America and WENR with its ocean-bridging place on the dial made Everett Mitchell a celebrity in New Zealand—was soon to end. The new era would be based on network broadcasting, in which a central radio facility created programs and fed them via telephone lines or other means of relay to a host of local and regional stations across the nation.

Most of the personalities who made radio possible in the Great Station Era—the amateur performers, the vaudeville artists, the local band leaders and announcers—would not cross over into the network era, but Everett Mitchell did. His contribution to the developing media would continue for three decades of network radio and television. He continued to be a "voice of service," providing education, information and inspiration to his legion of listeners in the United States and around the world.

29

The network era brought the specialist to broadcasting—the newscaster, the meteorologist, the sportscaster and many others. Mitchell, too, developed a speciality, one that to this day remains unique. This special service stemmed directly out of his childhood on the Moreland Prairie. Broadcasting through a critical era of the nation's history that spanned the Great Depression, the greatest of all wars and the intense post-war growth in this country, Mitchell became the leader in removing the isolation that from the beginning of time has blanketed and handicapped rural families. In the process he earned a recognition not before or since conferred on another. He was honored by millions of Americans, to whom he spoke daily for years, and by Presidents of the United States as "The Voice of American Agriculture."

### FOOTNOTES

(1) The only comparable peacetime news event up to this time, was on May 10, 1869 when through the magic of the telegraph people all over the nation waited for the moment the first transcontinental railroad was completed above Great Salt Lake in Utah. Western Union held open its lines and telegraph stations in every city, town and hamlet in the United States so that the crowds gathered around their offices could know within seconds when the last spike had been driven. When Governor Leland Stanford of California hammered the last historic golden spike into place, the prearranged telegraphic signal was flashed to every point in the United States simultaneously, touching off firing of cannon, speeches and parades from coast to coast.

(2) Our family lived on a farm at Macomb in western Illinois, 250 miles from Chicago. The only family in the farming community who had one of the new "super-heterodyne" radio receivers with its many dials and separate standing loudspeaker invited us to spend the evening at their home so we could follow Lindbergh's flight. I was very young but I remember two things: the distressing fact that there was no news of the flight and the prayer service. Not until my research began on *Radio's Beautiful Day* did I become aware that this was my first contact with Everett Mitchell. (--Richard Crabb)

(3) Theodore W. White, *In Search of History: A Personal Adventure* (New York, N.Y., Harper and Row, 1978), p. 16.

30

# Part 2
# Bucket in the Well

Everett Mitchell and radio were "born" in the last half of the same decade, the Gay '90's. The inventions that were to make broadcasting an indispensable part of American life took place in just the twenty-five years between 1895 and 1920 when Everett was growing up, first on a small farm near Chicago and later in a northwest Chicago neighborhood.

Just three years before Everett was born, Guglielmo Marconi, at his father's estate in Italy, had demonstrated that he could transmit messages through the air without wires. During Everett's pre-school and grade school years, inventors including John A. Fleming, Lee De Forest, Reginald A. Fessenden, Arnst Alexanderson, Edwin H. Armstrong and others were advancing the knowledge and technology that made the transmission of the human voice across great distances possible. In 1911 the name "radio" was first applied to the wireless telegraph..

When Everett was fourteen and singing the invitation songs at the revivals of the famous evangelist, Billy Sunday, radio was used for the first time to save lives in a disaster at sea. On the night of April 14, 1912, the Titanic hit an iceberg and sank in the North Atlantic fourteen hundred miles from New York. Young David Sarnoff, the Marconi wireless operator in the Wannamaker department store, stayed at his post for seventy-two hours contacting ships in the area and sending them to the rescue. The wireless saved the lives of hundreds who otherwise would have perished.

To show how the highlights for young Mitchell and fledgling radio moved along together, a summary of important advances in radio has been placed before the beginning of each chapter in Part Two. The summary covers roughly the time span in each chapter.

Everett Mitchell's childhood is also an illustration of the spectacular advances in the American standard of living which have taken place in this century. Everett and his brother and sisters spent their early years living in a house where there were none of the comforts and conveniences we take for granted today: no gas or electricity for light and heat, no telephone, no plumbing or running water, no window screens, no furnace, no automobile. The children slept in an unheated second story above the first floor living quarters on mattresses filled with straw. When Everett was six, one of his chores was to bring in enough water from the well in the back yard for all the needs of the family of eight. The well had no pump. The bucket, tied to a rope, had to be dropped in the well and pulled up by hand.

Those were difficult times for children. A brother and sister died as infants. Another sister succumbed to "children's complaint" and was left unable to walk for life. But the Mitchell parents were capable and hard-working, sustained by an unwavering faith in God and His personal concern for those who believe. They spared no efforts to give their children advantages they themselves had not had and to prepare them for rewarding, constructive lives.

"God was good me," Mitchell says now. "He gave me as fine a father and mother as anyone could have. He prepared me for the opportunities to come. Without the advantages of those early years the 'Beautiful Day' would not have been possible."

# Chapter 4
# Mighty Thunder Over The Prairie

Late in February and in the early days of March, 1898, young Dr. Fred Glenn of nearby Oak Park had made a point to stop his buggy regularly on the Moreland Prairie at the small truck farm of George Mitchell. George's wife, Lucilla, was expecting another baby, and the time was drawing close.

The Mitchells were one of the young families earning a living on the prairie near the west edge of Chicago producing vegetables for the city markets.[1] There were four daughters in the truck gardener's family awaiting the event. All of them had been given names that began with the letter "E," although George and Lucilla always said they selected the names they thought best for their children without regard to what the first letter might be.

Eva was thirteen and a great help to her mother, even though

33

Lucilla Bacon Mitchell, Everett's mother, whose unusual abilities, hard work and deep religious faith held the family together despite poverty and illnesses.

she had no use of her legs. While still a baby, Eva had been stricken by a malady which doctors did not understand but which they called "children's complaint" because it usually struck only children. There was no treatment and no cure for children's complaint, which was undoubtedly a form of polio.

Lucilla's next two children, Eban and Elizabeth, had died in infancy before the family came to the Moreland Prairie. Ethel, who was petite like her mother, was six. Four-year-old Edna was fun-loving and strong for her age. Two years before, Lucilla's sixth child, Edith, had been born. Two years later Lucilla would give birth to her eighth and last baby. He would be named Ellsworth.

Now it was Monday evening, March 14, 1898. Lucilla had suspected during the day that the birth was near. The three older girls were looking forward to the event in hopes that it would bring them a baby brother. Even Edith, not old enough to fully understand, knew that something important was about to happen in the Mitchell home.

Lucilla cooked and served supper, as usual, but soon after the evening meal she told her husband it was time to send for the doctor. Since the Mitchell family did not have a telephone (and would not for another ten years), George Mitchell decided to walk the three miles to Dr. Glenn's home in Oak Park. He would harness the doctor's horse and hitch the animal to the buggy while the doctor was getting ready. The buggy with Dr. Glenn and the expectant father arrived at the Mitchell farm between 8:30 and 9 p.m. It was warm for mid-March and the men agreed that there might be rain sometime during the night.

Dr. Glenn examined Lucilla and said he was sure there would be a baby born before morning. There were no complications, he assured Lucilla, and he complimented Eva, who had assisted him at the births of both Edna and Edith, on the preparations. The water was already hot and the clean towels were laid out. This would be a large baby, he observed, and the birth was still some hours away. But everyone in the family was excited over the news, since the doctor allowed that a larger baby could mean a better chance of its being a boy.

By 9:30 everything was in order. Lucilla had been made reasonably comfortable and there was nothing to do but wait. Since George Mitchell was a quiet man, Dr. Glenn was left largely with his own thoughts.

The doctor's thoughts were filled with concern for this unusual family, which had known better times. The impending birth added to his worry. He had spent many hours in the Mitchell home since the family moved to the prairie five years before, delivering two babies and attending to the many illnesses that inevitably come to any family with small children. He had come to know George and Lucilla better than anyone else on the Prairie and had developed fondness and respect for them. But he wondered how much longer their health would enable them to cope with the poverty that had closed in on them since they had been forced to leave a comfortable home in Chicago and retreat to the vegetable farm. The odds facing them now seemed impossible.[2]

Everett Mitchell's father, George, had been born on a farm north of Portland, Maine, of Scotch-Irish parents who were devout Quakers. Early in the 1880s when he was twenty-one, George Mitchell did what many young people in New England were doing at that time. He started west to establish himself in the country west of the Great Lakes.

He traveled the lake route and ended up in Chicago, where he soon found a job in the shops of the Michigan Central Railroad, whose main line connected Chicago and Detroit. It was not long before he was riding on the trains handling various jobs. In a short time he became an engine fireman and then an engineer, the most important job on the tracks except for conductor.

George Mitchell would pull his train out of Chicago early in the morning, stop at each northern Indiana and southwestern Michigan town along the Michigan Central route and by evening arrive at the railroad's division point in Niles, Michigan. He would overnight in Niles and bring his train back to Chicago the following day. At Niles he went to a boarding house not far from the railroad yards where the food was especially good. It was here that he met the young and vivacious Lucilla Bacon. She was serving the tables.

Lucilla had been born and reared on a farm in Canada near Winnipeg by devout Protestant parents. An older sister had married an American and come to live in Niles, where she operated a boarding house for railroad men. Seventeen-year-old Lucilla was living with her sister at the time she met George Mitchell, a quiet man with a ready smile.

George and Lucilla recognized, almost at first sight, that there was something special about each other. George began looking forward to the days his train would bring him back to Niles, and Lucilla was soon marking the calendar for the times he would be coming to the boarding house. Within months after their meeting they married and established a home in Chicago. Their first child was born the next year. Soon there were three happy little girls and two very pleased parents in the house.

Then in the early months of 1894, a disaster not of their own making overtook the Mitchell family. Most of the railroad men on the Michigan Central lived in Michigan, where several years before the Michigan Central workers had formed a union, the Knights of Labor, to seek better wages and working conditions.

George Mitchell told Dr. Glenn that he had refused from the first to join Knights of Labor. His Quaker parents, he said, had taught him that differences between either individuals or organizations should be settled through discussion and deliberation rather than by force. Too, although he worked for the Michigan Central Railroad, he lived in Illinois and did not want to be involved in the labor ferment in Michigan.

The climax came after Christmas in 1893. The Knights of Labor set a date on which they would attempt to shut down the railroad unless the owners met their demands. As the day for closing the railroad approached, the owners remained adamant. The Knights of Labor responded by telling workers like George Mitchell that if they attempted to go to their jobs on the day set for closing the railroad, they would do so at their own risk.

A Quaker and a man of peace, George Mitchell was torn. He felt he should report for his job as he had contracted to do, but he abhorred violence. Lucilla took the practical view. George could not settle this fight, but he could be hurt or even killed.

When the day came for the shutdown, George Mitchell stayed at home.

The Knights of Labor were able to shut down the Michigan Central Railroad, but the controversy exploded into the great Pullman Strike, the first United States transportation strike with nationwide impact.[3] In the violence, centered in Chicago right where George Mitchell might have been had he elected to become involved, lives were lost. President Grover Cleveland called out federal troops to avert further bloodshed and to prevent a nationwide paralysis. The owners of all railroads operating out of Chicago as well as many others joined in a pact of drastic measures in an effort to rub out what they regarded as rebellion on the part of their workers.

The most vicious of these steps was to blacklist all employees of the Michigan Central and the other strikebound railroads who did not make an effort to cross the picket lines to get to their jobs. This meant, to all intents and purposes, all the workers. These men were not only denied the opportunity to return to their former jobs, but they would also never be hired again by any of the blacklisting railroads. In effect, the blacklist instantly wiped out the chance for these men ever again to work for a railroad in the United States.

With no chance of returning to work on any railroad and with the generally widespread unemployment everywhere created by the 1893 recession, the Mitchell family was facing a desperate situation. Contributing to the severity of the crisis was the fact that neither George nor Lucilla had parents or other relatives close enough to help.[4]

The only other skill George Mitchell had was his knowledge of farming. Before coming to Chicago from Maine, he had all but operated the family farm for several years. So he rented the small truck farm on the Moreland Prairie, spent his meager savings to buy a team of horses and farming equipment and moved his family into a "hired man's house" that was badly in need of repair.

George and Lucilla had kept their family together with tremendous effort, but what Dr. Glenn wondered now was how much longer they could continue. He knew that most years during the winter, before there were vegetables to sell, the family food supply fell very low. There was not enough food on the family table to meet the requirements for growing children, and the parents just managed to endure. Now there would be another mouth to feed.

As Dr. Glenn had predicted, Lucilla's labor did continue for several hours. After midnight, he and George were aware that a storm was developing in the west. Within an hour it was evident that the first violent thunderstorm of the early spring season was at hand.

At almost exactly 2 a.m., and to the accompaniment of lightning flashes so continuous that the prairie was lighter than day and a mighty thunder that shook the house, Lucilla's baby was born. Her new baby, his mother always recalled, was a highly vocal child from the beginning, an excellent qualification for the successful career he was to begin a quarter of a century later.

The storm had moved off to the east and the morning sun was shining before a weary Dr. Glenn had the mother and baby in clean beds and resting comfortably. He would be back in the evening or early the next day to see that all was going well. Also, he

George Henry Mitchell, Everett's Quaker father, has remained a dominant influence in his son's life to this day.

would have the county records to fill out.

As he climbed into his buggy, he reminded the father that he would need the name as soon as one had been selected. Yes, attention had been given to the name in the event the baby was a boy, George Mitchell reported. The newcomer on the Moreland Prairie would be given the name Everett George Mitchell.

### FOOTNOTES

(1) What was the Cook County Moreland Prairie in Everett Mitchell's youth is now the Austin neighborhood of Chicago's west side. The farming area was urbanized after World War I when Chicago took over the Moreland acres, but the city's permanent western boundary was set when the village of Oak Park immediately to the west voted down a proposal to come into the city.

(2) This report on Dr. Glenn's thoughts is based on an interview given by the physician at his Oak Park office in 1951.

(3) The Pullman Strike of 1894 took twenty-six lives and resulted in sixty-eight injuries. It was also the most costly transportation strike in American history in terms of property damage. Entire freight trains were burned in Chicago rail yards. The strike was the first in which U.S. courts intervened in the public interest and issued orders and injunctions.

(4) There were no federal government assistance programs in the 1890s or for many years after. The welfare, food stamps, children's aid and unemployment relief came into being in this century, just before World War II and after. Before 1935 it was common practice when a parent or parents were lost in illness or accident to put the children with neighbors or relatives, if any were willing to take them, or to send them to an orphanage until they were old enough to fend for themselves.

# Chapter 5
# The Bank Was In The Sugar Bowl

```
┌──────────EVENTS THAT LED TO RADIO──────────┐
│                                             │
│   In 1900 when Everett Mitchell was two years old,  │
│ R.A. Fessenden, who earlier had worked with Thomas  │
│ Edison, was given a research contract by the U.S.   │
│ Weather Bureau to see if the new wireless could be  │
│ used to deliver weather information quickly. Fessen- │
│ den, already convinced that wireless could be har-  │
│ nessed to transmit the human voice, advanced a new  │
│ theory that wireless waves need not be in bursts as in │
│ the Marconi system. Wireless waves should be con-   │
│ tinuous, Fessenden reasoned, so that the voice could │
│ be superimposed on them. His theory became the      │
│ foundation of radio.                                │
│   When Everett was three in 1901, Marconi made yet  │
│ another important contribution. His wireless flashed a │
│ message entirely across the Atlantic. Two years later │
│ President Theodore Roosevelt and King Edward VII    │
│ of England exchanged greetings over the ocean via   │
│ Marconi's wireless.                                 │
└─────────────────────────────────────────────┘
```

In his childhood, Everett did not know there were such things as banks or checks. His mother handled all of the family's money, and her "bank" was the sugar bowl, backed up by a shoebox she kept under her bed. The shoebox figured in transactions only occasionally, but Lucilla went to the sugar bowl, which occupied an almost mystical place in the corner of the second shelf in the kitchen cupboard, nearly every time a purchase was made.

The family's total income flowed through the sugar bowl in nickels, dimes, quarters and occasional dollars. When George Mitchell took vegetables to the Chicago market, he was paid at once and in cash. When weather permitted and he could work at the Moreland lime quarry during the winter, he was paid in cash. He brought all of the money home to Lucilla. Together they planned every purchase.

The income problems that worried George and Lucilla were inherent in the vegetable farming business. The vegetable business was seasonal: there was never anything to sell before the last of May and again nothing to sell after the middle of November. Further, there was no way of knowing in advance what prices the vegetables would bring. On rare occasions when there was a general shortage, prices could be good. But most often, there would be a surplus. Then the money received would seem a very small return for the hard work George Mitchell and his children had done.

Lucilla's job was the most difficult of all. She knew that every posssible cent must be put away during the summer and fall so there would be money for food during the winter and spring. For those months, there would be little or no income.

Week by week, especially after the New Year, Lucilla would have to take sugar bowl money to buy necessities. Everything had to be paid for in cash. The stores extended no credit.

When the money was gone from the sugar bowl, food purchases stopped completely. Then all the family had to eat was what Lucilla had canned and stored from the garden the summer before, along with what potatoes, flour and sugar she had on hand.

At these extreme times potatoes and soup were the mainstays: potatoes because they were cheap and soup because the main ingredient was water from the family well. Lucilla had to give up any thought of serving balanced meals and concentrate on preparing the minimum amount of food she thought would get her children through to the next meal. The test was to keep the smaller children from crying with hunger. The older children understood and did not complain. By the time he was six, Everett was one of the "older" children; though he might be constantly hungry for days at a time he learned to say nothing.

The Mitchell family's home during these years on the Moreland Prairie was a four-room farmhouse. The rented house faced south on a dirt road which was dusty in summer and muddy in winter. It had not been lived in for several years and needed repair, especially the roof. George Mitchell, handy with tools, did what he could to make the house comfortable without spending money. The four rooms were all on the first floor, but above

42

them, under the exposed roof, was a floored storage area. There was a narrow stairway from the first floor to this attic. The children, except when they were babies, slept upstairs.

The rooms were large, consisting of a kitchen, a dining room, a parlor and a bedroom used by Lucilla and George and the babies. In the kitchen was the cookstove, one of the two sources of winter heat, and a large table on which food was prepared. In the dining room was a large dining table and the heating stove, the other source of heat in the winter. There was also a piano, a rare piece of furniture in a farmhouse in the 1890s.

The parlor or "front room" had the family's best furnishings and was rarely used except at Christmas and when there were special guests. In the parents' bedroom was a bed, a baby bed, a bureau for storing bedding and a washstand with a white pitcher and matching wash bowl.

Like most midwest farmhouses of the time, the Mitchell house had no electricity, no gas, no running water and no bathroom. The only source of water for all household use was the well. Light came from kerosene lamps that could easily lose half their lighting power from dirty chimneys. Heat for cooking, heating water and keeping the house warm came from wood or coal. There was no washing machine or sewing machine and the windows and doors did not have screens.

An outdoor toilet was located in the very back of the yard. It could be hot and sticky in summer and bitterly cold in winter. Bathing was done on Saturday before bedtime in the kitchen, in a wooden tub wide enough so that the children, at least, could sit down while bathing. Because it was time-consuming and difficult to heat water, the entire family used the same bathwater. The smallest child bathed first and the parents bathed last. To keep the water warm, very hot water from the teakettle would be added from time to time.

The summer after Everett's second birthday, in 1900, he moved out of the baby bed in Lucilla's bedroom downstairs and began sleeping in the attic with his four sisters. He was getting too big for the little bed and besides, it would soon be needed, for his mother was expecting another baby.

The underside of the attic roof was in full view from the children's beds. It was in such disrepair that during a rainstorm, buckets and pans had to be set under it to catch water. In places the cracks between the shingles were so big the children could see the stars. At times the heat in summer and the cold in winter were vicious. These problems were fought in different ways.

There was only one window in the attic. It faced south, an advantage because the summer breezes usually came from the south. There was no screen, but in summer Lucilla would place mosquito netting over the window to keep out the insects. In winter the window would be closed and covered with heavy paper to shut out the cold.

There were many winter nights when the temperature was zero or below. On these nights, bricks were heated to put at the feet of each child. The bricks would stay warm until nearly morning, a source of comfort, but the children's legs would cramp at times from keeping them in the same position near the bricks for so long.

On cold mornings the moment that required the most fortitude came when Lucilla called the children to get up. Laying back the warm covers and braving the cold in a dash for the warm downstairs was not something to look forward to. The children took turns so they would not get in each other's way in their race down the stairs. One by one they would rush down to dress near the kitchen stove or the heating stove in the dining room. The choicest spot was the place between the dining room stove and the warm wall behind it.

Everett and his sisters slept on mattresses filled with either straw or hay, which the family got from a farm neighbor. George Mitchell would get fresh bedding straw at least twice and sometimes three times each year.

Besides planning the family's menus, buying supplies, canning and drying produce all summer long and handling the family finances, Lucilla also made everyone's clothing. Everett Mitchell recalls: "My mother made all of my clothes. Of course, we specialized in hand-me-downs as did most families where there were several children. She even made my father's clothing, and, naturally, her own, besides the clothes for my sisters. The only items bought at the store were stockings and shoes.

"During our years on the truck farm she had no sewing machine and did it all by hand. She would also knit our sweaters and caps. If she could, she would put puffy tassels on the caps, but she couldn't always make the tassels because yarn was very expensive to buy.

"She was always cheerful about her work and rarely complained, though when sewing with black thread on black cloth she often said, 'This kind of work will put my eyes out.' "

44

Each of the children had important chores assigned by Lucilla with great care. If anyone was ill or absent, Lucilla reassigned the missing child's chores immediately. Stoves could not go without fuel and chickens could not go without feed and water for even a single day.

Doing chores was work, and it was sometimes tiring and unpleasant. But it could also be a special kind of fun. Lucilla gave the children jobs that were especially suited to them. They kept the same chores over long periods and became expert at their tasks, and the parents took every opportunity to praise them.

Edith and Edna were Lucilla's kitchen crew for food preparation. By the time they were six and eight, they were able to prepare complete meals. But there were several important duties in the kitchen in which they took no part. Neither washed the dishes nor cleaned the kitchen floor, which Lucilla insisted be washed three times a week. Despite her handicap, Eva handled these difficult assignments. She scrubbed the kitchen floor by hand from a sitting position, using her strong arms to move about the floor. She also dusted the furniture in the entire house, with some help from Edith.

In the evening, after supper was over, Eva would use a high stool at the kitchen table to wash and dry the entire day's dishes. This was necessary because the water in the hot water reservoir in the stove would not be hot enough for doing dishes until late in the day.

After his fourth birthday, Everett was given many chores of his own. By the time he was five, he was given the chores that required outdoor work. Most important were taking care of the chickens and the family cow, bringing fuel into the house, carrying out the ashes, carrying out the garbage and providing water for household needs.

The ashes had to be removed from the kitchen stove regularly and from the heating stove every day it was in use. There was a fuel saving phase to this job. Everett put the ashes through a coarse sieve to save any unburned pieces of wood or coal. The family's coal supply had to be transported by wheelbarrow from the Carlson Feed and Supply Store a mile away. Two scoops of coal, which would fill the wheelbarrow, cost ten cents.

By far the most difficult and time-consuming of Everett's chores was bringing water into the house. This had to be done not only every day the year round but often several times a day. Each evening Everett would bring in enough water to fill the heating tank on the stove, the teakettle and the pitchers that held the drinking water. On wash days and bath nights additional water had to be carried in.

The family's source of water was an open well about three feet across at the top, the type of well used in Biblical times and commonly in use in this country until the Civil War period. The well was twenty-five feet deep, and it was about fifteen feet down to the water level. Instead of a pump, there was a ground-level platform on which rested a wood casing. Mounted on this casing was a large wheel with a flange on its rim to retain the well rope. The water bucket was fastened to this rope, which passed over the flanged wheel in a pulley-type arrangement, making it easier to pull the heavy bucket up out of the well.

Drawing water was a time-consuming and difficult task, but Everett became as dependable at it as an adult. There were days when the boy had to pull twenty or thirty buckets of water from the well, a major undertaking for the arms of a six-year-old. Occasionally, he would lose his grip on the rope while pulling up the bucket, and bucket and rope would in an instant be down in the well. His father would then have to use a special hook on a string to bring rope and bucket back to the well casing, a delicate task, especially in winter. Everett seldom did things that brought displeasure from his father, but letting the water bucket rope fall into the well was one of them.

As in all families, there were at times confrontations, bitter words and tears. It was Lucilla who dealt with such matters. One recurring difficulty among the children concerned Ethel's chores.

Ethel, the second oldest girl, was a delicate, beautiful child with an exceptional singing voice. There was no doubt among the children that a special relationship existed between Ethel and her father. Lucilla understood this and must have approved.

But it was not easy for the other children to understand and accept what they regarded as preferential treatment sometimes given to Ethel by their parents. Especially in times of stress, her sisters and brothers would believe that Ethel was taking advantage of her special status.

The feeling of unfairness about Ethel's chores stemmed from two earlier parental decisions. One was especially evident when school was out in the spring. The day after school ended, all the children except Ethel were given the extra chore of working in the vegetable fields. While they worked in the hot sun weeding, Ethel stayed in the house to help her mother.

46

The second decision was an example of George and Lucilla's aspirations for their children and their ability, even in hard times, to look toward the future, although it was hard for the children to see it in that light then. Before the phonograph, radio or television existed, music in the home was provided by members of the family. It was an important part of family life. George and Lucilla had sacrificed during the railroading years to buy a piano. All the children, as they grew older, sang well, and the piano corner became a favorite place.

By the time Ethel started to school it became obvious that she had an unusually fine voice. Despite the family's always critical finances, George and Lucilla decided to go to the sugar bowl for money to give their daughter voice lessons. Ethel could lead the family singing and when she was older she might get to sing solos in the church choir. So when Ethel was seven, Elmer F. Bubb was engaged to teach her to sing and play the piano. The teacher walked the two miles across the prairie from his home in Chicago.

Lucilla made it plain that Ethel must practice regularly and exactly as her teacher directed. She announced to all the children that both the lesson time and the practice periods would count as part of Ethel's chores.

Lucilla undoubtedly knew there would be unhappiness among her children over the decision, but it was plain from the first that it was not subject to appeal. When her sisters complained too vigorously that Ethel was not carrying her share of the workload, Lucilla would descend upon them and say, "Ethel is your father's gentle child." With that, everyone accepted that the final word had been spoken.

Though Everett already had chores of his own, shortly before he was four he volunteered to share in another because of his affection for his oldest sister, Eva. It seemed unfair to him to leave Eva alone in the kitchen after supper to do the entire day's dishes. Gradually, he began pulling up a chair to the dishwashing table, at first just to keep her company. Soon he was picking up the dish towel and helping by drying the silverware.

The dish-drying chore led to the discovery that Everett was developing a singing voice with a remarkably deep tone. Eva had a good alto voice herself, and she made the time pass more rapidly by singing hymns and teaching them to her little brother.

"The first song she taught me was 'Let Jesus Come Into Your Heart,' and how she could sing that hymn," her student recalls.

By the time he was six, Everett had learned a number of

hymns, including "Tell Mother I'll Be There," "Must Jesus Bear This Cross Alone?" and "What a Friend We Have in Jesus." He learned other songs, too, such as the popular "I've Been Working on the Railroad" and the inspirational "When Day is Done," which was always his father's favorite. Neither he nor any of his family could know that the songs he learned before he was old enough to go to school would be the first step toward a career in radio two decades later.

Everett George Mitchell taken from his eighth grade graduation picture when he was twelve years old. He had begun his career with Evangelist Billy Sunday by this time.

# Chapter 6
# "One Boy — Ten Dollars"

---

**EVENTS THAT LED TO RADIO**

Twenty-nine-year-old Dr. Lee De Forest, a Yale graduate whose inventions would open the way to today's radio, moved to Chicago to continue his experiments in wireless communications.

In 1904 when Everett Mitchell was six, John Ambrose Fleming, stimulated by an earlier talk with Thomas Edison, invented a glass bulb up a wireless signal, enabling broadcasting to be done over greater distances.

Within months De Forest worked out a major modification of the Fleming tube detector which made it not only several times more sensitive but also gave it much greater capacity to amplify the signals. This De Forest invention ultimately opened the way to the production of a home radio receiver.

---

When Everett Mitchell was growing up, the Moreland Prairie still looked in places as it did when the buffalo grazed there. Native prairie grasses grew in lush profusion, standing taller than the boy. During the summers when he was three and four, Everett often went with his father to these stands of open prairie.

George Mitchell's truck farm did not provide land for pasture for the team of horses and the family cow. These animals could graze in the unfenced prairie during warm weather, but in winter they had to have hay. Hay could be bought at the Carlson Feed Store in Chicago, but that drew upon the all too scarce cash needed to feed the family. To avoid this expense, George Mitchell, with Everett tagging along, would go during the late summer and fall to the prairie and cut hay with a cradle scythe, an American improvement on the ancient sycthe used in Biblical times.

When Everett was five, one of the Mitchell's farm neighbors bought an early version of the mowing machine. Pulled by two horses, the mower could cut more hay in five minutes than George Mitchell could cut in an hour with his cradle. George and Lucilla regarded the new machine as one of the wonders of the age in which they were living. After the mowing machine was available, George paid the neighbor to cut his hay and hung up his cradle scythe for good.[1]

At about the same time, Everett was also making his first trips to the family garden with his mother and sisters. George and Lucilla planted a large garden near the house where they raised vegetables which were not sent to market, like potatoes and beans. From this garden, and from the regular vegetable fields, Lucilla would can, dry and store food to get the family through the long, spare winters. The younger children and even, at times, Ethel, would help tend the family garden.

A major cause of George Mitchell's financial difficulties was that the family lacked one of the assets needed to farm successfully in the pre-World War I era—children old enough to do a major part of the farm work. The reason farm families in that era were generally large was that only large families had the dependable labor force necessary to plant and harvest the crops and tend the livestock.

The two oldest Mitchell girls were unable to help with the field crops. Eva, the oldest, could not walk and Ethel, the next, was deemed too small and frail. Lucilla had all she could do to keep the house, prepare the meals, tend the cow, chickens and pigs, make the family's clothes, work in the family garden and preserve food so there would be something to eat in the winter. By working from dawn until dusk George Mitchell could get the land plowed, the seed bed prepared, and the vegetables planted. With the team, he could plow out the weeds between the rows. But there was no way he could, by himself, pull the weeds within the rows, and unless that was done the crops could be worthless. So Edith, Edna and Everett were put to work at an early age weeding the truck farm crops and even helping with the harvesting.

By the time he was three, Everett was going to the fields with his sisters. He liked being outdoors and even at three he could do a little weeding. By the next summer, he was able to do more, especially the onions and tomatoes, which were easy to distinguish from the weeds. By the time he was five he could weed the lettuce, beets, radishes and carrots, more difficult to tell from some of the weeds. When he was six he could weed any of the garden crops dependably.

"The weeding was real work," Everett recalls. "The rows would look like they stretched out of sight when you started at one end. But I did enjoy being outdoors, and I learned a lot about the soil and the weather that would help me later.

"The best moments came when mother brought the morning and afternoon snacks to the field. We'd have a little rest and some interesting conversation at snack times."

The three children also had an important role preparing the vegetables for market. All except the lettuce and tomatoes were pulled from the ground, sorted for uniformity and tied in bunches of one dozen. George Mitchell did the pulling, which took more strength than the children could muster. Everett began tying when he was five and took his full turn at the work when he was six.

The highlight of the week came on Saturday evening, when everyone but Eva and baby Ellsworth made the trip to market. Preparations and the actual trip required most of the family's attention on Saturday afternoon.

The evening meal would be served early so the family could get started on the mile-and-a-quarter trip to Schultz's Grocery and Bray's Dry Goods Stores. Because the Mitchells had no buggy or other personal transportation, the trip was made on foot except in the winter when the snow was deep enough to support a sled.

Going to the store was much more than just a trip to buy supplies; it was the social highlight of the week. The neighbors would be there with the latest news of births, deaths, triumphs and tragedies of the Moreland and Austin communities.

For Everett and his sisters it was an exciting time when they could see such strange sights as mountains of food. The prepackaging that is universal in the supermarkets of today was still far in the future, and going up and down the aisles the children would see open barrels of coffee, sugar, flour, crackers and other foods.[2] Eggs, when available, were kept in bins. Butter was scooped out of a tub, weighed and wrapped in just the amount the customer ordered. A huge block of cheese stood on the counter and the clerk would slice off the amount wanted.

After spending an hour or more in the grocery, Lucilla and the children would go two doors west to the dry goods store. George usually stayed at Schultz's to talk to the other men who gathered there. In winter, they sat around the pot-bellied stove with the mica door, through which they could see the fire burning merrily inside.

The dry goods store was operated by a young couple, C. D. Bray and his wife. It was here that Lucilla bought the cloth, thread and sewing supplies she needed to make the family's clothes. Besides bolt after bolt of yard goods of many kinds and colors, Bray's had a limited stock of ready-made clothing, stockings, shoes and other merchandise. When the children had to have shoes and stockings, they were bought at Bray's.

After the visit to Bray's Lucilla and George would gather the children together and start for home, everyone carrying, according to his or her size, some of the purchases. If the Mitchells had bought flour or potatoes, Mr. Shultz would deliver them in the grocery wagon on Monday. With eight people coming to the table, the Mitchells bought their flour by the barrel and their potatoes in hundred-pound sacks.[3]

During the Moreland years the Mitchells did not attend church. Because the family did not have a buggy, it was impossible for Eva to make any kind of trip and it was difficult to carry a baby. Instead, on Sundays the daily Bible reading and prayer service was expanded into a family worship held just after the noon meal. The service would begin with a hymn and a prayer. Then George Mitchell would read from the Bible, explaining to the children the meaning of what he had read. In the mode of a Quaker service, a general family discussion of the Bible reading would follow, with the fullest attention given to the children's questions. During this commentary, George Mitchell would explain to his children the tenets of his Quaker faith. Violence only causes more violence, he would caution. People must never hurt one another. Disappointments do lead to God's appointments, he would counsel again and again, especially when there were problems that had to be faced. Finally, there was a family prayer, often given by one of the children, and the service would close with another hymn.

In the evening, if George was not too tired, there would be family singing of hymns and songs of inspiration. As Ethel's lessons with Mr. Bubb progressed, she would often take over some of the piano playing from Lucilla. Eva's student, Everett, would do an occasional solo stanza.

Although for the young children life on the Moreland Prairie was generally a happy time, in spite of the occasional sparse

Members of the alumni of H. H. Nash School were known for
their dramatic and musical presentations in the neighborhood.
The producer Albert Huthens is shown at the left. Everett
Mitchell is on his knees in the front row in the presentation,
"The Mouth of the Cannon".

table, for the parents the future appeared bleaker and bleaker. The summer of 1904 was especially grim. Unfavorable weather had made truck farming less profitable than usual. And, what was worse, George Mitchell was not well. At times he could stay in the fields only half a day. Lucilla grew increasingly concerned. She saw that her husband's formerly robust health was gradually being eroded by the oppressive workload. The need for more food and clothing steadily mounted as the children grew older, and she did not know how she could provide for them if George's health were to fail. Although they managed to keep the full reality of the situation from the children, George and Lucilla knew they would have to be helped if the family was to remain intact.

Then came amazing news. The Mitchells heard it on a Saturday evening in August during a visit to the Schultz store.

George Mitchell's career as a vegetable farmer was soon to end. The North Western Railway, one of the major rail lines in the midwest, had agreed to make an exception to the pact it had made never to hire a man who had been blacklisted and give George Mitchell a job. He would have to start as a fireman, but he would have the chance to work back up to an engineer's job just like any other employee.

The key figure in bringing about this good fortune was Ward Committeeman Irwin Ross Hazen, an influential Republican leader on Chicago's west side whose district included the Austin community where the North Western's huge switch yards were located. A lawyer and a sympathetic and understanding man who would go on to to become a distinguished judge in Chicago, Hazen knew that Quaker George Mitchell had had nothing to do with inciting the labor troubles on the Michigan Central. At every opportunity he urged the North Western officials to take Mitchell's name from the blacklist and give him a chance to support his family by railroading.

Finally, before the heavy fall work began on the railroad in 1904, the North Western officials granted Hazen's appeal and offered George Mitchell a job as soon as he could close out his farming operation.

The job offer was regarded by Lucilla as an act of God, a direct answer to prayer. Even though her family would still have to face financial problems, she could keep them together and the new job would surely be better for her husband's health. It was a time for rejoicing and a prayer of thanks.

The family's precarious circumstances during the Moreland

Prairie years were forcefully and unexpectedly brought home to Everett Mitchell nearly fifty years later. Unable to get a passport for his first trip overseas in 1951, he returned to the Moreland-Austin community to see if the office records of Dr. Fred L. Glenn might still be intact. To his amazement he found Dr. Glenn, at ninety-five, still practicing in Oak Park. He went to the doctor's office and explained his need to verify the his birthdate.

The meeting was a joyous one for both men.[4]

"Well, son," said the doctor, "I've kept track of you ever since I first owned a radio at least twenty-five years ago. I've heard and enjoyed your broadcasts and followed your progress."

Then, after they had talked for a while about old times and old acquaintances, Dr. Glenn asked, "What year were you supposed to have been born, Everett?"

Mitchell said he had always understood his birth date to be March 15, 1898.

With that, the doctor got up from his desk, went to his book shelves and with some difficulty took down from the top tier a leatherbound ledger, obviously much used at some previous time. He brought it back to his desk and turned to the page marked at the top in large figures "1898." Then, with Mitchell looking over his shoulder, he began reviewing the reports of his office and house calls day by day in that year, more than a half century ago. For each entry there was noted alongside the amount of his fee.

There were many entries during the winter of 1898 for the Mitchell family. After each entry was noted the fee, which ranged from fifty cents to two dollars, and after each notation was written the word "paid."

"Lots of illnesses in your family that year, your father and some of the girls, and your mother expecting a baby," the elderly physician observed.

The two men looked through the January columns and then those for February. "Here it is, Everett, on March 15, 'One boy, ten dollars.' "

Everett leaned over to look. Then something unusual struck him. "But Dr. Glenn, I notice that after each entry for our family there is always written 'paid', but after 'one boy, ten dollars' there is no such notation. Is it possible the bill was never paid?" Everett asked.

"No, it was never paid, Everett, and there is a story behind that which I've never told to anyone," Dr. Glenn answered. "But considering all the time that has passed, I think I might as well

Everett Mitchell and his sister, Edith, are shown here in a photograph taken in 1904. Everett was six years old and Edith was eight.

explain it to you.

"I knew times had been hard for your family ever since they came to the Moreland Prairie, and this particular year had been very bad, with your father ill and sometimes unable to work.

"I thought another little one to take care of . . ." the doctor hestitated, then continued, "Yes, I thought she would have a hard time feeding you, things had been so bad. So about a month after you were born, I went over and asked if she would consider allowing me to adopt you. She knew that I had lost a son a few weeks before.

"I'll never forget her reaction. She stood up straight and looked me right in the eye and said, 'No, doctor, some way, somehow, God has always provided for the rest of the children and I don't think He is going to slight this one. I think He will help us so we can take care of him.'

"It was an embarrassing moment. I felt so ashamed of myself that I never sent your parents a bill," Dr. Glenn explained.

Mitchell told Dr. Glenn that while he did not think he could stand paying the ten dollars and compound interest for half a century, he would like to give the doctor a check so he could write "paid" after the March 15, 1898 entry. Later Mitchell learned from a member of the West Suburban Hospital staff that Dr. Glenn had proudly showed the check to his associates and told them in his seventy years of practice it was the largest fee he had ever received for delivering a baby.

### FOOTNOTES

(1) The cradle scythe, now seen only in museums in the United States though still used in less developed countries, consists of a frame of wood with a row of long curved teeth projecting above and parallel to a scythe. It leaves the cut hay in rows, making it easier to gather and tie into bundles. In a day a man can cradle and cut an acre or more, but the heavy hand implement is especially hard on the mower's back. Everett, who saw his father use the cradle, would later during his radio broadcasts describe mechanical mowers capable of cutting more hay in ten minutes than the most expert mower could cut with the cradle in an entire day.

(2) Cracker Barrel Era is a term coined to describe American society generally between the post-Civil War period and World War I. The term had its origin in the grocery store. The term might have been "flour barrel" or some other food sold in bulk, but crackers had a special significance. It was common practice for the grocer to take a cracker from the barrel, cut a little cheese from the block on the counter and hand it to the customer with the compliments of the store. As a result, "cracker barrel" took on the meaning of hospitality and good cheer.

(3) Until after World War II, Saturday night in town was an established tradition for farm families. This permitted farm work to go on all week without interruption. Merchants remained open until the rural families went home, some-

times after midnight during the season of heavy farm work.

(4) Dr. Glenn had changed as much as the Moreland Prairie. He was one of the first to buy an automobile to get to his patients more quickly. He was a leader in establishing the first hospital in Oak Park. When the present day West Suburban Hospital was opened, he was invited to join its staff and was still a member when Everett Mitchell visited him in June 1951. Within weeks after Mitchell's visit, Dr. Glenn was dead, victim of an automobile accident while on vacation with his wife in Indiana.

# Chapter 7
# The First Nickel

┌─────────────EVENTS THAT LED TO RADIO─────────────┐

On Christmas Eve, 1906, when Everett Mitchell was eight, R. A. Fessenden, using his specially built "alternator," for the first time used the wireless telegraph to broadcast the human voice over more than a thousand miles of ocean. From the Brant Rock station on the coast of Massachusetts, Fessenden played a violin solo and read from the Bible. Astonished wireless operators at sea called their officers to verify what was happening on the New England shore.

When Everett was eleven and again when he was fourteen, the wireless telegraph was used to save lives at sea. When the S.S. Republic passenger ship sank off the U.S. coast after a collision, most of those aboard were saved. When the Titanic went down in 1912, land-to-sea radio wireless saved hundreds.

Bringing the electronic age a step closer, AT&T bought the rights to the De Forest patents, including the magical "audion" tube, which was used to extend long distance phone service to San Francisco and the West Coast.

└──────────────────────────────────────────────────┘

All of the Mitchell children were excited about moving into Chicago from the Moreland Prairie, but the three girls attending school, Ethel, Edith and Edna, were beside themselves with joy. No longer would they be living in the country, isolated from school and community activities. Now they would be able to entertain their friends and go to parties.

Lucilla had been looking for a house even before George began working. To keep the rent low, she chose a small house at 5012 West Superior Street, two blocks west of today's Cicero Avenue, then known as 48th Street. The new home was within easy walking distance of the Chicago and North Western Railway yards. It was only two blocks from the Schultz Grocery Store and other stores where the Mitchell family regularly traded. Also, it was in walking range of the 49th Street Methodist Church, which Lucilla and the children would attend regularly.

The children would continue to go to the Henry H. Nash School at 49th and Erie Streets, just as they had while living in the country. From their new home they would walk a mile and one-quarter to school, almost as long as the mile and one-half walk from their former home. Even young Everett had been making the trip to school from the Moreland Prairie. In the fall of 1902, after he was four, he was enrolled in the kindergarten. The teacher found that he had been taught so much by his older sisters (he could read before he entered kindergarten) that he was promoted to first grade in mid-year. So when the family moved to Superior Street Everett, although only six, was in second grade and would soon be ready to begin third grade work.

Although today 5012 Superior Street is deep in Chicago's west side, in 1904 the Mitchell family saw only a slight change. There were just six houses on that section of Superior Street and then more open prairie. The street itself was a dirt road, if anything in worse condition than the lane in front of the Moreland Prairie house because the traffic was greater. Even heavy wagons would get stuck in the spring mud, and buggies raised clouds of dust during dry weather.

The new home had been built more recently and was in good repair, but structurally it was almost identical to the small house the Mitchells had left. There was no water, no electricity and no gas in the house. The well was located in about the same position in the back yard, but there was an important difference. This well was fitted with a pump. No longer would Everett have to raise water from the well in a bucket. The young Mitchells still slept in a rough-finished unheated upstairs with a single window, but it was no longer possible to see the stars through cracks in the shingles. The roof did not leak.

Although the change in the family's fortunes was an occasion for jubilation, Lucilla and George recognized the realities they were facing, which they did not stress with the children other than Eva, now old enough to understand. They regarded the new job as an act of God, an affirmation of their prayers and their faith. But they also knew that even the steady income from George's railroad job could do little more than avert the financial disaster that had been gradually closing in on the family, especially in the last two years with Everett and three girls in school. Although the new job did mean the family could remain together in slightly more comfortable circumstances, difficult times were still ahead. The family's financial strength had been so drained that it would be months before Lucilla could do more than purchase absolute necessities in food and clothing. She dreaded the coming winter.

The children would, soon enough, have to be made aware of the limitations of the new job, but for the moment the parents kept the details to themselves and joined the children in the exciting experience of beginning a new life on Superior Street.

The children's first indication that family finances were still critical came when it was necessary to buy school books. There was just not enough money to buy them at the beginning of school. Some of the more expensive books could not be purchased for weeks, until Lucilla could scrape together enough cash to buy event the most heavily used, and therefore least costly, from the Waller sisters, who operated a small book and candy store directly across the street from the school. To have to go to classes without books day after day stamped the Mitchell girls and their small brother as children of a poor family.

There was another unfortunate aspect of buying school books, one which divided all students as coming from affluent homes or from poor families. It was the practice at the Nash School during these years to furnish books without charge to families who owned their homes, while children of families who rented had to pay for their own books and supplies. This policy was widely practiced at the time and was based on the idea that property-owning families paid real estate taxes from which public schools were supported.

But the real financial pinch came when it was necessary to outfit the four children in winter clothing. Lucilla worked at her sewing table for many late nights to get her daughters and son outfitted. Among the ingenious creations she made out of scraps and hand-me-downs was a coat for Everett that could be fortified with newspapers to provide an interliner effect. The colder the weather, the more pages of newspaper the boy could wear under his coat.

A tobacco auction in Kinston, North Carolina, complete with the auctioneer's chant, was broadcast in the fall of 1935 on the National Farm and Home Hour. Presented by Everett Mitchell, the crowd filled the auction barn, the street and a lumber yard lot.

But despite Lucilla's efforts, when the weather turned cold Everett encountered his first really painful experience of deprivation, the first to leave permanent scars. While it was warm, he had been able to get by with a pair of inexpensive sandals. But with the coming of cold, damp mornings and muddy walks, his sandals were no longer adequate.

Lucilla, struggling to buy books, did not have the money to buy her son a pair of heavy winter shoes. The only solution was for him to wear hand-me-down shoes that had been worn by his sister Edith the year before. They were high-button shoes, stamping them immediately as girls' footwear. His teacher and the motherly Waller sisters at the book and candy store understood the situation, but many of the students, especially those he met on the playground from other classes, were heartless in their ridicule. Nor would some of them ever the let the boy forget his plight. He became known as the little boy with girls' shoes. Even his sisters in the higher grades were aware of the difficult time their little brother was having.

Yet another matter made 1904 a hard year for young Everett. He was still trying to cope with his first experience with the death of someone close to him, his first-grade teacher Isabel Idarius. She had helped smooth the transition from kindergarten to first grade and she had always found time to praise his work and encourage him in many ways. The previous year, when he returned to school after the Christmas vacation, his beloved Miss Idarius was not there. She had decided to attend the Wednesday matinee between Christmas and New Year at Chicago's new Iroquis Theater to see the famous Eddie Foy in the children's classic, "Mr. Bluebeard, Jr." She was among the hundreds who died in the tragic theater fire that day.[1]

As the winter passed it was clear that the problem of not having books and clothing like most of the other children was the first real challenge of the boy's short life. A turning point was at hand. The situation was either going to break the boy's spirit and force him to retreat into chronic smoldering resentment, or he would have to find some means of rising above it.

His father sensed that his small son was at a dangerous crossroads. When the family was together for Bible reading, George Mitchell would begin by telling his children several things that Everett has never forgotten, truths which became the guideposts around which he fashioned his life.

"Disappointments do lead to God's appointments if you have

the faith and courage only to wait," the father told his children.

"We must never forget that everything which is important and good has to be worked for constantly and hard. We can't expect God to do it all.

"Finally, we have the opportunity to talk directly to God about our problems, as often as we wish, and prayer helps in many ways," he would say.

Then a word of caution. "In our prayers we must go beyond always asking God to help us. We must realize that we have many blessings and give thanks for them. Just counting one's blessings brings a special kind of happiness," the Quaker father would tell his children.

There were other, private talks between Everett and his father. Soon it seemed natural for the six-year-old to take up both his problems and his blessings in his prayers. He prayed that God would make it possible for his sisters and himself to have school books and clothes like other students. He thanked God for his mother and father, his sisters, especially Eva, and his brother.

Nothing changed immediately, and at times during the winter at school matters seemed to be even worse. But the crisis was passing. Somehow the boy felt more confident, better able to counter his disappointments. He gradually developed the conviction that his prayers would be answered and that somehow things would get better.

On March 15, 1905, Everett was seven. One day at the end of April of that year, his mother asked him to stop at the Harris Drug Store to pick up a prescription for her. Druggist Harris, who had known Everett even before the family moved in from the prairie, greeted him by name as he reached for Lucilla's prescription on the back shelf.

Everett noticed that there were several other prescriptions on the shelf. He knew that the druggist, who was not a young man, would be delivering them on foot after he closed the store. It just came naturally for him to say, with nothing more in mind than being helpful, "Mr. Harris, I would be glad to deliver those other prescriptions for you on my way home."

Harris was silent for a long moment, undoubtedly wondering whether he could depend upon such a little boy to deliver something as important as a prescription. Then he reached back to the shelf behind him.

"Yes, I'd be glad to have you take this prescription to Grandma Schmidt, since her house is right on your way home. It would be good to get it to her quickly because I'm sure she needs it. You might stop in and see me after school tomorrow. Maybe you can help me with another prescription or two that ought to go as soon as possible."

On the way to Grandma Schmidt's house, which was on Superior Street just "two doors" from his own home, Everett began to wonder if Mr. Harris might pay him something, a penny or maybe two. It was an exciting thought and he told his mother what had happened. She said he must not expect pay for doing such a kindness, but she was proud that Mr. Harris would trust her seven-year-old with such an important errand.

The boy found it hard to wait for school to be over so he could go see Mr. Harris. When he got to the drug store, he told the druggist how surprised and glad Grandma Schmidt was to have her prescription early. Mr. Harris nodded, then told the boy he would like to have him stop in after school every day and deliver any prescriptions that needed to go quickly. He would pay Everett a nickel for each one he delivered.

As he spoke, the druggist reached into the till, took out a nickel and handed it to Everett, pay for taking the prescription the day before. Them he went to the shelf, looked over the several packages and selected two which he handed to Everett for quick delivery. After thanking Mr. Harris, Everett fairly ran out of the store.

On his way out the boy looked at the nickel again and again, just to be sure he had really understood Mr. Harris. Then he began to think of the many things he could buy with his first nickel. How often he had been tempted by the candy displayed at the Waller sisters' little store! Then he thought of his mother, who worked so hard and had such a difficult time paying the bills. It was late in the week and the family was without bread, since Lucilla baked bread only once a week, usually on Saturday. So after making his two deliveries, Everett went to Schultz's Grocery Store and bought a loaf of bread (at that time the large loaves cost only a nickel). Then he went home to present it to his mother and tell her about his first job.

Lucilla, who seldom allowed anyone to see her cry, gathered her son into her arms and wept. With his first nickel, her little boy had passed the candy counter to buy bread for his family.

His first job taught Everett many things, discoveries that would mean a great deal to him in later years. He learned how important it was to earn even a little money, he found that a job could be fun since it enabled him to meet new and interesting people, and he discovered the pleasure of being depended upon to do important tasks. Although Mr. Harris did not always have prescriptions for him to deliver, some days there were as many as five or six. Then he would have twenty-five or thirty cents to take home to Lucilla, who always put the coins in the sugar bowl.

The job led to a close friendship between Everett and Mr. Harris, and the next fall the druggist helped to buy his school books at the Waller sisters' store. And Lucilla did not wait for cold weather before buying her working son a pair of heavy shoes. It was never again necessary for him to wear hand-me-down shoes.

The job also put Everett into a situation that, had he not been able to resist temptation, might have been troublesome. In the window of the Harris Drug Store were the latest Wild West thrillers, colorfully-illustrated magazines that sold for a dime. In them were tales of soldiers, Indians, highwaymen, lawmen, cowboys and saloons where scantily clad women entertained. Their action-packed climaxes featured six shooters and long guns and language which young children were not supposed to know. Concerned parents feared that reading them would encourage their children, especially the boys, to emulate the western heroes' use of violence and of profanity.

Most parents ruled out the western thrillers, and the teachers at Nash School, concerned for the moral training of their students, rigidly banned them. If a student was caught with one of the magazines, it was confiscated and burned. Waiting for Mr. Harris' prescriptions gave Everett the opportunity to regularly examine the illicit literature and his job would have provided him money to buy it. But though he read the covers of the magazines, found some of the stories looked interesting and often wondered if they were true, he never bought even one Wild West magazine with his money.

As the word got around that George Mitchell's little boy was entrusted with the delivery of prescription drugs, there were other opportunities for after-school jobs. Grandma Schmidt, to whom Everett had made his first delivery, asked him to become her yard boy. He mowed her lawn in summer, cleaned her porch and walk of snow in winter, washed her windows, carried the coal and kindling for her stoves and cleaned out the ashes. He was paid ten cents a week, and Grandma Schmidt always saved hot bread for him when she baked.

In the summer of 1906, when Everett was eight years old, there was another important development. Grandma Schmidt's son lived only a few houses away on Superior Street. From his home he operated a wholesale coffee business. In a large carriage house, he maintained two teams of horses and delivery wagons. That summer the man who took care of the horses and wagons left the essential transportation job.

Schmidt was so impressed with Everett's work for his elderly mother that he offered the job to the small boy. Although some tasks, like putting the harness on the big animals, were difficult, Everett liked working with the horses. He even learned to jack up the wagon, remove the wheels and grease the axles.

This was not a boy's job but man's work, and for it Everett was paid two dollars a week, more than he earned from all his other jobs put together. Now, there were times when he brought three dollars or more a week home to his mother for her sugar bowl, an important addition to the family income. Lucilla began shifting her son's home chores to the other children so he would have more time to do his jobs well.

As the season turned from fall to winter in 1906, the boy took on still another job. He became stock boy and floor sweeper at the Carlson Feed and Supply Store. The store was located on 49th Street just south of the Nash School. Like the Harris Drug Store, the Carlson store was operated by an older owner who had known the Mitchell family when they lived on the Moreland Prairie. The family still bought coal from Carlson's.

Everett liked his new position because it provided inside work during cold weather which he could do on Saturdays or after dark. He would go from school to the drug store, deliver his prescriptions, do whatever work was needed for Grandma Schmidt and her son, then go to the Carlson store and do the sweeping. Most of the stock work was done on Saturday. The merchandise usually came in wooden boxes which Everett opened with a claw hammer. The boxes, made of white pine logged in Wisconsin and Michigan, were such good lumber that customers would buy the larger ones to use in building projects around their homes.

There was one more memorable development that winter for Everett. One afternoon on his way home from his jobs, he passed Schlager's Barber Shop on Chicago Avenue. (At that time, haircuts cost fifteen cents.) From under the front steps came a whimpering sound that no small boy could disregard. Everett searched for its source and found a little brown and white puppy that appeared to be only a few weeks old.

Barber Schlager allowed that someone must have abandoned the puppy by shoving it under the shop's steps. Everett decided to take it home and ask his father if he could keep the little dog, even though he felt fairly sure the answer would be no. He was well aware that George Mitchell had turned down all such petitions in the past, on the very good grounds that the family could hardly afford enough food for themselves and had none to spare for a pet.

That evening Everett showed the puppy to his father and asked if he might keep it for a family pet. George Mitchell did not say no immediately, as his son had feared. He realized that his son was making an important contribution to the family income and that his children had long wanted a pet. After some deliberation, he gave his approval, provided three things were clearly understood. Everett must take care of the dog and see that it was fed, the dog would be housed in the dirt-floored cellar in bad weather and would never be in the house itself, and finally, if the puppy cried in the night Everett would have to get up and take care of it.

Everett willingly agreed. He named the puppy Prince.

Prince was half grown by the time school was out in the spring, and by then boy and dog were inseparable. When school began in the fall, Prince quickly learned the new schedule and would join Everett as he came from school. Together they would deliver the prescriptions, feed the Schmidt horses and attend to any other chores of the day.

"I never understood how that little dog knew when it was three o'clock, but as I would come out the front door of the school I would invariably see my friend racing toward me across the meadow north of Chicago Avenue," Everett Mitchell recalls.

In the fall of 1908, when the family had been living in the house on Superior Street for four years, the city of Chicago brought the first gas mains to the community. At first Lucilla used the gas for just one fixture, a two-burner hot plate that she placed on the counter next to the kitchen sink. The little gas burner revolutionized her meal preparation. No longer was it necessary to start the fire in the big kitchen range to cook or to heat water. A turn of the tap and the strike of a match and there was instant heat. Lucilla thought it was a marvel. Later a gas light fixture was installed over the dining room table.

Another marvel came for Lucilla while the family was living on Superior Street, her first sewing machine. Lucilla's dressmaking

Everett Mitchell holds the microphone for Secretary of Agriculture Henry A. Wallace at the dedication of the Northern Illinois Research Laboratory in Peoria October 13, 1939. Within three years this laboratory discovered how to mass produce penicillin. The dedication was broadcast to the nation on the National Farm and Home Hour.

and tailoring chores were becoming more complex and time-consuming as her family grew, and at last she decided she must have the labor-saving device. Putting aside her lifelong aversion to buying "on time," she purchased a White treadle machine on credit, paying it off at one dollar a month. The machine increased by several times the amount of sewing she could do in one day, and she often described it, like the gas burner, as a marvel. Even in a time when almost every housewife was a good seamstress, Lucilla's accomplishments with needle and thread were outstanding. The sewing machine opened the opportunity for her to "take in" dressmaking for an extra source of income.

Everett worked for the Schmidt family for two years. Then he was offered a job grooming the Carlson Store teams and servicing the wagons. He did not think he could do both jobs, so because he was already working many hours at the Carlson store he decided to take over the care of the horses and wagons there. The Harris Drug Store moved, ending the prescription delivery job.

The spring he was eleven, Everett took over another job which did not conflict with those he already had because of the time element. He went to work for the Puertz Brothers on Lake Street, who distributed all the newspapers that circulated on Chicago's west side. Everett was a morning carrier; it was necessary for him to get up at 4 a.m. to deliver papers to one hundred customers before breakfast. He delivered the *Chicago Tribune*, which sold for two cents, and the *Chicago Examiner*, which sold for a penny. In addition, he delivered the popular German language newspaper, *The Abenpost*, and also a Polish language newspaper. He was paid $1.20 a month. On Sunday after going to Sunday school he made extra money by selling papers from a newsstand near the 49th Street Methodist Church.

One of the reasons Everett did not mind getting up early to deliver papers was that Prince could go with him. But after three years of loving companionship, Everett lost his pet. Prince was found dead, obviously by poison. The Mitchell family believed that a neighbor was responsible for destroying the dog. Everett was inconsolable for many weeks.

When he was twelve Everett began working for the William Schultz Grocery Store, where during his high school years he handled practically every job except the buying. On occasion, he even did some of that, when Schultz would send him down to the South Water Street produce market with a team and wagon to buy vegetables and poultry.

The same year, George Mitchell found an opportunity to move his large family from the small house on Superior Street a half mile away to a nine-room completely modernized house at 732 Laramie Avenue. Owned by a plumber who needed to move to another part of the city, the house had the latest appointments available—bedrooms both upstairs and downstairs, a central heating system with a furnace, water piped into the house, a bathroom, a hot water heater and both gas and electricity. In addition, it had a large back yard and an equally large side yard. The rent was $27.50 a month, more than three times the $8 a month the family was paying for the house on Superior Street. But the Mitchell children were getting far too old to sleep in a single attic room, and George and Lucilla believed they could find ways to make the new home an economic asset.

The house changed the lives of everyone in the family. Lucilla said it cut her work in half. Completely gone were Everett's chores of carrying in water, carrying out wastes, cleaning the lamp chimneys, bringing in wood for the stoves and carrying out the ashes. Even George Mitchell got another half hour of rest because he did not need to get up and start the kitchen stove.

But the development that would make the greatest change in Everett's life was much more subtle. The first evidence began to manifest itself in the month before Christmas in 1910. The twelve-year-old boy's voice began to change rapidly to an unusually deep and rich adult baritone. George and Lucilla hardly knew what to make of it. The sisters tended to be amused, all except Eva. More than anyone else, she realized the importance of the change and encouraged her brother to be proud of his new voice. She began going back over all the songs she had taught him since he first climbed up beside her in the kitchen of the house on the Moreland Prairie so he would stabilize the new voice tones.

Also impressed with the boy's new voice was his Sunday school teacher at the 49th Street Methodist Church. Mrs. Alvin McDonald recognized that her student was developing a vocal asset that could earn him wide acclaim as a soloist. Before he was thirteen in March of 1911, Mrs. McDonald had offered to pay for music lessons for Everett, and she said she would see if the leading church choir director on Chicago's west side, Miss Ida Belle Freeman, would take him as a pupil.

·The channel had been opened that would make Everett a featured boy soloist at the famous Billy Sunday revival and later serve as a passport to a career in radio broadcasting.

## FOOTNOTE

(1) The Iroquois Theater fire of December 30, 1903 still stands as the greatest theater tragedy in Chicago history. The theater was regarded as completely fire-safe. The December 30 performance was completely sold out and there were hundreds of standees. Midway through the second act some paper backstage caught fire from a defective floodlight. The asbestos curtain jammed about halfway down, allowing the flames to sweep through the theater. There were 603 deaths, 212 of them children.

# Chapter 8
# The Most Important Day

┌─────────── EVENTS THAT LED TO RADIO ───────────┐

By the time Everett Mitchell was ten years old, radio broadcasts were taking place over short distances in isolated places. Some were made from engineering schools and later led to important commercial broadcasting stations.

What is believed to be the earliest of these regular broadcasts took place at San Jose, California. In January of 1909 Charles David Herrold, a classmate of Herbert Hoover at Stanford, began voice broadcasts with a 15-watt spark transmitter of his own invention, using the code name SJN. Years later SJN figured in the founding of Station KCBS in San Francisco, today's 50,000-watt CBS feeder station for the West Coast.

By 1917 Professor Earle M. Terry and his University of Wisconsin engineering students had developed a radio telephone transmitter to send weather forecasts to farmers. In 1922 Terry's experimental station's call letters, 9XM, were changed to Station WHA in Madison, Wisconsin, which noted its sixtieth anniversary in 1979.

└─────────────────────────────────────────────────┘

Should anyone ask Everett Mitchell if there was one day in his youth that influenced the rest of his life more than any other, he would answer immediately.

"It was March 15, 1912, the day I was fourteen. Perhaps as much as a month before, my father surprised me by saying that I would soon be observing an important birthday. On that day, he

73

added, he and I were going to spend the evening together and do some things which there had been too little time for in our busy lives, have a little fun and a chance to talk."

On this special occasion, George Mitchell had continued, he and his oldest son would go all the way to State Street, heart of the great city's main business district, to have dinner at Kohlsaat's Restaurant, considered by many to be Chicago's finest dining establishments.

"So I was excited about my birthday dinner for some time, undoubtedly exactly what my father wanted," Mitchell says now.

Other than the obvious reason that Everett had reached the turning point from boyhood to manhood, George Mitchell gave no clue as to why he and Lucilla were tapping the family sugar bowl for money that would have purchased half a week's groceries to arrange for this special evening for their son. There were other considerations.

Everett's voice lessons with teacher Ida Belle Freeman had started, and his progress had been remarkable. For the first time George and Lucilla recognized that their oldest son was becoming something of a prodigy. They saw that he had the musical talent, the personality and the capacity for hard work that could lead to his becoming a well-known public performer. The "special occasion" was a step in preparing him for such possible opportunities and responsibilities.

"The day finally arrived and father, who by this time had worked his way up through the ranks and was again an engineer, brought his train in from Clinton, Iowa, in good time," Everett recalls. "I had arranged to finish my jobs early. We left shortly after 3 p.m. for the hour streetcar trip to State Street. I remember that father's fare was five cents and mine was three."

The trip in itself was an adventure for Everett, since the Mitchell family rarely ventured so far from home. Eight years ago, soon after the Moreland farm days, George had taken the children to ride the State Street cable car. Now, Everett noted that the cable car was gone, an electric streetcar having taken its place, in the city's Loop.

The visit to Kohlsaat's afforded fourteen-year-old Everett his first opportunity to see how Chicago's affluent dined. Kohlsaat's operated on several floors. The high, ornate ceilings, the brilliant electric lights, the carpeted floors and the elegantly dressed people who were dining there left permanent memories. And the food! There was so much and it was all so good. George explained

74

that Kohlsaat's was famous for its pie and bakery goods and assured his son that he could have his favorite pie for dessert.

The dinner was served leisurely in courses, with plenty of opportunity for conversation. George Mitchell had carefully thought out what he wanted to say to his talented son, who although still a boy had been doing a man's work since he was ten.

He wanted his son to be happy, happy in his personal life, in his business life and in his moral and religious life. He wanted to share with his son the convictions he had formed about the right way to live to find that kind of happiness. It was a creed he had developed and lived by over the years, in good times and bad. Through it all ran a religious thread based on his Quaker faith.

\* \* \*

When you have to make a decision, if your conscience troubles you, don't do it.

\* \* \*

Make up your own mind about what is good for you. Be very slow in allowing friends or strangers to influence your decisions.

\* \* \*

Avoid loaning money or other items of value to a friend, because you often end up losing both the loan and the friend.

\* \* \*

Treat girls the way you want other boys to treat your sisters.

\* \* \*

God's greatest gift to man is a good woman. Your mother is a good woman. A woman who does not walk in the way of the Lord and who is lax in her morals is to be avoided.

\* \* \*

Many things will tempt you. Just go slow and listen to your conscience.

\* \* \*

No matter how favorable a proposal may come to you, sleep on it before acting.

\* \* \*

George Mitchell had some other advice, as well. "You know how I feel about the use of liquor and tobacco. Tobacco can destroy your health. Drinking changes the personality, causes people to do things they would not otherwise do and makes them weaklings. I would urge you not to use tobacco or liquor until you are twenty-one. In fact, if you will refrain from using tobacco or liquor until that time, I will give you a lifetime watch, not as a bribe but because of the happiness you will have given me."

Mitchell asked his son to promise him just one thing. "Promise me that you will not do anything that will make your mother ashamed of you."

Finally, as time for dessert drew near, he offered the last words of advice from a loving father to his young son.

"If you do get into trouble, I want you to come to me and explain the problem. I will do everything that can humanly be done to help you."

The waiter came to inquire about dessert. Along with his son, George Mitchell, who all through his life had abstained from eating desserts, ordered apple pie. It was the only time Everett ever saw his father eat dessert.

The bond of devotion between father and son, already close, grew even closer as the months and years allotted for them to be together passed. Everett fashioned his life around the creed his father had taught him at Kohlsaat's. All his life he avoided tobacco in any form and he never allowed liquor to become his master, even for an hour. He did on occasion loan money to friends and, just as his father warned, at times lived to regret it. He treated the sisters of others as he would have his own sisters treated, and his mother was never ashamed.

## Chapter 9
# Rabbits, Doves and Old Bill

---

### EVENTS THAT LED TO RADIO

Everett Mitchell was eighteen in November of 1916, when De Forest broadcast election returns throughout the evening and night from his New York laboratory. On Tuesday, November 7, United States Chief Justice Charles Evans Hughes went to bed believing he had been elected President; the next morning he woke to find California returns had swung the election to Woodrow Wilson.

After the United States entered World War I in 1917, the U.S. Navy required all citizens owning radio equipment to either seal and box it or turn it over to ? the government. All patents were suspended, permitting the government to use all known radio technology and to make great strides in broadcasting techniques.

The first use of radio to influence the course of war and peace on an international scale occurred in 1918 when the historic Wilson Fourteen Points were heard all over Europe from the Navy's station NFF in New Jersey, on the same day the peace proposal was presented to the U.S. Congress. NFF was the first and only station to be equipped with the latest General Electric Fessenden-Alexanderson alternating current transmitter. The era of worldwide broadcasting had begun.

---

By the spring of 1912, after Everett was fourteen, his singing had begun to attract wide attention. The previous fall, his Sunday School teacher, Mrs. Alvin McDonald, had been able to interest Ida Belle Freeman in accepting the boy with the man's baritone voice as one of her pupils.

Miss Freeman, who was director of two church choirs on Chicago's west side, had been to Germany to study music and was considered one of the city's eminent teachers. She was reluctant to add to her pupil list, but when she learned that Mr. and Mrs. McDonald believed so strongly in the youth's future that they were willing to pay for a year's music instruction, something that was beyond his family's means, she agreed to accept Everett Mitchell as one of her students in the fall of 1911.

To accomodate her new student Miss Freeman had to lengthen her teaching day on Thursday afternoons from four o'clock to four-thirty. This had the advantage that he could do some of his jobs after school and before his lesson. Since there were no students to follow, the teacher was free to extend Everett's lesson time from ten to thirty minutes more, something she did regularly for him.

Miss Freeman was a stickler for the fundamentals. She insisted on hearing every word distinctly and properly pronounced both when Everett was singing and when he was speaking. She taught him a method of breath control using the diaphragm, which, she explained, would enable him to sing in large halls and even outdoors and be heard for great distances. In addition to the lessons, she provided him opportunities for "on the job" practice. These started with solo assignments with her church choirs, where as a boy in knickers but with a man's baritone voice he was a special attraction. Soon his services were increasingly in demand. Whenever he was given an honorarium, he always took it home to his mother.

When the year of lessons provided by the McDonalds was about to end, Miss Freeman insisted that some way be found to continue the boy's training. She met with Mrs. McDonald and Lucilla, and the three of them devised a plan. Everett would become Miss Freeman's yard boy and Lucilla would do some dressmaking for her to pay for the lessons. The McDonalds would seek more opportunities for Everett to sing in public. Alvin McDonald owned his own printing business, and he could take time to accompany the youth to singing assignments when it was not possible for George Mitchell to go. The arrangement enabled Everett to continue his study with Miss Freeman for another three years.[1]

The singing and elocution lessons also benefitted Everett's work at school, especially in speech classes and dramatics. During his upper classmen years at Austin High School, he appeared in most of the school plays. He soon became recognized because he could be heard distinctly even in the last row of seats.

Everett's increasing involvement in a musical career added a new outside interest for the Mitchell family, but still the problem of meeting the family expenses had to be faced. George Mitchell's salary increases were modest and infrequent. With four or five children in school, there was always a need for money for clothing and books; these expenses had to be met by after-school jobs for the children and Lucilla's expertise as a seamstress.

George and Lucilla had gambled that the move to the modern house at 732 Laramie Street would have financial advantages that would more than make up for the $27.50 rent they paid. The large yard at the new house was one important reason for the move; it was almost the equivalent of renting a small farm with the house. The family's flock of chickens, for both eggs and meat, could be increased from what had been possible on Superior Street. There was room for a very large garden where an important part of the family's food could be produced. Unlike the days on the Moreland Prairie when the children were small, George and Lucilla now had the manpower to produce, with ease and at home, most of the family's eggs, meat and vegetables.

In spite of the increase in the home food supply, the pattern of the Mitchell family meals was still based on economic considerations. "We had lard instead of butter so much that we got used to it," Everett recalls. "Actually, we got to like it."

On Tuesday evenings the family had a liver supper (liver cost only three cents a pound). On Fridays the main dish was baked beans flavored with a ham bone Everett brought home, free of charge, from Schultz's store. Saturday was the big day in the kitchen, because the food was prepared for both Saturday and Sunday. The Sunday noon meal usually featured chicken.

Lucilla adjusted the chore schedule so that Everett no longer had any responsibilities inside the house and could become the family's "chicken farmer" in the big yard. George Mitchell enlarged the chicken house so there was room for fifty laying hens and quarters for raising the roosters for meat.[2]

Everett's busiest time of year was in the spring during hatching time. "When a hen was unmistakenly 'broody' I would gather fifteen of the largest eggs from the nests and start the hen setting. Three weeks later her chicks would begin to hatch. If we got less than twelve chicks, we would put a band on the old hen's leg so we would know not to let her set again.

"In about a month we could tell the little pullets from the roosters. We would save the pullets for replacements in the laying flock, and the roosters would go to the fattening pen to have an important role later in one of our Sunday dinners. I always handled the slaughtering and dressing of the roosters."

Except for arranging for the garden to be plowed and laid out for planting, Everett had little to do with the production and harvest of the vegetables. His sisters, with an occasional hand from George and Lucilla, became expert vegetable gardeners, as well as expert in drying and canning the produce.

The chickens, however, were but one of Everett's livestock projects. Shortly after the move to Laramie Street, Everett asked his father to build him a dove cote. George, an artist with tools, built a cote large enough to hold fifteen pairs of pigeons.

At school, students were encouraged to keep doves or pigeons as an educational hobby, and there was an abundance of literature on how to keep the birds healthy and beautiful. Students often visited one another's cotes and exchanged or sold birds. Everett decided he would like to specialize in white doves.

When Mr. Carlson at the feed and supply store learned of his young friend's interest in white doves, he invited Everett to take his pick of the pairs in the store stock. Eventually Everett had more than a dozen pairs of the beautiful white birds.

When the florist and the undertaker in the Austin area learned that Everett had a large dove cote, they offered to buy all the white doves he wanted to sell at fifty cents each. It was a common practice at this time to mount a white dove at the center of important floral pieces, expecially those made for the funerals of children and young people.

Still another livestock enterprise also provided important funds for Lucilla's sugar bowl. Like the dove project, Everett's rabbit enterprise began as a hobby but became a money-making business. His original pair of rabbits, like the doves, came from the Carlson store, and again his father stepped in to build a battery of hutches.

When Mr. Carlson learned that Everett had access to an almost unlimited supply of food for his rabbits-vegetable trimmings, outer leaves of lettuce and carrot tops from the Schultz

M. L. Wilson (right), director of the Extension Service for the United States Department of Agriculture, as they planned future features to be broadcast on the *National Farm and Home Hour.*

market-he reported that there was a constant market at a nearby pharmaceutical research laboratory for rabbits for experimental work. He even made the contact for Everett. George built more hutches and in a short time the laboratory was sending a specially equipped horse buggy to 732 Laramie Street each month to pick up the rabbits. Everett was paid twenty-five cents each, and there were months when his sale of rabbits amounted to ten dollars or more. The Mitchell's large backyard was paying another major dividend.

The income from his rabbit project paid most of Everett's high school expenses; to cover the rest he cleaned the manual training room floors and equipment for the loan of the expensive manual training books and lumber for woodworking. To pay for his noon meal, he cleaned tables in the school lunch room and carried out the garbage.

As Everett's reputation as a vocalist grew, he began to need more and more time for singing engagements. He also began to need greater flexibility of working time so he could work longer at his music lessons or accept engagements at church programs or funerals. Gradually he phased out his work at the Carlson Feed and Supply Store to concentrate on his backyard projects and his work at the Schultz Grocery Store, which had been steadily increasing as he grew older.

The store's owner, William C. Schultz, had just started his business when the George Mitchell family moved to the Moreland Prairie. Now, in expanded quarters at Chicago Avenue and 51st Street, he had four full time clerk-salesmen and a fleet of small wagons that enabled him to deliver groceries to an area of five miles along Chicago Avenue.

Willie Schultz did not ordinarily hire small boys. But because he had known the Mitchell family for years and had seen Everett, despite his small size, handle many jobs successfully, he made an exception in this case. He started the twelve-year-old boy opening hundred-pound bags of potatoes just as they came from the South Water Street Market, removing the sprouts and rebagging them to be sold by the peck. Schultz was impressed with the boy's dependability, his capacity for hard and tedious work, and his confident "I can do it" attitude. As a result, Everett went from one assignment to another, until during his high school years he was the chief backup for every person on the staff except Schultz and the butcher, and for the butcher he killed poultry and skinned beef carcasses. (Beef was delivered to the store in half carcasses with the hide still on.)

The Schultz store was on a corner, with a single wide window across the front where the fresh vegetables were displayed. Shelves for holding and displaying merchandise ran all the way to the ceiling. Floor to ceiling ladders that operated back and forth on small steel tracks imbedded in the floor were used to restock the shelves.

Clerks secured the cans above their reach with the aid of a special pole equipped with a "grabber" at the end; with this pole they could pick single cans off even the highest shelf. To save time, the clerks often released a can in the air and caught it as it fell toward the floor. The clerks might be filling orders they had taken on their rounds of the neighborhood or they might be waiting on a customer who came in with his grocery list. In those days, self-service was unknown; customers told the clerks what they wanted and the clerks got it for them.

In the open center of the store were the bulk foods--barrels of flour, cylinders of cheese, open sacks of potatoes, beans and other staples. There were bins for coffee and sugar and buckets of butter and lard and other items sold in small amounts, according to the customer's wishes. The coffee came as whole beans and had to be ground in the coffee mill mounted on the counter. Often customers wanted to see their coffee ground to be sure it was fresh.

The entire back of the store was taken up with a huge walk-in ice box, cooled by blocks of natural Wisconsin ice. The ice was hauled by wagon directly from the railroad car where, packed in sawdust, it had been shipped from southern Wisconsin's lake region ice storage silos.[2]

The large lot behind the store was completely enclosed by a high fence. The horse and wagon barn was at the back of the lot. The poultry killing was done in the yard, and there were special garbage and manure dumps.

Of the several wagons, all but one were the small single horse type. One larger team wagon was used to bring unusually heavy loads of produce home from the South Water Street Market. The horses were gentle and well-trained, but everyone's favorite animal was an especially gentle elderly mule known as Old Bill.

Schultz's operational plan was simple but exhausting. Monday through Friday each of the four neighborhood clerk-salesmen came to the store at 7:30 in the morning, harnessed a horse, hitched the animal to a wagon and spent the time until noon calling on customers and taking orders. The daily sales routes were patterned so that by week's end the hundreds of families that depended on Schultz's store had been visited at least once and the institutional customers even more often.

In the afternoon the men would return to the store, fill the orders and place the groceries in the wagon for delivery late in the afternoon or early in the evening. The deliveries were made either by the clerks themselves or by a special driver who came in just for that purpose. Also, at least one clerk would stay in the store during the evening to wait on walk-in customers. The store had no fixed closing time but remained open as long as there were customers. Monday through Friday it might close as early as 8:30 p.m., but on Saturday nights, when most of the rural people did their shopping, an 11:30 or midnight closing was not unusual.

Everett's responsibilities soon expanded to a seven-day-a-week job. He often took the horse and buggy and made afternoon deliveries. On Monday, and usually on another day later in the week, he would drive to the South Water Street market, seven miles to the east on the Chicago River, and pick up produce. Schultz would ride down with Everett and pick out the produce, then he would take the Lake Street streetcar back, leaving his boy to supervise the loading of the wagon and handle the drive back to the store. The horses knew the way back perfectly, down to the last turn.

When time was available, especially on Tuesdays and Wednesdays, Everett would fit in a long list of jobs which constantly needed to be done. He would place canned goods on the shelves, using a small basket to carry the cans up the movable ladders to the highest spots. He would sack potatoes, remove carrot tops, or whatever else needed to be done to get the vegetables ready for sale. He operated the coffee grinder, one of his more difficult tasks, since he was so short that in order to reach the handle on the large, heavy balance wheel he had to stand on a box. He fed the horses, checked their feet for broken shoes, cleaned the horses' stalls, checked their harnesses and brought them hay and clean bedding.

The boy's entire time on Thursday and Friday evenings was often spent killing the poultry for the heavy trade on Friday and Saturday. He took the birds from the crates in which they had been purchased at the South Water Street Market and with a sharp knife severed the large blood vessel on the neck. Then he dropped the birds into a shallow barrel until they stopped jumping and became quiet. He would then dip them in hot water and remove the feathers. The heads remained intact, something the customers insisted on.

At holiday time killing turkeys could be difficult. "I had one turkey that was so powerful he kicked the quieting barrel apart," Mitchell recalls. "Another time I had a turkey that flew out of the barrel with his throat cut, over the fence at the back of the store and over three or four back yards before he collapsed."

Sunday was the day he gave special attention to the horses and wagons, which were worked constantly the other six days. Everett worked so regularly in the barn that he knew what harness needed to be repaired, when a horse's feet needed attention and when a wagon needed mending. He would make an appointment with the blacksmith for Sunday work so that all would be in readiness for Monday morning business.

There were other special jobs that could only be done conveniently on Sunday. One of them Everett detested. Especially in fall and winter, customers would order a load of horse manure for the family garden. Everett would borrow a wagon from the blacksmith (to avoid hauling manure in a vehicle used to deliver groceries) and deliver the garden fertilizer. There was another Sunday chore he disliked, as well. Since there was not yet a city garbage service on Chicago's west side, the store had to remove its own garbage. There were garbage dumps farther east in the city, but Schultz considered them too far away. Much of the Austin-Moreland area was still open prairie. So, although there were city laws against it, one of Everett's tasks when he had the borrowed wagon was to take a load of garbage out to an open area, making very sure there were no Schultz sales slips that would enable a sanitary official to trace the garbage, and dump it.

Everett's rate of pay at Schultz's was not as high as he had earned on some other jobs, but there were fringe benefits that made it more than worth while. On most weekends Willie Schultz would send him home with an armload of food that substantially reduced the drain on Lucilla's sugar bowl. Often on Friday evening unsold fish which Schultz did not want to keep in the store's big cooler over the weekend went home with Everett. On Saturday fruits and vegetables that would not keep until Monday went to the Mitchells. Daily Everett brought home one or more sacks of carrot tops and other greens for his rabbits and chickens. Most food was shipped to the store in wooden boxes, and regularly Everett would borrow the wagon and bring home a load of boxes for repair lumber and kindling for the kitchen stove.

Of the hundreds of memories from the Schultz era, none stands out more clearly for Everett than a particular Saturday night. For regular customers the store would make deliveries in the evening. Some people took advantage of this opportunity, and one woman, the wife of a prominent saloon keeper on Lake Street, did so often. She would call as late as 10 p.m. Saturday and order just one or two items. On this particular night she ordered a loaf of bread and a can of kerosene. The thankless job of driving the three miles to the saloon keeper's home on streets that were lighted poorly or not at all fell to Everett. To make the drive even more of a chore, the trip required going over the high arching overpass that took 52nd Street (now Laramie Avenue) over the big North Western Railway freight yards.

On this Saturday night Everett elected to drive the mule, Old Bill, because he had not been used earlier in the day. With the loaf of bread in the wagon and the can of kerosene at his feet, so that if it dripped it would not contaminate the part of the wagon where the groceries were carried, he urged Old Bill on at top speed. Still, by the time they had made the delivery it was after 11 p.m. Everett was not looking forward to the return trip on the overpass, which had seemed difficult for the mule to negotiate the first time. When he got to the overpass Everett stopped and rested Old Bill several times on the long, steep grade up to the top. Then, right at the peak of the bridge over the railroad, with the worst of the trip behind him, Old Bill paused. He took a few steps more, then collapsed in the total darkness. Everett could hear, but could not see, the wagon shafts and mule hit the overpass floor.

Old Bill had never done anything like this before. The boy pulled on the reins in the darkenss, trying to urge the mule to get up, but there was no response. Everett climbed down from the wagon and went to the animal's head. In the next instant he discovered that the mule was not longer breathing. Old Bill had dropped dead.

The fourteen-year-old delivery boy sat down by the mule's head, grieved because of the animal's death. But he also had to consider what he could do in the total darkness of a moonless night with a grocery wagon and a dead mule. He was still more than two miles from the store, and he had not seen a buggy or a wagon for half an hour.

Everett decided to walk to the end of the long overpass and go to the first house where there was still a light, in hopes that the

William A. Roberts of Allis-Chalmers Corporation, entertainer Fran Allison and Everett Mitchell, master of ceremonies, look over a salute to twenty-five years of broadcasting the *National Farm and Home Hour*.

owner might have a telephone. There were a few lighted houses at this hour, and at the first two the occupants refused to answer his knock. Finally, after walking a half mile farther, he found another house with a light on. Here, at last, a man came to the door. No, he told Everett, he did not have a phone, but about two blocks away there was a house that did have. He knew the family. The house might be dark, but the man would go with the boy and rouse the family so the boy could call the store.

Willie Schultz was still there, waiting and wondering what had delayed the usually dependable delivery boy. He brought a horse and another wagon to the overpass. Together he and Everett removed the harness from Old Bill, rolled the carcass over to the side, hitched on the empty wagon and returned to the store.

### FOOTNOTES

(1) Although she never sang in public until after she married, Everett's sister Ethel continued to study voice until she finished high school. Then she married and moved to Ohio, where she became a soloist in her church choir.

(2) Only the size and intensity of the Mitchell poultry program was unusual. At that time Chicago was the home of countless small family "chicken ranches." The practice of keeping a flock of chickens was common across much of the United States even after World War I, as families produced their own eggs and much of their own meat.

(3) Although production of ice mechanically had been demonstrated as one of the chief attractions at the Chicago World's Fair in 1893, until the 1930s it was still cheaper to bring in natural ice from Wisconsin. For years Everett Mitchell used a small, homemade wagon to go to the freight car, always on a siding in warm weather, to buy fifty pounds of ice for ten cents. The Mitchell's home ice box held a fifty-pound block; as it slowly melted it would fill the drip pan, and he would receive a quick and severe reprimand from his mother if he let it overflow onto the kitchen floor.

# Chapter 10
# Sing It With All Your Heart

┌─────────────EVENTS THAT LED TO RADIO─────────────┐

A decisive moment in United States broadcasting
occurred in 1918 even before the guns fell silent in Europe, when the United States Congress rejected the
Navy's proposal to permanently retain its wartime
control over radio in America. Everett Mitchell was
twenty years old.

Recognizing the potential of radio broadcasting, the
federal government insisted that U.S. radio facilities
be American owned. Station NFF, operated by the
Navy during the war, was owned by the British firm
American Marconi. In 1919 General Electric formed
the Radio Corporation of America (RCA) and made it
possible for RCA to acquire the American Marconi facilities. Seven years later RCA would organize the National Broadcasting Company (NBC).

└──────────────────────────────────────────────────┘

In a time so short it filled them both with amazement, George
and Lucilla had a concert soloist in their family. They began to
wonder what lay ahead for their oldest son, who performed before large audiences looking like a boy in his knee-length knickers
but singing with a remarkably adult baritone voice.

In this period before radio, movies or even, in most homes, telephones, church gatherings were the major social events in the
community. Moreover, they often provided the only entertainment, in the form of concerts of sacred music, that most people
were able take advantage of. In the churches on Chicago's west
side, there was a demand for Sunday afternoon and weekday evening concerts. Ida Belle Freeman arranged many performances in

these churches for her star pupil. The practice in most of the churches was to take a free-will offering and give it to the soloist; sometimes the amount Everett took home was as much as twenty-five dollars, a large sum in a time when a working man's wages were about two dollars a day.

Most churches also held yearly or twice-yearly revival meetings to bring back members who had strayed from the congregation and to add new ones. Often groups of churches in a community or city neighborhood would join together to bring in one of the "big name" revivalists. So each spring and fall the best-known evangelists in the nation would be preaching in Chicago on their city-to-city tours. Those who came to the west side churches were astounded when they heard "the little Mitchell boy" whose voice carried to the back of even the largest churches.

Two of the best-known of these evangelists, Gypsy Smith and the Rev. Ely Zollar, heard Everett sing after he had been studying with Miss Freeman for about a year. Gypsy Smith was born of gypsy parents in a tent near Wanstead, England. He became a Christian speaker and was persuaded to come the United States by Chicago evangelist Dwight L. Moody (founder of the Moody Bible Institute). When he met Everett, he had been in America for twenty-five years and was a very popular speaker. When the Rev. Zollar first heard Everett, he was approaching the end of a long career as a minister, educator and evangelist, much of it spent in Texas. He had also served as president of Texas Christian University.

Both evangelists wanted Everett to join them on their revival circuits; the Rev. Zollar especially wanted the youth to return with him to Texas and offered to assure him of a university education. But George and Lucilla did not think he was old enough to leave home.

However, they were glad to allow him to sing at revivals in the Chicago area. In the spring of 1912, when he was fourteen, Everett sang with both Smith and the Rev. Zollar when they were in the city. Both evangelists worked with the Pacific Garden Mission, located at State and Madison streets in the heart of Chicago's Loop. Everett, accompanied by either his father or Alvin McDonald, sang at the Mission with both evangelists.

Affectionately known as "God's flophouse," the Mission served the downtrodden — the drifters, the hungry, the sick, men without jobs and girls who wanted to escape the life of prostitution. It did much more than provide religious services. It was a counseling agency for those who needed guidance; it would provide meals or pay for a night's lodging in a cheap hotel for those down on their luck; it was an employment agency for those who were capable of holding a job. The Mission had gained widespread public recognition after baseball player Billy Sunday was drawn to it through a street service to begin his epic career as America's best-known evangelist.[1]

Services at the Pacific Garden Mission were held between 6 and 9 p.m. From time to time a minister and a group of musicians, both instrumentalists and singers, would leave the Mission and conduct services on State Street. These sidewalk services would attract people off the streets and bring them into the Mission where longer religious meetings would be held. Everett frequently accompanied the evangelists on these sidewalk services.

Not everyone welcomed the evangelists and their message, as Everett remembers quite vividly. One evening while he was singing "Where Is My Wandering Boy Tonight?" a woman opened a window in a third-floor apartment directly above him, shouted "I'll tell you where your wandering boy is tonight!" and poured a bucket of cold water on Everett and the other musicians.

His work with the evangelists also took Everett into the notorious Bucket of Blood saloon on North Clark Street, but only after it had been closed. The Chicago police shut down the old tavern after a series of murders had been committed there. But before it could be dismantled, the innovative Gypsy Smith rented it with the furniture still in place and held a highly successful revival. When Everett sang, he stood next to the bar, which was almost as tall as he was.

During the spring of 1912 Gypsy Smith visited with Billy Sunday and told him about the Chicago boy in knickers who sang hymns in an impressive baritone voice that could be heard in the back of even the largest churches. The boy was too young to travel far from home, Smith reported, but he could be useful in revivals in Illinois and Indiana. Billy Sunday was interested. Smith agreed to pass along the message that Billy Sunday would like to meet Everett. George and Lucilla wrote to Sunday, suggesting that Everett come to Sunday's home at Winona Lake, Indiana, for a visit and audition. The evangelist responded quickly. He suggested that Everett come "any time after the morning New York train arrives the last Thursday in June."

The whole family was excited about Everett's meeting with the famous evangelist. Sunday was then at the peak of his career,

Billy Sunday was a well known evangelist and former baseball player who had a young Everett Mitchell sing the invitational songs at his revivals.

which had begun with his conversion in 1886 and would not end until his death in 1935.

Sunday had been born in Iowa during the Civil War and had never seen his father, a Union soldier killed in battle. When he was in high school his talent at baseball became evident. Later he joined the Marshalltown, Iowa, town baseball team. When they played the Chicago White Stockings (predecessors of the Chicago Cubs) the Stockings' manager Cap Anson was so impressed he invited young Sunday to join the Chicago team. For nearly ten years Billy Sunday was the outstanding base runner in the National League. In 1886 Sunday and several White Stocking teammates were on State Street, where they heard an evangelistic group from the Pacific Garden Mission conducting a street service. Sunday was so impressed that he accepted the invitation to return with the evangelist to the Mission. He began his Christian work immediately, and by 1891 had given up baseball entirely.

By 1912 Sunday was being talked of as the greatest evangelist in American history, perhaps the greatest since Biblical times. Huge crowds came to hear the spectacular and forceful preacher whose sermons were delivered with such energy that he might pound on the pulpit, jump up on a chair or even do handsprings. His revivals drew so many people that existing church auditoriums and meeting houses could not accomodate them and it became necessary to provide other facilities. First, large tents were used, but later these gave way to the Billy Sunday tabernacles, temporary wooden buildings put in the large cities that could seat from twelve to eighteen thousand people. The tabernacles were comparable to the biggest meeting halls of today but without benefit of electronic amplification.[2]

George Mitchell wanted to take his son to Winona Lake, but the date fell on a day his train was on the road so Alvin McDonald escorted the youth instead. They took the Lake Street streetcar to the old Chicago Union Station and boarded the New York Central's Cincinnati Express for the two-hour trip. Although his father was a railroad engineer, this was Everett's first ride on a passenger train. McDonald took the youth to the dining car, where they were served a meal such as Everett had only seen the evening his father took him to Kohlsaat's to celebrate his fourteenth birthday. Lucilla had decided that Everett would wear his best knicker pants, long stockings, a white shirt and a small, light waistcoat to sing for the famous evangelist.

"Boys at this time usually changed at fourteen from short

pants and knickers to long pants," Mitchell recalls, "but we didn't have the money for long pants."

As promised, Billy Sunday's buggy and driver met the Chicago train at Warsaw to take Everett and his escort to Winona Lake. At Winona Lake there were fifty or more houses, many of them summer cottages, a large meeting hall and recreational facilities. (Winona Lake had been a Methodist church summer campground for many years.) Billy and Mrs. Sunday, universally known as "Ma" Sunday because Billy addressed her that way, had for some years lived in a modest but comfortable six-room house on the lake. Because the Sundays spent their summers at Winona Lake, the community had become a noted center for religious activities, including evangelistic training.

The driver escorted Everett and McDonald into the front room of the Sunday home. Everett saw immediately that there was a piano in the room. In a few minutes Billy Sunday himself came in; he was in shirtsleeves but wearing a vest. He greeted Everett and McDonald warmly, saying how good it was of them to come all the way from Chicago "so we could visit." After chatting for a few minutes, Sunday turned to Everett and said he had been looking forward to hearing the youth sing. He asked Everett if he would be nervous singing without the piano. Everett said he would prefer to sing that way.

Then Sunday asked if Everett had a particular hymn he would like to sing. Everett and Miss Freeman had agreed that if Billy Sunday left the choice up to Everett, he would sing "Face to Face." Billy Sunday said he would be pleased to hear that hymn, which had always been one of his favorites. Everett stood up across the room and sang all of the verses. When he finished, Billy Sunday wiped tears from his eyes.

The great evangelist's decision came quickly. He asked if Everett could come back for a week, perhaps two, later in the summer to sing at the Winona Lake summer revival services.

Billy Sunday said he particularly liked the way Everett was dressed and he wanted Everett to wear knickers whenever he was appearing in a Billy Sunday revival. Then he revealed what he had in mind even before Everett arrived: he wanted the youth to sing the important invitation songs which would help bring people up to the stage to be saved. Sunday had wanted to hear Everett sing without the piano because the invitation soloist would not be able to have any kind of accompaniment. He had to be able to change instantly from one hymn to another during the tense, emotional climax of the revival service, when there was no opportunity to coordinate the songs with an instrument.

Shortly before Everett and McDonald were ready to leave, Mrs. Sunday came home. Billy Sunday told her how impressed he was with Everett's singing, that he had invited the youth to come back and sing at Winona Lake later in the summer and that he wanted Everett to stay in the Sunday home.

Everett was immediately drawn to Mrs. Sunday. The evangelist's wife welcomed the Chicago youth and said she would be happy to have him stay with her and her husband.

"I liked Mrs. Sunday from the first," Everett recalls now. "I was immediately impressed with her sincerity and her concern for her husband's work. They were a very close couple. I am sure that he consulted her on every major decision. She was completely in charge of the revival finances."

Everett and Mrs. Sunday soon developed a warm regard for each other. When Everett returned to Winona Lake twice that summer and again in the two years following, he always stayed at the Sunday home. "Ma" Sunday always made sure she had time to spend with the youth. Everett continued to keep in touch with her until her death forty years later.

Over the next two years, Everett sang the invitation songs at fifteen Billy Sunday revivals, either at the Winona Lake meeting house or in midwest towns such as Bourbon, Indiana, or Monmouth, Illinois. The revivals took place in the spring and fall and were either four-day affairs or lasted for an entire week, starting on Sunday and continuing through the following Sunday.

Singing with Sunday's revivals was an experience unlike any the fourteen-year old Everett had had before. Just listening to the sermons of the famous evangelist was a moving and dramatic event, but from his vantage point on the stage Everett could see the audience's reactions the way Sunday did, and he could see how sensitive the evangelist was to his audience's mood.

"Billy Sunday was a psychologist. He made a great study of human beings, their actions, reactions and their way of thinking. As he was preaching, he could monitor his audience and know exactly how they were feeling and thinking", Everett says.

Sunday's sermons were delivered with such energy and vigor that the evangelist would have to take an occasional break. When working with Everett, Sunday found him so reliable and attentive that he could count on the youth to help him make these pauses without slackening the pace of the sermon or losing the interest of the audience. Everett, one of up to fifty persons who would be seated onstage, would be where Sunday could always see him, usually in the second row close left of the pulpit. During the sermon, Sunday would give the youth a signal with his hand and Everett would come to the pulpit. Sunday would mention a single word, audible only to Everett as he came forward, to tell the youth what hymn he wanted. If, for example, the word was "Mother" it meant that Sunday wanted the hymn "Tell Mother I'll Be There." Everett would thus momentarily become the song leader, with the audience frequently joining him in the singing.[3]

The finale of a Billy Sunday sermon was something to behold, Everett recalls. Like William Jennings Bryan, Sunday talked so rapidly that he baffled even veteran court reporters, yet he could be heard to the last word. As he moved into the finale, he often took off his coat and tie and sometimes his shirt as well. If the devil had figured in the sermon, and the devil usually did, Sunday would jump up on a table on the stage and challenge the devil to come up and fight in the open. He would peer down from the table, as if looking for the devil, and shout to him to come up and fight fair.

The climactic part of the service came when Sunday asked for those who wanted to be saved to come up to the stage and confess their faith publicly. Then, as the evangelist urged, pleaded, exhorted and prayed for those who were not saved to come up to him, the invitation songs were sung. Everett would choose his selections to match the mood of the sermon at that point, and he would change to another number if he felt it would be more effective. Sunday would counsel with him ahead of time on possible numbers, but he left to his youthful soloist the actual selection of the songs and the number to be used. Among the gospel hymns Everett sang regularly were "Softly and Tenderly Jesus Is Calling," "Face to Face," "Come Now, Come Now," "Rock of Ages," "Where Is My Wandering Boy Tonight?" and "Let The Lower Lights Be Burning."

Often when Everett was singing the invitation, the energetic former major league baseball star would pace up and down behind him, saying almost unconsciously but in tones loud enough so that those in the first rows could hear, "Sing it, son. Sing it with all your heart."

After each of Everett's engagements with Sunday, Mrs. Sunday would write a word of appreciation to his parents and in-

"You old Hypocrite"

Striking a familiar pose of shadow boxing with the Devil, Billy
Sunday spread the gospel for fifty years.

clude a check which would cover his expenses of attending the revival and leave a generous sum toward his school costs.

At home, as friends learned that he was singing in the revivals of the famous Billy Sunday, Everett received considerably more attention. The attendance at his concerts increased, and his audiences would expect him to include some of the revival hymns of invitation in his programs. He and Ida Belle Freeman continued to work hard on his breath control to increase the distance over which he could project his voice.

No one was as proud of Everett's being chosen to sing for Billy Sunday as his first music teacher, his oldest sister Eva. She would rehearse with him the hymns he used in the revivals, and on summer evenings when the windows were open the neighbors would be treated to duets blending Eva's alto voice with her young brother's baritone.

About this time Everett was able to crack the isolation imposed on Eva by the paralysis of her legs. At the Schultz store the Fels-Naptha soap came in long, rather narrow wooden boxes. Everett mounted one of these boxes on a set of wheels from a discarded baby carriage so that he could take his sister, who had been housebound for more than twenty-five years, to church. Being able to go to church opened up a whole new world for Eva. Everett also took her to school programs, some of his concerts and other places. When winter snow made the carriage wheels useless, Everett mounted the box on sled runners.

Eva became a member of the Forty-Ninth Street Methodist Church and rejoiced in being able to attend regularly. A few years later, members of the church's youth group, the Epworth League, raised the considerable funds needed to buy her a wheel chair to replace the little cart. Thereafter, Everett took her to church and other places in her wheel chair.

Everett's growing musical career changed his thinking about his own future. Now he knew that he would not remain at the Schultz Grocery Store indefinitely. He began making inquiries and learned that the big Charles A. Stevens department store in Chicago's Loop was paying its wagon boys considerably more than he was earning at the grocery store. He needed the extra income, too, because vandals had destroyed his rabbit hutches and dove cote and he no longer had income from these projects.[4] Everett was also attracted to this job because of the impressive green and gold Stevens delivery wagons, always manned by two boys, one to drive the team and the other to "run" the parcels to customers. So during his junior year in high school he applied at the personnel office at the Stevens store for a job as a wagon boy. He was interviewed by J. H. Stevens, one of the brothers in the company. Upon learning of his work at Schultz's store, Stevens discouraged Everett from applying for the wagon boy's job.

"The job is one without much future," Stevens told the young applicant. "You should come into our purchasing department as a stock boy where there will be a real chance for advancement. Also, your starting pay will be more than we pay wagon boys." As it turned out, the purchasing department was the one J. H. Stevens himself headed.

So in the spring of 1915, when he was a high school junior, Everett took a job in the Chicago Loop. As stock boy at Stevens, he spent his time unpacking clothing, attaching price tags and hanging the garments for display in the big store that had and still has entrances on two Loop Streets, State and Wabash.

On Saturday morning, July 24, 1915, shortly after he had left the Schultz store and started working for Stevens, Everett witnessed what still stands as Chicago's greatest tragedy in terms of loss of life. He had just gotten off the elevated train on the north side of the Chicago River, across from the South Water Street Market where he had so recently picked up produce for Schultz's store, when he found himself in the thick of the chaos following the sinking of the Eastland excursion boat. The boat, carrying twenty-five hundred Western Electric Company employees and their families bound for a company picnic at Michigan City across the lake, had moments before overturned, throwing hundreds of people into the main channel of the Chicago River and trapping hundreds more below deck.

"I saw what appeared to be four or five hundred people struggling in the water, many of them obviously unable to swim. Mothers were trying desperately to keep their small children from drowning. People on the riverbank were screaming in terror," Mitchell recalls.

"I could see the commission men of the South Water Street Market, many of whom I recognized, frantically hurling chicken crates as far out into the water as they could. People were clutching the crates and managing to stay afloat that way. How I wished I had been on the south side of the river, where I could have helped! I knew exactly where those crates were kept. But my way to the nearest bridge was already blocked by the panic-stricken crowds."

99

The tragedy, which Everett has never been able to forget, took the lives of nearly eighteen hundred people.[5]

Before the summer was over, J. H. Stevens made Everett an unusual proposition. If Everett would decide not to return to high school for his senior year, Stevens promised to personally train him to become a buyer, so that in three years or less he would be assured of a management job at a good salary. After talking to his father, Everett declined the offer. He had two reasons. First, he wanted to finish high school, something both George and Lucilla were anxious that their son do. Also, although Everett liked Stevens and was sure he could do the job projected for him, he did not want to work inside the rest of his life. He did continue as a part-time employee at Stevens until he finished high school and he kept J. H. Stevens' friendship.

The next year, in February of 1916, the first great tragedy came to the Mitchell family. George Mitchell had not been feeling well. He was often so tired on returning from his train run that he had to rest before he could eat. On this February morning he left to walk to the railroad yard as usual. It was the last time Lucilla or the children ever saw him walk unaided. Even before he took his train out of the yards, George Mitchell collapsed, the victim of a severe stroke that ended his railroading career and left his left side permanently paralyzed. After a time he became fairly comfortable but he was bedridden for the rest of his life.

There were no sick benefits for railroad engineers in 1916. George's salary simply stopped. Although the need for income was acute, the family decided that Everett must finish high school. Everett made another decision regarding the use of the family's limited income, as well. George Mitchell found his enforced idleness a heavy burden. To lighten it as much as he could, Everett bought him one of the newest Wurlitzer phonographs on monthly terms at the Stevens store. The music was a great source of pleasure for George Mitchell. His favorite recording was "The End of a Perfect Day."

Once again the Mitchell family found help forthcoming from their former alderman, now Judge Irvin Ross Hazen. After Everett graduated from high school, Judge Hazen helped him to obtain a position at the First Trust and Savings Bank in the Loop, Chicago's largest financial institution. In this emergency Everett set aside his objections to working inside and became a bank clerk at an attractive beginner's salary. This he took home to a grateful Lucilla, who issued him carfare and lunch money weekly and clothing money as needed. Everett spent his money as frugally as possible. Soon after he began working at the bank, the institution began free lunch service, and he no longer needed lunch money. Sometime there was night work at the bank, but for this employees got a twenty-five cent meal allowance. Usually, Everett spent five of the twenty-five cents, buying a large bowl of soup with crackers instead of a full meal.

The bank was almost totally a man's world, but gradually a few women were being added to the staff. After Everett had been working there for several months, the head of his department introduced him to an attractive young bookkeeper, Mildred Roddoz. From the first day Everett knew there was something special about this young woman. The quiet yet confident newcomer enjoyed the company of the outgoing young man who had sung with Billy Sunday. She had been reared in a devout German family on Chicago's north side and had strong ties to her neighborhood Lutheran Church, where she was the pianist.

In a short time Everett invited Mildred to come to his home and meet his family. This was the first time he had brought a girl home to meet George and Lucilla; both of them soon became fond of Mildred. The girl took a special interest in George Mitchell and his Quaker philosophy. Lucilla urged Everett to take forty cents a week from the sugar bowl, twenty cents to take Mildred to the Friday evening movie and twenty cents for chocolate sundaes afterward.

Despite all that could be done, George Mitchell's condition continued to worsen. As a Quaker and the grandson of a Civil War chaplain, he was saddened by World War I and America's involvement. His greatest pleasure came from having Lucilla and the children close to him and reading his favorite passages from the Bible. Although he maintained his calm judgment and faith in the rightness of God's plan, there was no question that he understood his illness was terminal. Shortly before his death he called for Everett. He seemed to have in mind the things they had discussed at Kohlsaat's restaurant when they observed Everett's fourteenth birthday.

"I've tried my best to help you work out a rewarding pattern for your life," he told his oldest son. "I had hoped to stay with you until you were a grown man, but I don't think, according to some of the symptoms I now have, that this will work out."

On another occasion when Everett was with him, apparently aware that he would not live another year to see his son become twenty-one, George Mitchell gave him his cherished Waltham railroad watch as he had promised he would do.

Everett was with his father "when he left us." There had been some conversation about the events of the day, then his father lapsed into silence. A few minutes later, George Mitchell said in a firm voice tinged with surprise, "Why Eban (George and Lucilla's first son, who died in infancy before Everett was born), I haven't seen you for a long, long time. I will be with you soon." He never spoke again.

### FOOTNOTES

(1) The Pacific Garden Mission was founded in 1881 and was only five years old when Billy Sunday's conversion occurred. It completed a century of service in 1981, having been in the same Loop location the entire time.

(2) According to Willliam G. McLoughlin, Jr., an authority on the evangelist, Billy Sunday preached to a hundred million people face to face. One million of them made a public profession of their faith. (McLoughlin, *Billy Sunday Was His Real Name*, University of Chicago Press, 1955, page 293). This was before paved roads, when trains were the principal means of travel. Only Billy Graham, with the advantage of air travel and the automobile age, has preached to more people in person.

(3) Homer Rodeheaver, Sunday's musical director for twenty years, resented the fact that Sunday always worked directly with Everett whenever he sang at a revival. Ordinarily, Rodeheaver, a well known composer and publisher of religious music, was in full charge of all musical arrangements.

(4) Although he could not prove it, Everett was sure the person responsible was a big boy who had been in his class at Nash School. The boy could never keep up with his studies and, to offset his shortcomings, turned into the school bully. Later he would murder another member of Everett's class and die in the electric chair.

(5) Everett Mitchell's life was also touched by the tragedy which took the second highest toll of human life in Chicago, the Iroquois Theatre fire of 1903, in which his first grade teacher and nearly six hundred others died.

# Chapter 11
# A Pleasant Summer Day

┌─────────────EVENTS THAT LED TO RADIO─────────────┐

By 1920 radio broadcasting was getting a foothold in every section of the nation. A dozen colleges and universities, including the University of Wisconsin, Cornell University and Loyola University in New Orleans, were broadcasting weekly or more often. In Detroit *The News,* published by the Scripps family, put in radio transmission equipment and acquired a permit with the call letters, 8MK. In the summer of 1920, results of the state primary election were broadcast and in November the little station broadcast the election returns for four hours.

The modern era of radio began the evening of November 2, 1920, when Station KDKA in Pittsburgh observed its grand opening by broadcasting results of the election in which Warren G. Harding was elected president, launching a programming schedule that continues to this day. Everett Mitchell was twenty-two years old.

└──────────────────────────────────────────────────┘

Some months after George Mitchell's death, over chocolate sundaes after the Friday night movie, Everett summoned the courage to tell Mildred Roddoz of his interest in marriage. She was both honored and interested. It was one of the great moments in her life but the banker in her ruled out quick acceptance. Together she and Everett would, without delay, think about it.

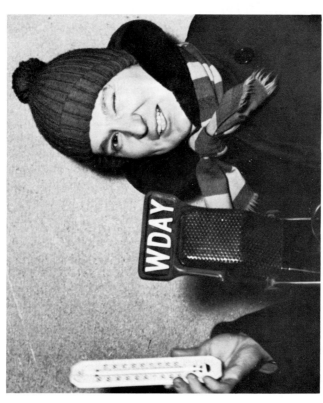

The stocking cap was standard attire for Everett Mitchell on fall and winter programs on location for the National Farm and Home Hour programs. Above he is in Fargo, North Dakota, when the outside temperature was 15 below zero. Below, Mitchell is seen at the National Corn Husking Contest near Davenport, Iowa, in the fall of 1940 attended by 145,000 spectators.

For Mildred this meant considering choices that would shape the rest of her life. She was one of the first of a relatively few women in Chicago with the opportunity of a promising career in banking. Were she to marry she would have to give up that career; in America after World War I married women did not work outside the home unless they were self-employed.

Then there was the question of income. Even though Everett had been advanced rapidly at the bank and his salary was now a promising $85 a month, his income was only at the minimum level at which the bank would permit its employees to be married.[1] The young couple must consider whether such a salary would enable them to maintain a home and still help Everett's mother, who had to provide a home for Eva, who would always need care, and young Ellsworth. (The other sisters, Ethel, Edna and Edith, were all married by this time.)

After a period that seemed long to Everett but was actually only two or three weeks, Mildred revealed her decision. Having thought and prayed about the matter and also talked to her pastor, she decided she preferred to be Mrs. Everett Mitchell, with a home of her own, rather than a well-paid single career woman. But she did have an important reservation. Her training in book-keeping and finance told her that Everett's current income was not adequate to maintain a home of his own and still help his mother. The young couple were confident that the income limitation was something that together they could overcome.

The first step was for Mildred to develop a budget. She found that they would need an income of at least $150 a month, or nearly twice what Everett was making at the bank. That made it clear that if they were to be married, there would have to be a better-paying job. The war ended and nearly a year passed. A lot of reading of the classified help wanted advertisements and a great deal of counseling together took place during these months. Then a solution came, as if an answer to prayer.

Soon after Everett had gone to work at the bank, he had joined the Masonic Lodge in Austin. One of the members, Charles Catlin, knew of Everett's need for a better job. So when a position opened at the firm where he worked, Catlin notified Everett. The firm was Continental Casualty Company on Michigan Avenue. The man in charge of the insurance office, Frank Hooper, was also a member of the same lodge.

With Catlin breaking the way, Everett went to see Hooper to ask for the job. Hooper needed an auditor and he was impressed with Everett's experience at the bank. He liked the idea, too, that the young man wanted the job so that he could get married to a woman who was a bookkeeper at the bank. She would be more interested in his work and more understanding when there were extra working hours. Within a month Everett Mitchell was the new claims auditor at the insurance company, at a salary of $175 a month. In addition, he could depend on some extra earnings from his singing engagements.

Six months later on a pretty summer day, June 18, 1920, Mildred Roddoz and Everett Mitchell were married in a ceremony held in the bride's home.

During the last days of his father's illness, when encouragement meant a great deal to Everett and his mother, an unexpected communication from Billy Sunday had arrived. He revealed that he was preparing for what he thought might be the greatest revival of his entire career. It would be held in Chicago and would last for ten weeks. He wanted to know if Everett, a young man now and no longer a boy in knickers, would like to handle some of the invitation songs. Sunday proposed a schedule of three evenings a week, heavy for a young man holding down a six-day-a-week job.

Everett, his parents, Ida Belle Freeman and Mr. and Mrs. McDonald were overjoyed. It had been a long time since Everett had sung at a Billy Sunday revival. They had each silently come to believe that Everett had received the opportunity to be with the greatest evangelist of his time because Billy Sunday liked the unique appeal of having a boy in knickers able to extend the invitation in a man's voice. Each of them had wondered, separately, if it was no more than the knickers that had done it, but no one had ever said so aloud.

Now Billy Sunday had refuted all such thoughts. The Chicago revival would be held in one of Sunday's specially-built tabernacles at Chicago Avenue and the Lake Michigan shore. It would seat twelve thousand people, the largest indoor assembly hall in the city.[2] Billy Sunday wanted even the people in the back rows to hear the invitation songs, and he was confident that Everett Mitchell could make that wish come true.

The Billy Sunday Chicago revival ended on Sunday evening, May 9, 1918. Despite an almost continuous spring rain, people began arriving in the afternoon to make certain they would be at the final service. By seven o'clock that evening all the seats were filled and standees were looking for room.

Everett, who had sung the invitation hymns three times in the final six evenings, was invited by Sunday to attend as a guest at the final service. The Rev. Sunday turned his last appearance into a sentimental journey.[3] Before the sermon Sunday paid a surprise tribute "to the man to who I owe more than anyone else my start in life." Sunday raced down to the front seats, not far from where Everett and Mildred were sitting, and led to the platform the famed captain of the Chicago White Stockings, A. C. "Cap" Anson, who had brought Sunday to the major leagues.

During his final sermon, Everett Mitchell recalls, Billy Sunday pulled off his coat, tie and collar and called for repentance now. "Every man in hell was warned, but he didn't heed," he said.

It was Sunday's practice to accept only the free-will offering on the last night of a revival for his personal use; other offering money went to pay the expenses of erecting the tabernacle, for other costs and salaries and for special bequests. From the time the revival in Chicago was announced, Sunday made it clear that he and his wife would accept only the final contribution in return for their months of preparation and for conducting the ten-week service. The final collection amounted to $56,000. Sunday, in a dramatic gesture that amazed his audience, announced that he was donating the entire sum to the Pacific Garden Mission, where his conversion had taken place thirty-two years before.

The next day, in the May 20, 1918 edition of the *Chicago Tribune*, religious editor Rev. W. B. Norton summarized the ten-week spectacle for its readers.

> The "trail hitters" (those who came up to be saved, so-called because they walked on "sawdust trails" up to the front of the tabernacle) numbered 49,165. The total attendance at evening, morning and afternoon sessions in the lakefront tabernacle and the many smaller services that had been held in Chicago churches totaled 1,300,000.

The *Tribune* also reported that 424 churches in the city had cooperated to make the revival possible. One hundred eighty-two special services had been held in churches near Chicago's high schools, and there had been forty-seven hundred conversions among the students.

Of the nearly fifty thousand people who had come forward during the revival, at least twenty thousand had responded to the invitation songs of Everett Mitchell.

One unusual feature of a Billy Sunday revival was the attention given to special groups, and on certain nights blocks of seats would be reserved for them. Every campaign had a businessman's night, a businesswoman's night, a students' night, and evenings devoted to older citizens, ethnic groups and clubs and lodges. Since Chicago was a great railroad center, Sunday held a special service for railroad men and their families. Appropriately, Everett sang the invitation songs at this service. Although saddened by the fact that his father had not lived to see his part in the great Chicago revival, particularly on the night dedicated to railroad men, Everett paid his own private tribute to his father by starting the invitation with "The Railroad Man's Hymn":

Life is like a mountain railroad,
With an engineer that's brave--
With his hand upon the throttle
From the cradle to the grave.

He will watch the bridge and trestle,
Never falter, never fail,
With his hand upon the throttle
And his eye upon the rail.

Precious Savior, I am coming.
We will reach the other shore,
Friends will be there to greet us,
Where we will live forever more.

### FOOTNOTES

(1) In order to prevent its employees from assuming personal obligations of a scope that might make them poor risks in handling its money, the First Trust and Savings Bank had a firm rule that married men must have an income of $85 a week if they were to remain with the bank.

(2) Everett Mitchell remembers that the lumber for the great tabernacle was loaned by the Edward Hines Lumber Company, and that one hundred tons of sawdust was used to keep the aisles clean and dry. The platform back of the extended pulpit and in front of the great choir was thirty feet long and at least ten feet deep. Newspaper reporters checked the number of times Billy Sunday walked, ran and at times crawled across the platform, finding it was not uncommon for him to move at least a mile and a half during a sermon.

(3) Although he was born and spent his boyhood in Iowa, Chicago was really home to Billy Sunday. The most important part of his baseball career took place in Chicago. His conversion, which he regarded as a direct visit from the Holy Spirit, occurred in Chicago. His first religious work, meeting his wife, the former Helen Thompson, and his marriage took place in Chicago. In 1935 his death would occur at the home of his brother-in-law in Chicago.

# Part 3
# Eyewitness To The Beginning

The first radio broadcast, as the term is understood today, took place on Christmas Eve, 1906. Reginald A. Fessenden, a Canadian, building on the work of Henrich Hertz and Guglielmo Marconi, developed a means for radio waves to transmit continuous sound, even the human voice. Fessenden conducted his broadcast from his wireless telegraph station on New England's coast at Brant Rock, Massachusetts. He himself was the only "live" performer, playing a violin solo and reading the Christmas story from the Bible. The transmission astounded wireless operators, used to hearing only the dots and dashes of the Morse Code, on ships as far away as the Caribbean.

In the same month the Yale-trained scientist, Lee De Forest, proved the practicability of his vacuum "audion" tube that increased by many times not only the capacity to detect radio waves but also their amplification. The De Forest tube opened a new era that led to the wireless telegraph transmission of continuous sound—radio—and eventually pictures—television.

Wireless amateurs who assembled and even built much of their own equipment became so numerous in the United States (an estimated forty thousand in 1917) that when the nation entered World War I the government had to order them all silent so the air might be exclusively available for military transmission. Many of these amateurs were pressed into wartime government service; consequently, radio development continued at an accelerated pace. The government's large orders for radio tubes attracted the attention of General Electric and Westinghouse, leaders in the making of light bulbs, turning them in a remarkably short time into leaders in the production of radio broadcasting and receiving equipment.

The war over, radio amateurs returned to much more sophisticated experimentation. Soon there were clusters of them in several states; they talked to one another regularly and even exchanged entertainment programs. One of these groups, backed by Westinghouse, launched the nation's first commercial radio station, KDKA, in Pittsburgh on Nov. 2, 1920, the evening that Warren G. Harding was elected President. Westinghouse was so impressed with the possibilities of commercial radio that during the next year it established four more stations, including KYW in Chicago, billed as "the first radio station west of Pittsburgh."

At the end of 1921 there were five radio stations, the four Westinghouse stations—KDKA, KYW, WJZ in Newark and WBZ in Springfield, Massachusetts—and one operated in Schenectady, New York, by General Electric. But in the next year the radio boom exploded, with a record number of three hundred fifty stations coming on the air. By 1925 the number had jumped to six hundred. In 1921 there were an estimated fifty thousand receiving sets (crystal and battery sets that could only be listened to through headphones). By 1925 the number had grown to an astonishing four million.

The listeners who tuned in on these sets were not hearing network broadcasting as we know it today. They were listening to single stations, often owned by individuals, which broadcast little but entertainment on irregular schedules. Radio was the nation's newest craze, but no one knew were the craze would lead.

Part Three deals with the beginning of broadcasting in the United States—The Great Station Era—and of Everett Mitchell's part in it. During his early career, before there were networks, he introduced concepts that have been used in radio and television ever since.

# Chapter 12
# Crystal Set Soloist

How did Everett Mitchell and radio meet?

The fact is, until less than twenty-four hours before his first appearance on the air, the idea of being on radio had never occurred to him.

It all started Friday evening, November 2, 1923. Mitchell had a singing engagement at a church on the west side, not far from his old home on Superior Street. When some of the friends who had gone to school with him at Nash Elementary and Austin High Schools learned he would be back in the old neighborhood, they planned a party for him at a home on Superior Street, in the heart of the community he knew so well.

The Mitchells arrived at the party, already in progress, shortly before 9 p.m. After an affectionate greeting for the guest of honor and his wife, there were games, reminiscences, refreshments and singing. Perhaps it was the singing that provided the inspiration that followed.

"The conversation turned to the 'newest miracle,' radio," Everett recalls, "what fun it was to listen to and what it could all mean. Quite suddenly, everyone seemed to think of the same thing at the same time. 'Why haven't you been on radio?' several of them asked me. 'Your singing would make a hit.' At first I thought they were joking, and maybe they were for a minute or so. But quickly the idea took on a serious and determined note.

"The idea was new to me, and my first reaction was disinterest. But my friends were determined that I would seek an audition and sing on one of the new radio stations, something they seemed to take for granted would happen if I went for the audition.

"I was still only mildly interested when the conversation took on a different tone. 'Come on,' someone said, 'we don't think you have the courage to try it.' Now, my reaction began to change.

111

Uncle Alex plays his three-string fiddle with Bradshaw's Band during a National Farm and Home Hour program that originated at the Kinston, North Carolina, tobacco auction in the fall of 1935. Everett Mitchell presented the program over the NBC network.

Then one of the fellows who knew me pretty well almost shouted, 'We dare you to try it.'

"That did it. At that age it was very hard for me to withstand a dare. My response now was 'If you are going to put it that way, I'll do it.' Someone brought up the question of which station I would go to and when. It was the concensus that I should go to the oldest and best known station, KYW. The next question was when I would do it. 'Immediately,' I said. 'Tomorrow evening.' "

On the way home from the party, Everett and Mildred discussed how he would make his presentation to Station KYW, whose studio was located just across the Loop business district from Everett's office. He would leave for the studio directly from work, buy a sandwich for his evening meal and arrive at KYW before 7 p.m. They discussed what his best number would be, and decided it should be neither too popular nor too classical. Mildred thought it should be sentimental, so it would have wide appeal, something like "The Sunshine of Your Smile," and, thus Everett's first song on radio was selected.

Offices in Chicago were open all day on Saturdays in the 1920s, so Everett was at his desk after the "I dare you" party. His insurance tasks took something of a back seat that day as he planned responses to the possible situations he might encounter at KYW that evening.

When he arrived he found that a line of people seeking to appear before the KYW microphone had already formed in the hallway outside the small studio. He wondered if he would even get an audition, but it proved to be much easier than he thought. He had not been waiting very long when he learned an acquaintance, Herbie Mintz, whom he had met through his appearances at church programs, was the station's pianist. Mintz, who was familiar with Mitchell's singing ability, saw him waiting and promptly called him in for the audition. It was only a few minutes after 7 p.m.

The "audition" consisted of a brief explanation from Mintz on how to appear before the microphone. Then, stepping up to the strange device, Mitchell began to sing his number to the radio audience. He thought he had done well with "The Sunshine of Your Smile." Evidently Mintz thought so, too; he complimented Mitchell, then suggested that he remain in the studio for a while and observe the broadcast. Within minutes Mitchell knew why. Mintz told him that his solo had swamped the studio telephone system with calls from listeners asking that "this Everett

Mitchell" be brought back to the program for another number.

Because of the large number of performers who were waiting, Mintz asked if Mitchell would like to come back the following week. The time was set, and Mitchell left for home to find out how his greatest admirer and critic regarded his first broadcast.

Mildred had been able to hear the broadcast well on the crystal set Everett himself had assembled, at a cost of just under four dollars. Since the landlord had not yet entered the radio age and would not permit the erection of an outside aerial, the Mitchells used the bedsprings instead. (Hooking the aerial attachment to the bedsprings was a common and inexpensive substitute for an outside aerial for many owners of early receivers.)

Mrs. Mitchell thought her husband had done a fine job with the broadcast. She thought his full baritone voice was a real asset, because, as she observed, radio transmission made everything sound "a little higher and thinner," so that at times Everett had sounded more like a good tenor. She thought a real tenor voice might have "gone through the roof."

Actually, the night was well over before Everett and Mildred were able to complete their evaluation because of the phone calls from friends, especially those who had been at the party on Superior Street the evening before. The phone comments made heady listening, and Mitchell enjoyed reporting that he had been invited back for another performance the following week.

On November 8, Mitchell was back at KYW for his second appearance. This time Mintz, who Mitchell learned was also the station manager, suggested that Everett team up with two other performers, each appearing at least twice, to fill a half hour segment. After the broadcast, Mintz invited Mitchell to come back and perform on Station KYW whenever it was convenient. Mitchell should just report to the receptionist when he arrived to avoid waiting.

When he got home, Everett acknowledged to Mildred that there was "a certain unusual stimulation and excitement about appearing on radio." He said he was interested in singing on some of the other Chicago stations to study the matter more closely.

The Mitchells were beginning to see something very significant about these small radio stations, generally operated by a manager, an engineer and a receptionist, with a microphone and a telephone as their major studio equipment. They wondered if this might be the beginning of a new kind of communication service, one that would mean new jobs. True, most of the Chicago stations in the fall of 1923 were owned by individuals, like Station WHT owned by Chicago mayor William Hale Thompson, whose initials constituted its name, or by small businesses like Station WEBH, operated by the Edgewater Beach Hotel, for which its call letters stood. But KYW was owned by the Westinghouse Corporation, one of the major firms in the nation.

Mildred and Everett concluded that they needed to know more about this new young industry, which had celebrated its fourth birthday the same week Everett made his first radio appearance. Mildred, who was just as interested as her husband, began clipping newspaper and later magazine articles on radio. In time the Mitchells pieced together how daily radio broadcasting began in Chicago and the United States.

A Pittsburgh retail store had provided the original spark that exploded into Station KDKA. Frank Conrad, a Westinghouse engineer who lived in a suburb of Pittsburgh, had, after the first World War, turned his garage into a studio and had advanced to the point of doing broadcasts that could be heard over the entire Pittsburgh area. To stimulate the sale of parts to build crystal sets, the Joseph Horne Department Store in Pittsburgh had installed a radio receiver in its basement sales floor so customers could hear Conrad's broadcasts and those of other amateurs. Early in the fall of 1920 the store inserted a small advertisement in the *Pittsburgh Sun*, perhaps the first radio advertisement ever printed in a newspaper.

"Air concert 'picked up' by radio here," the advertisement read. The statement that followed explained, "Victrola music, played into the air over a wireless telephone, was 'picked up' by listeners on the wireless receiving station which was recently installed here for patrons interested in wireless experiments."

Harry P. Davis, Westinghouse vice president, who had casually followed Conrad's experiments, suddenly realized that there might be a tremendous opportunity in radio, one that could mean a great deal to his company. With regular broadcasts, there could be a vast demand for home and business receiving sets, the kind of equipment Westinghouse could easily produce.

Davis met with Conrad and asked how soon he could assemble the equipment for a Westinghouse-sponsored radio station in Pittsburgh. It was only a few weeks before the 1920 national election on November 2. Could Conrad get a radio station assembled in time for a grand opening on election evening? Conrad said he could. So Station KDKA, located atop Westinghouse's tallest building in Pittsburgh, began broadcasting in time to carry the election results as they were relayed from the nearby *Pittsburgh Post* newspaper.

The station came on the air at 8 p.m. November 2 and interspersed phonograph music with bulletins on the election returns from the *Post*. There were telephone calls from listeners that first evening, most of them complaining that there was too much music and not enough election information. Broadcasting continued until after midnight, by which time it was possible to announce that Ohio's Warren G. Harding, the Republican, had defeated his Democractic opponent Governor James M. Cox, who was also from Ohio.

Although the *Detroit News* radio station had also broadcast the 1920 election returns, there were important differences that made KDKA the first broadcasting station in the United States as the term is understood today. On October 16, Westinghouse had applied to the U.S. Department of Commerce for a license to operate a privately-owned for-profit radio station daily beginning November 2. The license was issued five days before the station's opening. The *Detroit News* station was operating under an experimental license, 8MK, and had not made a commitment to broadcast after November 2. The *News'* experimental station did continue to broadcast, however, and later became the powerful Station WWJ of Detroit.

Station KDKA touched off a national preoccupation with radio that rivaled the nation's interest in Babe Ruth and the Charleston. In the months that followed the election broadcast, a parade of nationally known personages appeared before the KDKA microphone to speak person-to-person to an audience known to exist in at least three states and perhaps more. Secretary of Commerce Herbert Hoover appeared early in January, followed by other members of the President's cabinet.

The next fall, at the time of the 1921 baseball World Series, Westinghouse launched its second radio station in Springfield, Massachusetts, where the firm operated another plant. This plant began making crystal set home receivers at about the same time. The next month, on November 11, 1921, Westinghouse unveiled its third radio station, KYW in Chicago. While the attraction used to introduce the Springfield station was World Series baseball, in Chicago it was opera.

The magnetic star of American opera, Mary Garden, had become the general director of the Chicago Civic Opera, and from the opening night until the opera season closed the next March KYW broadcast little else. The magic of radio was overwhelming regardless of the program menu, and it was known there were between twenty and thirty thousand home receivers in use in Chicago by the spring of 1922, with hundreds being added every week. Listening to the radio had become the thing to do.

Until the opera season ended, the Opera House was the only studio KYW had. Then a small studio was opened nearby in the Commonwealth Edison building at 30 West Adams Street; the station's antenna was on the Edison building's roof. Because of its size and central location, the parade of celebrities to the KYW microphone was even more impressive than it had been in Pittsburgh. Al Jolson, the storied Rudolph Valentino, and Madame Schumann-Heink were among the famous persons who graced the station's register in 1922. But the big name era for KYW was definitely over by the fall of 1923 when Everett Mitchell made his debut. Now, stations had to find their attractions locally, and talented amateurs were much in demand.

After his two appearances on KYW, Mitchell decided to audition at the Calumet Baking Powder Station, WQJ, whose studio was in the Rainbow Gardens, a Loop area restaurant and night club. He went to the station the week before Thanksgiving and was immediately offered an opportunity to sing that evening in the classical music program with some of the best amateur musicians in Chicago.

His singing drew the attention of the radio reporter for the *Chicago Daily News.* In his notes on current radio programs, the *News* reporter commented, "Station WQJ's 8 to 10 program (last evening) presented extraordinarily fine radio voices that were indeed a joy to hear. . . Also for Everett Mitchell, a baritone, and Catherine Diepenprock, pianist, many words of praise." Everett's first press review had been complimentary, and Mildred's young scrapbook had its first newspaper item about radio in which her husband's name appeared.

Early in December Mitchell went to Station WMAQ, whose studio was in the LaSalle Hotel. When he reported that he had appeared on Station KYW twice and on WQJ, he was automatically invited to come to the microphone.

In the two months since his first appearance at KYW, Mitchell had participated in six broadcasts, and Mildred was monitoring closely what was being done on all of the Chicago stations. Everett was bringing home the Chicago newspapers that regularly

117

carried reports on radio programs and news of developments at the city's radio stations. Six Chicago newpapers had appointed radio reporters and were printing radio news each week, some almost daily. They were the *Chicago Daily News*, the *Chicago Evening Post*, the *Chicago Herald Examiner*, the *Chicago Daily Journal*, the *Chicago Times* and the *Chicago Tribune*.

Shortly after the New Year holiday in 1924, Mitchell had developed a schedule that would take him to one of the Chicago radio stations at least every two weeks. At the end of the year he and Mildred would evaluate the career possibilities in radio and act accordingly.

Mitchell decided he would concentrate on those stations that presented programs that would offer him the most opportunity in the future. He would regularly appear on the singing programs of KYW, WEBH and WMAQ. He would go to WIBO, the Nelson Bond and Mortgage Company station, at least to get acquainted with the manager.

There were radio stations on which he would not appear. One was WBBM, a station that focused entirely on popular music. While Mitchell could sing popular songs and enjoyed some of them, he did not want to become known as a singer of popular music. These songs generally enjoyed but a brief period of popularity and were then forgotten. Mitchell wanted to be known for his singing of the proven longtime favorites and for the classical music which had been popular with his concert audiences.

Nor would he go to Station WHT in the Wrigley Building, but for an entirely different reason. The owner, Mayor William Hale Thompson, was in Mitchell's view a pitiful and despicable person. Mitchell had been present at a gathering at which Thompson appeared, apparently intoxicated, and made indecent and vulgar remarks in a loud voice in the presence of children and women. Some of the leading Chicago radio stations of today, such as WGN (the World's Greatest Newspaper, which is still owned by the Chicago Tribune) and WLS (World's Largest Store, started but no longer owned by Sears, Roebuck and Company) were not yet on the air in early 1924.

Mitchell also decided he needed to find out how wide his appeal was to audiences who did not already know him. To determine this he adopted an assumed name, George Bass, and entered amateur contests, which were popular in the big Chicago Loop theaters, especially on Monday evenings when the radio parties were held. He entered a dozen of these contests and won the first prize on every occasion, which ranged from $25 to $50. The test was positive.

Every station that Mitchell visited in 1924 was open to him for repeat performances. Some station receptionists, like the young woman at WQJ, would call from time to time and ask if he would accept a place on a particular evening or weekend program.

By the fall of 1924, Everett and Mildred were convinced that radio was not only here to stay but that it would get bigger and bigger. Everett was convinced from his year-long study that he had something to offer the new medium, not just as a singer of great songs but in the field of planning and policy for any station interested in enlarging its audience. By the time he and Mildred celebrated his first anniversary in broadcasting with a dinner out on November 2, they were agreed that the next thing on the agenda was to study the stations to determine where the opportunity for jobs, both short range and longer range, might exist.

Just before the anniversary dinner, a new station had come on the air with the call letters WENR. The station had probably the clearest signal of any in Chicago. Its studio was located on Belmont Avenue in the All American Radio Building. The firm was a major Chicago producer of home radio receivers and radio parts. The Belmont studio was outside the Chicago Loop and within walking distance of the Mitchell's apartment on Nevada Street. The young couple agreed that they must listen to WENR more intently.

One evening early in December when Everett came home from the insurance office, Mildred had a proposal regarding WENR. This station was new and its programming was not up to the standard of most of the other stations, especially its announcing, which was sometimes hard to follow. The station needed help, she concluded. Also, the station was having a hard time attracting good amateur performers, probably because it was a considerable distance from the other studios, which were clustered close together in the Loop business district. This might be the place for Everett to find a job in radio, and Mildred had a plan for making the initial contact.

Everett, she suggested, should give up being with her and his family on Christmas Eve and instead go to WENR and offer to sing. There would probably not be many other amateurs who would leave their families on Christmas Eve to go to the radio studios, especially to the remote WENR. His appearance could not help but make an impression on the manager. Everett liked the strategy, though he grumbled a little about giving up Christmas Eve with his wife and family.

When Everett arrived at WENR that Christmas Eve, he found that Mildred's plan had been exactly right. There was not a single performer at the station, and Frank Westphal, the leader of the small WENR orchestra and manager of the station, was overjoyed. Westphal could hardly believe that Everett Mitchell, who he had heard on many other stations, would come to WENR at all, much less on Christmas Eve. Mitchell explained that the station was within walking distance of his home, so he had just decided to come over.

Westphal quickly devised a routine for the studio orchestra accompanying Mitchell's solos, and Everett finished the impromptu evening concert with the ever-popular "Prisoner's Song."

There were a number of calls following the performance, a large number for Christmas Eve. One of them was especially important. It was from E. N. Rauland, owner of WENR.

"Everett, I admired your perfomance for us tonight. I hope you will come back soon. Merry Christmas to you and Mrs. Mitchell."

# Chapter 13
# Putting The Gold In WENR

On Halloween evening in 1925, E.N. Rauland, owner of Station WENR, stopped by the studio, a single large room in the All American Radio Corporation building at 4201 Belmont Avenue on Chicago's near north side. Rauland also owned All American Radio, a major Chicago producer of radio receiving sets and parts. It was Saturday, and he usually came to the station before going home on Saturday evening. He brought the weekly paychecks for Station Manager Frank Westphal, members of the eight-piece studio orchestra, the studio receptionist and the still relatively new announcer-soloist, Everett Mitchell.

It was after 7 p.m., so the performers had all returned from dinner to put Station WENR back on the air. (In 1924 Chicago radio stations generally were silent during the dinner hour, usually resuming broadcasting at 7 or 7:30 p.m.) Rauland enjoyed chatting with the members of his staff and he often stayed to watch some of the evening broadcasts. On occasion he would even handle the announcing.

Except for Westphal, with whom he met from time to time in his office down the hall, Rauland's Saturday evening visits were his primary means of keeping in personal touch with the studio staff. Since he had hired Everett Mitchell some months before as a soloist and backup announcer, Rauland had made a special point of visiting with him.

Before leaving the studio this Saturday evening, Rauland asked Mitchell if it would be convenient to come to his office on Monday immediately after the afternoon broadcasting ended at 5 p.m. Mitchell agreed. Although this was the first time Rauland had asked him for a meeting in his office, Mitchell was curious but not apprehensive.

During the previous month, Mitchell and Rauland had talked

over a number of ideas Everett thought would be interesting for future programs. These ideas were different from the musical entertainment that made up most of Chicago's radio fare at this time; there would be programs offering services to listeners, perhaps inviting listener participation or presenting information of general interest. Mitchell though it likely that Rauland wanted to explore in more detail some of these new ideas.

At their meeting, however, Rauland indicated that the subject for discussion now was very much broader. Within two weeks, he confided, the contract with Westphal would be up; it would either have to be renewed or terminated. Westphal had a drinking problem, Rauland said, that at times must surely be obvious to WENR listeners.

With that brief introductory observation, Rauland came directly to the point.

"Everett, do you think you could manage this radio station?"

Mitchell was completely taken by surprise. Quickly he collected himself to weigh his answer. His thoughts turned to the many times, during his nearly two years of singing on Chicago radio stations, he had observed studio practices which he felt could have been improved. There was probably no one in the city, he thought, who had seen and studied the management of so many Chicago stations at such close range. While unexpected, Rauland's question seemed almost a logical culmination of his radio experience.

After a considerable pause, Mitchell replied, in a thoughtful but firm voice, "Yes, I could manage a radio station. In fact, I would like to have the opportunity."

Rauland did not seem surprised at Mitchell's answer. He moved quickly to his next question.

"What kind of salary would you want for managing, announcing and performing on the station?"

This time Mitchell's answer came quickly.

"One hundred and fifty-three dollars a week."

Mitchell has never been able to explain how he arrived at that particular figure, especially the last three dollars. It was about twice what he was being paid as an announcer and soloist, and his only explanation is that he believed being manager would at least double the amount of time and energy that would have to be invested in the job.

This time, Rauland seemed amused. "Well, I guess there is no reason why we should not pay you $153," was all he said about the salary. He told Mitchell to begin making preparations to take over as manager on November 16.

Mitchell then asked Rauland about the goals he had set for his station. Rauland replied that he believed radio broadcasting would follow the general pattern of any new business. Some stations would grow stronger and some would disappear. He pointed out that already some Chicago stations had closed and he was sure more would follow. The stations that gave the best service, Rauland said, would grow; he was determined that WENR, small as it was in 1925, would become one of Chicago's outstanding radio stations.

But Rauland acknowledged that he needed more than a good station in Chicago. His All American Radio business, the sole source of WENR's financial support, had to sell its products all over the country. Rauland was aiming at markets both east and west of Chicago. He wanted a station that could be heard and would interest a significant audience from New York to Denver and all points in between. He had some ideas about solving the engineering problems; he wanted his station manager to be thinking about innovative programs that would be of interest to such a wide audience.

Mitchell saw that his decision to manage the station was a sharp turning point in his radio career. From now on, his most important role would be decision making. He would have to create new programs capable of building a larger listening audience. His role as a soloist, the special talent which had given him his chance for a career in broadcasting, would disappear. But the rewards would be immediate. Never again would he have to be concerned about enough money to pay the rent or meet unexpected bills. His $8,000 annual salary would enable him to live comfortably, help support his mother and Eva, and even set up a savings program. Bread could be bought for a nickel, a new Ford touring car, the most popular in America, could be bought for $300, and except for the wealthy, no one paid income taxes.

The conference had lasted until early evening. Mitchell looked up at the calendar hanging on the wall of Rauland's office. The date was November 2. Almost to the hour five years before, Station KDKA in Pittsburgh had introduced continuous broadcasting in the United States. The anniversary of U.S. broadcasting and Everett Mitchell's becoming a radio station manager would fall on the same date, with only five years in between, for all time to come.

Soon after Rauland's announcement of the new management, Mitchell let it be known there would be no staff changes and that Westphal had agreed to stay an additional two weeks to direct the orchestra and give the new manager time to get organized. Even so, there was a degree of uncertainty and tension the first day, when Mitchell had scheduled a staff meeting at 5 p.m. following the afternoon broadcast.

The new manager did his best to put everyone at ease. He said he looked upon the staff as a family, and this meeting was merely a family meeting to consider some new plans. There would have to be some changes, Mitchell added. Radio in Chicago was growing rapidly, and growth and change always went hand in hand. WENR would be a leader in change.

The immediate changes, he continued, would be in the musical arrangements. William Fantozzi, a member of the station orchestra and formerly violinist with the Minneapolis and Chicago Symphony Orchestras, would become the new WENR music director. A new music ensemble would be formed, known as the Rauland Lyric Trio. It would be headed by Fantozzi, with cellist Joseph F. Novy and pianist Vin Lindhe the other members. The trio would bring an entirely different type of music to WENR; each evening it would present a program of classical and semiclassical music at the peak listening hour from 8 to 9 p.m. Mitchell would on occasion appear with the trio as soloist.

This was only the beginning, the new manager promised his staff. There would soon be other new programs that would give everyone in the WENR family fresh opportunities.

The difficult first meeting with the staff went well, Mitchell thought. There were questions and comments, some of them indicating enthusiasm for the new plans.

Immediately after the staff meeting, Rauland sent news releases, including Mitchell's picture, to all of the Chicago newpapers. The releases included news of the new trio and noted that there would be more new programs coming soon.

All the Chicago newspapers carried the story. The *Chicago Times* carried the pictures of both Mitchell and Westphal. Some of the editors added comments of their own. The *Chicago Daily News* observed:

> It seems strange indeed to have the announcement from WENR, 8 to 9 p.m., that a Schubert program is being given over the station . . . We hadn't been used to anything classical like that, you know.

There were some laudatory references to Mitchell's announcing. The *Herald Examiner* commented that it was "worthy of special note that a portion of the announcing on WENR's new program was being done by one who has perfect breath control and a pleasing voice."

The *Evening Post* carried the announcement, and the newspaper's radio editor, Harry Lawrence, came to the station to interview the new manager. The *Post* artist also prepared a special cartoon to illustrate the changeover. The cartoon showed Westphal and Mitchell holding up the studio, complete with its microphone, piano and receptionist desk. Under Westphal were the words "Retiring Director" and under Mitchell "The New Boss." The legend beneath read "Programs for every taste—classical, popular and religious."

While Mitchell was pleased with the newspaper attention to the announcement, Rauland was downright delighted. This was the first time his little radio station, located in a manufacturing district outside the Loop, had "made all the big papers."

But Rauland saw an even greater significance to the publicity. He said the comments by the radio writers would "tell us what we need to know" to become a more important station. The attention the papers had given to the new classical music program was really saying, he pointed out, that WENR had been so largely a popular music station that it could only appeal to a fraction of the potential audience.

Mitchell was excited about Rauland's desire to raise WENR to the ranks of Chicago's top stations. Also, he believed he knew how to achieve such an end. The key, he knew, was more listeners. But more listeners could only be attracted by offering more programs that were new and different and that expanded the present role of radio in Chicago. Also, WENR needed to be on the air on a regular schedule, one which listeners could depend upon. Mitchell wanted to see WENR broadcasting from 2 p.m. to 2 a.m. six days a week, with a sign-on time even earlier, noon, on Sundays. (Studies indicated that there were not enough listeners to justify being on the air before early or mid-afternoon during the 1920s.)

All this was possible, but there was one huge stumbling block. Mitchell knew that his small staff could at best provide programs for only half or two-thirds of a twelve to fourteen-hour broadcasting schedule. The only way to cover the remainder would be to recruit amateur entertainers to provide part of the day's enter-

Everett Mitchell who as a child watched his father cut hay with a cradle (scythe) checks (above) on the operation of a hay baler at his Beautiful Day Farm at Wheaton. Below, Mitchell and his farm manager, John Kupjack, determine when the alfalfa hay is ready to harvest.

tainment, just as they were doing for the other full-schedule stations in Chicago. This could not happen as long as the WENR studio was on Belmont Avenue. The amateurs simply would not pay for transportation to come to a station that was not known when in the main Chicago business district they were within walking distance of several prominent stations.

The idea of renting space and creating a studio in the Loop's high-rent district seemed completely beyond reality. Faced with a situation that seemed hopeless, Everett Mitchell turned to his father's approach to difficult problems, "work hard, pray hard and don't forget to give thanks for your blessings."

Then something of a miracle occurred. In only two weeks WENR had exactly the kind of fully equipped studio it needed, in the place the studio needed to be, with no expense for rent and little of any other kind. Nor was that the end of the miracle. Confronted with another of those "disappointments that lead to God's appointments," within a year Mitchell would be able to maneuver WENR permanently into one of the finest radio studios in Chicago in a Michigan Avenue building facing the lake.

The solution to the problem began when Mitchell spoke to one of the newpaper radio writers about the matter. "Do you know that the studio in the Kimball Building is just being vacated by Station WTAS?" the writer asked.

The Kimball Building, headquarters for the makers of the famous Kimball organs, was at the corner of Jackson and Wabash in the very heart of the Loop. Mitchell knew the building well. The radio studio was on the seventh floor, but also available for broadcast use was the big Kimball organ in its own studio on the third floor. The seventh floor studio had a private line to the Edgewater Beach Hotel Marine Dining Room, making it possible during the evening to present the music of the big name bands playing there.

What Mitchell did not know was why such an excellent studio was suddenly vacant, and before going to see the building's manager he made some inquiries. Station WTAS, he learned, was owned and at times personally operated by attorney Charles Erbstein, better known as Charlie. Erbstein specialized in handling divorce or alienation of affection suits filed against wealthy Chicago men. The WTAS call letters stood for the names of Erbstein's four children, Willie, Tommy, Annie and Sammy.

There was always some question, even in Erbstein's mind, whether WTAS was a Chicago or an Elgin station. Elgin, forty miles west of Chicago on the Fox River, was where the Erbstein family lived, on a country estate called Villa Olivia just east of the city. Erbstein had been an avid radio amateur. By 1922 he was broadcasting from Villa Olivia under the amateur license 9AWK. When he opened the station, in an ornate studio fashioned like the radio control room of an American ship complete with navigation lights and illuminated portholes, both the studio and transmitter were located on his estate.

But Erbstein had his law offices in the Chicago Loop, and he made an arrangement with the Kimball Building to locate a studio there and feed programs, especially from the Kimball organ and the Edgewater Beach Hotel, to his Elgin transmitter. A man who did nothing by halves, Erbstein also had plans to build a major radio station in Elgin. He even created his own "Edgewater ballroom" type facility near his estate. This was a popular restaurant formerly known as The Motor Inn (widely rumored to be one the retreats along the Fox River for Al Capone, the Chicago crime king, and his friends when they had to be "out of town"). Erbstein bought the Inn and transformed it into a fashionable eating place and ballroom, which he named The Purple Grackle. There was a private line from the Grackle to the WTAS studio, so that music from the restaurant could be broadcast by the radio station. It was at this time, when he was ready to draw on programs from The Purple Grackle, that Erbstein decided to leave his studio in the Kimball Building.

Mitchell went to the Kimball Building manager to ask if it would be possible for WENR to take over the studio and also have access to the Kimball organ studio. Yes, the manager said, the owners would be glad to have WENR locate in the studio. The station would have to pay for any alterations, but there would be no rent if Mitchell would make certain that each time the station was identified on the air the announcer would add that its studios were in the Kimball Building and that the organ music was played on the Kimball organ. The agreement could be indefinite, the manager added, probably as long as WENR wanted to stay. Mitchell could not get a formal lease, which was something he would learn more about sooner than he wished.

The move into the Kimball Building studio brought the amateur performers needed to flesh out the station's schedule, just as Mitchell had predicted. This gave him the time he needed to concentrate on creating more programs and finding the resources to put them on the air. Everything seemed to be going well for the new manager. Then one day during the holiday season, about eight months after the move to the downtown studio, Mitchell had an unexpected visitor.

The visitor was Charlie Erbstein. Jovial and friendly, Charlie pulled a flask from an inside pocket and offered Mitchell a drink. Although Mitchell declined, Erbstein took a swallow, then went on to explain the reason for his visit. He was finding it difficult to maintain enough broadcasting time on his Elgin station without access to the Kimball Building studio and its conveniences. He needed to "take back" his studio in the Loop. Now Mitchell understood why he had never been able to get a written lease agreement. Although Erbstein left the studio intending not to return, he retained the right to do so in case he changed his mind.[1]

Faced with the prospect of returning to the remote Belmont Avenue studio and oblivion, Mitchell began urgently searching for a solution. Again, it came through his friendship with Chicago's radio writers. The day after his conference with Erbstein, Mitchell arrived early at the studio and began calling a number of reporters.

One of them confided that he was sure that soon, in a few weeks at the most, the Chicago Station WSWS would be going out of business and as a consequence the Spanish Garden Studio at the Straus Building would be open.

"The Spanish Garden Studio is as good as there is in the city," Mitchell pointed out. "Surely it must be spoken for."

The reporter said that he did not think even the Straus Building management knew of the impending development at WSWS and urged Mitchell to investigate.

Aided by a call from Rauland to the Straus Brothers, whose investment business occupied the building's street level offices, within two weeks Mitchell had a lease for the Spanish Garden Studio, this time in writing and renewable.

When Mitchell went to look over the studio, he was delighted to find it was even better designed than he had thought and was equipped with some of the newest broadcasting equipment available. In addition to having a much larger lobby and reception area, the Spanish Garden had a main studio large enough to accomodate an entire symphony orchestra. And no longer would it be necessary to go outside of the studio to the organ. The Spanish Garden was one of the few studios in the nation with its own organ. Most important of all, it had a place for a studio audience, which would provide an exciting theater atmosphere.

Mitchell and his staff planned every step of the move with care. On Sunday, February 20, 1927, with ceremonies that included even the radio audience, WENR began broadcasting from the Straus Building. The entire evening programming was devoted to a dedication of the new WENR home. The *Chicago Daily News* announcement story not only described the event, but showed that sweeping changes were taking place in Chicago radio as stations struggled for leadership or just to stay alive.

> In celebration of the opening of its new studio, the Spanish Garden in the Straus Building, Station WENR will present a gala program Sunday evening when a number of well-known entertainers, a glee club and an orchestra will be heard.
>
> WENR is the third radio station to occupy the studio. WJAZ, its first occupant, made the studio known all over the country in advance stories before the building was completed. While WJAZ was still occupying it, WSWS opened another studio in the same building and moved to the Spanish Garden when WJAZ moved to the Chez Pierre.
>
> According to Everett Mitchell, director of the station, the public will be welcome to visit the new broadcasting rooms at any time.

Although there was no effort during the gala to seek audience mail, nearly three thousand letters of congratulation were received. Some of them commented on the improved reception. Half of the mail came from Chicago and other points in Illinois, but there were letters from twenty states and Canada.

Mitchell was elated when a close check of the letters showed the great variety of WENR listeners. They came from people in villages as well as cities, from farm families as well as those in town, and from people representing a broad range of educational and social backgrounds and holding a variety of jobs. Many came from professionals, and often the correspondents were ministers. WENR was on its way to reaching the wide audience Mitchell and Rauland had hoped for.

In the midst of this rapid progress, there were major disappointments. The most painful involved two members of the regular WENR staff, persons who had worked closely and apparently harmoniously with Mitchell since he was appointed to succeed Frank Westphal.

In one of their twice-weekly management meetings, still held at the All American offices on Belmont Avenue, Rauland reported the disturbing news. The two staff members had come to Rauland and asked to be appointed co-managers of the station should he be seeking to replace Mitchell. They were both members of the WENR orchestra, William Fantozzi and the popular young woman pianist, Vin Lindhe, two of the three musicians Mitchell had promoted to the new and very successful Rauland Lyric Trio.

"They are not loyal to you, and I think you had better get rid of them," was Rauland's advice.

Mitchell called James C. Petrillo, Chicago head of the American Federation of Musicians, and explained what had happened. Petrillo, who was later to become national president of AFM, immediately cancelled the WENR contracts with the two musicians and directed Mitchell to call him at once if there were any further difficulties with AFM members.

"My musicians know that they are not to intrude in management matters," Petrillo said.

To this day Mitchell does not know what caused the two musicians to seek his job, especially when they might well have suspected it would cost them theirs. Most radio stations in Chicago were still managed by members of the station's musical staff. Apparently Fantozzi and Lindhe continued to believe that radio's function was only to entertain and that Mitchell's innovations would in time disappear and he with them.

Within a month the public response to the invitation to visit the new WENR studios in The Straus Building overwhelmed the staff and the facilities. Not only were the seventy-five seats for guests filled much of the time, but on occasion the large reception area, from which the broadcasts could be seen through a window and heard through a loudspeaker, was also crowded. Mitchell instituted a new plan by which reservations could be made by phone and were required at least one day in advance.

With the station solidly in place in the Straus Building, Mitchell began the most intensive days of his entire career in broadcasting. He personally presented all of the WENR programs, which were now on a solid schedule starting at noon on Sunday and at 2 p.m. the other six days and running until 2 a.m. His seven-day-a-week schedule left him little time even for sleep. He left for home immediately after the 2 a.m. sign-off, slept for sometimes as few as four hours and then started his next working

Everett Mitchell is greeted in Madison, Wisconsin, by Miss Wisconsin at Wisconsin Cheese Day in 1949. The Badger State's beauty queen was featured on a salute to Wisconsin as the nation's No. 1 cheese producer.

day. He always insisted, however, on a leisurely breakfast with Mildred. He would be back at the Straus Building by about 11 a.m. to hold conferences on programs coming up that day or in the future. On rare occasions he would accept a lunch invitation.

Even with such a busy schedule, Mitchell did take time to contribute to the advancement of the broadcasting profession. He helped to organize the Chicago Broadcaster's Association and served as one of its early officers. In 1927 he served as the association's vice-president. William Hay, manager of WGN, the *Chicago Tribune* station, was president.

As early as mid-summer, 1927, there were rumors that the Insull utility empire, headquartered in Chicago and with customers in twenty states in the nation's great mid-section, was soon to move into radio. Mitchell gave them little heed. With radio stations being started, changing owners and going out of business regularly, there were always fresh rumors, most of them proving to have no substance.

But in October there was evidence that the Insull rumors might be true after all. In one of their management conferences, Rauland reported that All American Radio had received a letter from a newly formed Great Lakes Broadcasting Company, owned by the Insull companies. Rauland regarded the communication as a routine questionnaire sent to all Chicago area radio stations. Along with questions about the station's operation, number of staff members, hours of broadcasting and program schedules, the query asked if WENR was for sale and if so, at what price. Rauland said he would respond, in polite language, that everything he owned, from All American Radio to WENR, was for sale if the price was right.

Three weeks later, at another conference, Rauland told Mitchell that he had received a response to his letter to the Great Lakes Broadcasting Company. The new communication asked additional questions about WENR and also requested a luncheon meeting with Rauland. Rauland told Mitchell that he was surprised by the letter and its tone, but that he still attached little significance to the matter. Great Lakes, he said, was apparently making an intensive study of the Chicago radio situation and "picking the brains of the existing station owners."

Perhaps wishing to allay any concern Mitchell might feel, Rauland added that he would accept the invitation to an over-the-table discussion, but he wanted to assure Mitchell that were he to sell WENR at any time, he would make it a condition of the transaction that Mitchell be offered a position of top management under the new ownership.

The luncheon meeting took place just before Thanksgiving. What happened during that three-hour lunch, served in a private room in a Loop hotel, surprised not only Chicago radio but sent shock waves for the first time directly to New York. Mitchell learned the details soon after the meeting was over, when Rauland called for him to come to his office as soon as he could.

Rauland was still somewhat bewildered by the luncheon developments. There were still major items to be worked out, he explained, but he had reached a verbal understanding for the sale of WENR. The proposal was of such magnitude and made in such a spirit, he told Mitchell, that he was left "little grounds for a refusal." The initial offer for WENR was $1 million, and even that figure was open for further discussion. (Rauland was eventually paid $1.5 million for his station.) All the conditions which Rauland had attached, including the assurance that Mitchell would be part of the executive staff under the new ownership, were acceptable to Insull.

Still trying to assess the developments, Rauland said he believed the purchase of WENR was but the first step to project the Insull utilities empire into a major role in radio broadcasting in the Midwest and possibly nationally. It was, perhaps, a challenge to the New York bid for leadership. Just a year before, the Radio Corporation of America and associated businesses interested in making radio receivers had formed the National Broadcasting Company, whose name revealed in the plainest terms that RCA and New York were determined to dominate radio broadcasting in the United States.

Rauland also could not help wondering why WENR was the station the Great Lakes Broadcasting Corporation had chosen to buy and why they wanted it enough to pay such a staggering price. There were Chicago stations, Rauland pointed out, that could have been acquired for a fraction of that figure; half a million dollars would have bought any station in Chicago with the possible exception of WLS and WGN, owned by two wealthy Chicago publishing barons, Brundege D. Butler, publisher of Illinois' leading farm magazine, *The Prairie Farmer*, and Col. Robert R. McCormick, publisher of the *Chicago Tribune*. How could Rauland's little station, which did not even exist three years ago, be worth $1 million? It would have had little, if any, sale value on the day Everett Mitchell took over as station man ager on November 2, 1925. The changes he and Mitchell had made in the station during the past two and one-half years, Rauland calculated, had increased its value more than $1,000 a day.

Rauland also shared another observation with his station manager. He was certain, he said, that Insull had personally made the decision to buy WENR. There had been references, during the luncheon, to the magnificent studios that would be provided for WENR in the new opera house Insull was building on the banks of the Chicago River on the west side of the Loop.

Mitchell found it difficult to focus on his announcing duties the rest of the night. When he arrived home after the 2 a.m. sign-off, sleep did not even occur to him. He had to tell Mildred about the momentous developments, which both excited and disturbed him.

It was overwhelming to think that Samuel Insull, acknowledged to be one of the ten most powerful men in the United States, had personally made the decision to buy WENR at a figure Rauland could not in sanity turn down. Insull could have bought any other radio station in Chicago at a fraction of the WENR offer, and he could have had some of them for little more than an offer to pay up their bills. What did he have in mind?

Then there was the disturbing side, as Mitchell explained in the middle of the night to his thoroughly wide-awake wife. What did Insull really want with the station Mitchell had come to regard as almost his own? Would he really honor Rauland's condition that Mitchell have a role in running the station in the future? Would Mitchell have the chance to continue to expand WENR's unique blend of service, information and inspiration when the other Chicago stations were still making entertainment their stock in trade? Would he ever have a chance to meet Samuel Insull personally?

Mitchell voiced some of these concerns later to Rauland.

"I don't think you have a thing to fear, Everett," Rauland said. "Things will be different but some of the changes will surely benefit you. For one thing, you won't have to work so hard. That has worried me. If you find you can't be happy under the new ownership, I will still be here. I am sure that I could, in a short time, find you an important job in radio. Your service concept of radio will always get you a good job. Don't ever give it up."

(1) Mitchell still does not know what long-range plan Erbstein had for his radio station when he insisted on reclaiming the Kimball Building studio. Shortly after Erbstein sold his station to the *Chicago Tribune*, and WTAS was closed so the *Tribune's* station, WGN, could have a clear channel. A year later, in 1927, Erbstein died, leaving his Elgin estate to his widow, who converted it into the Villa Olivia Country Club.

A member of the Park Ridge Masonic Lodge for more than sixty years, Everett Mitchell reminisces as he shows off his Masonic ring.

# Chapter 14
# A Firestorm Between Giants

The last weeks of 1927, during which the details of the transfer of Station WENR from Rauland to Insull were being worked out, were anxious but exciting for Everett and Mildred Mitchell. At their breakfast talks, the only leisure Mitchell's seven-day schedule permitted, they tended to assume that Everett would continue to manage the radio station. Who else could the new owner find with so much proven experience?

The Mitchells reviewed Insull's alternatives. He could have brought Station WEBH, they reasoned, the Edgewater Beach Hotel station, with its fine musical program format. Or there was WHT, Mayor William Hale Thompson's station, with its impressive studio in the new white skyscraper just built by William Wrigley on Michigan Avenue's Magnificent Mile. This station had no clearly identified program format, affording a new owner the opportunity to develop whatever kind he wished. The fact that it was WENR that had been acquired, and at such a price, could only indicate that the Insull group was interested in the station's unique programming.

In their discussions this serious young couple - Everett with his sense of history and Mildred who kept scrapbooks about radio - recognized that the nation was undergoing a spectacular change. Spurred by a prosperity that continued at a constantly rising tempo during the 1920s, more and more people were buying motorcars, radios and electrical appliances. Electricity was no longer being used in homes solely for lighting; it was also providing central heating, and power for new appliances that made cooking and keeping house easier that it had ever been. Average families now had advantages and comforts that had not even existed just a few years before. Clearly, the nation was at an important turning point.

Events in 1927 dramatized the great changes. Lindbergh's solo flight across the Atlantic made Americans realize that the airplane was not just a machine to give thrilling rides at country fairs but a new kind of fast transportation, one that might someday even replace passenger trains and steamships.

Just a week after Lindbergh's flight in May, Henry Ford stopped the production of his famous Model T Ford and closed the Ford factory near Detroit. There had been fifteen million Model T Fords made since the first one in 1908; in fact, more than half the cars on the road in United States were Model Ts. But in the general prosperity Americans were turning to more expensive automobiles like the Cords, the Chryslers and the Jordan Playboys. (Ford would re-enter the automobile market more than a year later with the new, more powerful, faster Model A.)

An unprecedented sports craze was also sweeping the nation. Previously, sporting events had only been accessible to the well-to-do, but now, with radio to carry sports news across the nation and automobiles to carry people to games, families in even modest circumstances were caught up in the excitement. Star athletes such as Babe Ruth in baseball, Red Grange in football, Jack Dempsey in boxing, Bill Tilden and Helen Wills in tennis and Bobby Jones in golf were becoming as famous as Hollywood movie queens or the President of the United States.

But nothing documented the great change like the 1,103 pages of the 1927 fall and winter Sears, Roebuck and Company catalogue. After the Bible it was the most important reference book in the Mitchell home. Nothing impressed Everett so much as the 450 pages of ready-to-wear clothing. Making of clothing in the home, which had claimed so much of his mother's time, was disappearing at an astounding rate. Buggies, once given an entire section, were offered only on page 1,044, but there were twelve pages of Ford accessories and two for the upcoming Chevrolet. The catalogue also explained in detail that anyone could install one of the new Sears radios by following the carefully-worded instructions.

Faster train transport and higher family incomes were transforming even the grocery stores, especially the fresh fruit and vegetable counters. Oranges and bananas that had been seen in Midwest homes rarely except in Christmas stockings were now sold most of the year.

The Mitchells viewed the marvelous era into which the nation was moving with wonder, but also with some concern. They were fascinated with the many new aids to comfortable living, but other things, in conflict with their childhood home and religious training, made them apprehensive. Lawlessness seemed to be on the increase everywhere. In Chicago, murder was becoming a common spectacle, much of it a spin-off from illicit liquor traffic. The public conduct of many young people did not seem to fit them for happy and useful lives, the Mitchells thought. Everett at times observed that he was glad his Quaker father did not have to witness the evidence of the weakening of family ties and the increasing disregard of brotherhood.

Partly because of Everett's demanding schedule, the Mitchells in 1927 continued to live modestly in their small apartment. They did not yet own a car. They continued to help Everett's mother, to maintain close ties with their church (Everett moved his membership from the Methodist to the Lutheran to be with Mildred) and to save all they could in hopes that in time they could own a house of their own.

Convinced that sweeping changes were soon to come to radio, Mitchell's most searching scan of the future was focused on broadcasting and his part in it. His convictions were more than hunches. E. N. Rauland's All American Radio Company business contacts kept him informed of the rapid developments taking place in the nation's communications headquarters.

Rauland's own wizardry in electrical engineering also enabled him to project what was to come from the developments rapidly unfolding in the laboratories in the east. In their WENR management conferences, he told Mitchell about the exciting things he had learned, many of them not yet public knowledge and some of them hard to believe.

One such report was about the development of picture radio - television. A Westinghouse engineer, Vladimir Zworykin, formerly a communications expert in the Czarist army, had in December of 1923 demonstrated a primitive but practical system of television for Westinghouse executives. On December 29 of that year, Zworykin and Westinghouse filed a television patent application. In 1927, American Telephone and Telegraph (AT&T) demonstrated that its long lines could also be used to transmit television when Secretary of State Herbert Hoover spoke in Washington and was seen and heard on an AT&T receiving set in New York. In the fall of 1927 a magazine called *Television* was published for a short time in both New York and London.[1]

The stage for the United States leap forward in radio and electronics had been set during the World War I years, when the federal government required that everyone in radio research work together in the war effort. Control of all broadcasting facilities based in the United States was turned over to the U.S. Navy. These included the important ship-to-shore stations owned by the British firm, American Marconi. By far the most powerful was Station NFF at New Brunswick, New Jersey. Powered by a newly-invented alternator produced by General Electric, NFF could broadcast the human voice to all of Europe.

After wartime broadcasting had demonstrated the potential of the new medium, the United States government made two landmark decisions regarding radio. It ruled that in the interests of national security all radio stations on American soil be American-owned. This ruling was aimed largely at American Marconi. Congress also denied the Navy's request that it be allowed to continue operating American radio facilities in peacetime, thus leaving the field open to private development.

To implement the ruling on radio ownership, in 1919 the Department of Commerce suggested that General Electric form a subsidiary company, Radio Corporation of America (RCA), and fund the new corporation so that it could buy American Marconi and its coastal broadcasting stations. The sensitive negotiations were conducted by Owen D. Young of General Electric.

As the new radio stations which sprang up after the war began to broadcast, a market for home receiving sets began to appear. Many small companies such as Rauland's began producing parts and sets for this growing market. Seeing the trend, General Electric and Westinghouse, who had worked together during the war on radio receiver research, entered into cross-licensing and marketing agreements under which they pooled their know-how and patents to produce receivers superior to those of the smaller companies. All of the parts and receivers the two giants produced were marketed by RCA, an arrangement which gave it a virtual stranglehold on the home radio market.

By 1922 the battle lines were being drawn for control of the new field of radio broadcasting. The contenders were RCA and its allies and AT&T, which by this time owned a vast communications web of "long lines" that reached every important town and city in the United States. Both contenders wanted to reshape radio broadcasting by developing a network of stations with programming capacities far beyong that possible for any one single station. Both were sure there would be room for only one

This sound truck made it possible for Everett Mitchell on November 27, 1951, to "feed" the first television program from Chicago to the NBC television network. Mitchell was master-of-ceremonies on a "Parade of Champions" program from the International Livestock Show.

dominant network.

AT&T established Station WEAF in New York as its primary feeder station. RCA countered by buying Station WJZ in Newark, New Jersey, and moving it to New York. RCA also bought a New York station, WJY. All three stations were in place and broadcasting by 1923.

As early as 1922 AT&T was discussing linking up stations via its telephone lines and late in 1924 was actually quoting the toll costs for a network of thirteen stations. AT&T's first network effort extended as far west as Station WOC in Davenport, Iowa, as far north as Station WCCO in Minneapolis and as far south as Station WASI in Cincinnati. In all there were ten cities, each with a single station, except for Philadelphia, which had three. There was no Chicago link in the AT&T network since its adversary, Westinghouse, had the leading station, KYW, in that city.

RCA was working along the same lines. It had access to the Westinghouse stations in Chicago, Pittsburgh and Springfield, Massachusetts, and the General Electric station in Schenectady, New York. These, with the New York City stations, also served as an embryonic network. But simply owning stations was not enough; RCA also had to be able to send programs from one to the other. By far the best way to transmit radio programs was AT&T's long lines.

AT&T, however, saw no reason to give up the advantage it had with the long lines monopoly; it refused to move any but its own programs. RCA and its allies tried everything they could think of to by-pass the telephone wires but without success. At this point, AT&T held a clear lead in the battle to build a dominant network.

The corporate giants had kept their preliminary skirmishes as secret as possible lest the federal government become concerned about the sensitive issue of monopoly. But in 1924, a new development touched off an all-out war between the contenders which threatened to become public. The incendiary issue had nothing directly to do with either broadcasting or moving programs from one station to another. Even in 1923, there had been rumors that AT&T, through its big manufacturing subsidiary, Western Electric, was planning to produce and sell a home radio receiver. By early 1924 the AT&T plans had been confirmed. This would be a blow to RCA and its virtual monopoly in the production of home radio sets.

RCA seized the challenge and sought to turn it to its own advantage. Within days after the company had firm evidence that AT&T was entering the home radio market, RCA attorneys took the offensive. They served notice on AT&T that as a public utility it would be in clear violation of the federal anti-trust laws if it entered a new field of manufacture already effectively served by private enterprise.

The contenders entered into private discussions in hopes of resolving the dispute without outside interference. But the only thing on which they could agree was the massiveness of the opportunity that lay ahead. Still, they sought a means to resolve the matter quickly and without fanfare. A court battle might take years, during which the other corporations would almost certainly move into the broadcasting business and reap the rewards that were within the grasp of the belligerants. Also, both sides wished to stay away from federal probes into what might possibly be interpreted as monopolistic practices. So RCA agreed not to fight AT&T in court. Instead, both agreed to submit the controversy to binding arbitration before a single referee. They retained a New York lawyer, Roland W. Boyden, who specialized in industrial law and government-business relations.

Boyden began taking closed-door testimony early in the summer of 1924. He listened to both sides, sometimes as much as ten hours a day, all through the summer and early fall. The issues were clear. AT&T owned the long lines and believed it was entitled to decide what radio programs would move over them. RCA contended that because the long lines were a public utility other companies, including RCA and its allies, should have the right to lease them with no strings attached by AT&T. RCA also continued to hold firmly to its stand that a public utility such as AT&T had no legal right to enter into the home radio receiver market. In addition, the details of the cross-licensing pacts between RCA, Westinghouse and General Electric which gave them the lion's share of the home radio market were laid bare for Boyden's scrutiny.

Boyden's final opinion was issued in the spring of 1925. RCA and its allies were jubilant. They found it difficult to believe the referee had so universally held for their side. Boyden agreed that AT&T would have to lease its long lines to RCA or any other broadcasting service and also that AT&T could not enter the home radio receiver market. It appeared to be a sweeping victory for RCA.[2]

Another blow had also been struck at the AT&T long lines monopoly. While Boyden had been deliberating, the Federal Trade Commission (FTC), without knowing about the AT&T-RCA controversy, had been doing a study of its own on broadcasting industry practices. Shortly after Boyden's announcement, the FTC also held that AT&T must lease its long lines to legitimate broadcasters, under a standard toll schedule. But AT&T was not ready to give up the battle. The FTC had taken note of the marketing agreements between RCA and its allies, which, it said, had the appearance of a monopoly. In a bold charge, AT&T's attorneys attacked the RCA group in this weak spot and once again the great controversy was stalemated.

AT&T contended that the information gathered by Boyden about the cross-licensing practices of the RCA group, now documented for the first time, constituted proof of a monopoly, the kind of "conspiracy in restraint of trade" that the FTC was so concerned about. Its case was made more formidable because it was presented by one of the most respected lawyers of the 1920s, John W. Davis. who had been the Democratic candidate for president in 1924.

AT&T said that it found no fault with the Boyden ruling, but that under no circumstances could it enter into agreements of any kind with RCA and its allies since it was now apparent they were operating outside the law.

Finally, it was David Sarnoff, president and spokesman for RCA, who devised a means of breaking the impasse.[3] Sarnoff made two sweeping proposals. First, he asked that both AT&T and RCA completely remove themselves from radio broadcasting and the development of radio networks; instead, they should approve the creation of an entirely new corporation that would develop not one but two networks, assuring a maximum of programming. RCA and the other corporations involved in the controversy would provide the financial backing to make the new corporation operational immediately.

The second proposal represented a major concession on Sarnoff's own part. He had been in the forefront of those seeking ways to move programs without AT&T's long lines. Now he proposed that the long lines be the preferred means of moving radio programs from city to city. His proposal projected a network linking fifteen eastern cities at a first year toll of $800,000. AT&T was offered a long-term contract that would involve millions more in tolls as other cities were added to the network. The various parties to the controversy gave Sarnoff's proposals careful consideration. By July 7 they were all ready to sign documents supporting the general proposal.

Sarnoff and RCA moved quickly to implement the new understanding. Fourteen days later, on July 21, RCA called a press conference and gave the public its first indication that guidelines for the future of broadcasting in the United States had been set. AT&T's future role in radio would be limited to moving radio programs from city to city, and RCA's role would be only to form the new corporation that would develop the nation's first broadcasting networks. The new corporation would have certain responsibilities, such as buying AT&T's New York radio station, WEAF.

In August RCA announced its plans for the new broadcasting company. It would have two separate networks, both originating programs from New York and sending them across the nation to other stations.[4] The proposed name left no doubt about the new company's goals for network broadcasting. The name was the National Broadcasting Company.

On September 9 NBC was incorporated under the laws of Delaware. One of its first acts was to send AT&T a check for $1 million as payment for Station WEAF.

Within days RCA ran a full page advertisement in the New York newspapers announcing the formation of the National Broadcasting Company.

The heart of the announcement was that national radio broadcasting with high-quality programming would be "permanently assured by this important action of the Radio Corporation of America in the interest of the listening public." NBC would produce and broadcast these "better programs" and make them available to other radio stations throughout the country.

The announcement revealed that RCA was aware its action in forming NBC was on the edge of monopoly. Half of the thousand-word announcement was devoted to assuring the public that there was no intent of monopoly. An advisory council, to be made up of "twelve members representing all shades of public opinion" would be formed to further assure that programming would be of the highest quality and in the best interests of the public.[5] Also announced was the name of NBC's first president, Milton H. Aylesworth of Denver, who was resigning his position as managing director of the National Electric Light Association to develop network radio.[6]

Athough Everett Mitchell was aware of these developments in New York and sometimes speculated on their importance with

Rauland in their management conferences, he could see no immediate impact on Chicago radio. The drama being played out on the East Coast seemed like a spectacular but small cloud in a distant sky. He had no way of knowing that Sarnoff and Aylesworth would in a short time become his associates and that he would have an important role in developing the NBC network.

## FOOTNOTES

(1) Everett Mitchell was fascinated by Rauland's reports of radio accompanied by pictures. Although the Great Depression soon crushed the television research effort, which would not begin seriously again until after World War II, Mitchell steadfastly insisted during the 1930s and 1940s that "radio will be accompanied by pictures and you will see what you are hearing during my lifetime."

(2) Erik Barnouw, *A Tower in Babel; A History of Broadcasting in the United States,* Vol. I (New York: Oxford University Press, 1966), pp. 182-82.

(3) David Sarnoff, born of peasant parents in southern Russia, came to New York as a child in 1900. He took a messenger's job at Postal Telegraph and after hours taught himself telegraphy. He became acquainted with Guglielmo Marconi during the inventor's frequent trips to New York and was given a job as a wireless operator in the network of American Marconi stations on the northeastern seaboard. When the United States government forced American Marconi, owned by foreign investors, to sell to the newly-formed Radio Corporation of America, Sarnoff joined RCA. In a matter of months, at the age of thirty, he was named RCA's general manager.

(4) Following the agreement providing for two NBC networks, lists of prospective cities in each network were developed. The engineers who prepared maps of the two networks connected the cities of one with red lines and of the other with blue. Thereafter, they were known as the Red and the Blue networks. The double network continued until 1944 when the federal government ordered NBC to divest itself of one of them. NBC kept the Red network; the Blue network became the American Broadcasting Company (ABC).

(5) Barnouw, p. 187. A facsimile of the original advertisement appears here.

(6) Barnouw, p. 188. Aylesworth became president of NBC without any previous radio experience. He had never even owned a radio.

# Chapter 15
# Mr. Insull's Personal Announcer

New Year's Day in 1928 found Mildred and Everett Mitchell with more questions about the future than they had ever had before. The talks between E. N. Rauland and John Gilchrist, president of the new Great Lakes Broadcasting Corporation, were dragging; they had, in fact, been completely recessed for the holidays. Rauland and Mitchell had the impression that Gilchrist was stalling, not because of any misunderstanding with WENR but because he was reluctant to face the responsibilities of taking over and operating the radio station.

There may have been some validity in that impression. Gilchrist was a capable young administrator in the Insull domain but without any experience in radio. He was faced with several difficult problems in reorganizing the new venture, all of which required his immediate attention.

Gilchrist had observed that WENR was operating on a low budget, cutting costs wherever it could, such as using volunteer performers and exchanging Straus Building promotion on the air for studio rent. He knew that with the Insull group as station owners, everyone would expect to be paid. New policies for station operation would have to be developed.

Another matter concerned the permanent facilities for WENR, Insull's new Civic Opera Building then under construction. At the beginning plans called for turning over the top floor, the forty-third story, for the studios and executive offices of WENR. As further planning was done, it was decided that the forty-second and forty-first floors should also be made available. All of these decisions had to be made quickly.

In addition, Gilchrist's directors were determined that WENR wuld become a "clear channel" station, which meant that no other radio station in the United States could broadcast on the

Mr. Insull's personal announcer was the title conferred on Everett Mitchell by the Chicago radio reporters during the period when Insull owned and operated Station WENR as a part of the Great Lakes Broadcasting network.

same frequency. Col. Robert R. McCormick's Chicago *Tribune* station, WGN, had already won clear channel status. WENR was operating on a good mid-dial channel, but local stations outside of Chicago also used the same frequency, creating interference for listeners outside the immediate Chicago area.

The new owners were determined that WENR should use the maximum power of 50,000 watts allowed by the federal government. A contract was being drawn up with Western Electric to build a 50,000-watt transmitter, on the assumption that the Insull organization could obtain approval for a clear channel with 50,000-watt transmission from Secretary of Commerce Herbert Hoover.

The conferences to complete the transfer resumed in mid-January but were not immediately conclusive. Always looking on the bright side, Mitchell regarded the delay as evidence that the new owners in general approved of the way in which WENR was being run. Mitchell continued his seven-day-a-week schedule as usual, hoping for the best.

One day late in February rumors and speculation came to a sudden end. Gilchrist met with reporters and confirmed that the final terms of an agreement had been completed for the sale of Station WENR to the Great Lakes Broadcasting Corporation. The purchase had been made, Gilcrhist said, after a study of all Chicago area broadcasting stations. WENR had been acquired because of its wide reputation for service programming. Under the new ownership, its official name would be "WENR of Chicago—The Voice of Service."

The schocking part of the news release for Everett Mitchell and the WENR staff came in the final paragraph. Morgan L. Eastman, conductor of the Edison Symphony Orchestra, had been appointed station manager of the new WENR. B. G. Swift was named assistant manager.

The announcement seemed to say in the most convincing way that Everett Mitchell would not be manager of WENR again.

Mitchell was grateful that he had been given some advance notice of the appointments. That enabled him to report the news to his WENR staff and speak some words of assurance. As he had done often at periods of crisis, Mitchell reminded his associates of his father's belief that "disappointments often lead to God's appointments," adding that he had repeatedly found it to be true.

There were many telephone calls after the newspapers carrying the announcement were out that afternoon. Two were especially important. One was from the manager of WMAQ, the Chicago *Daily News* station whose studios would soon be located in the just-completed Daily News Plaza directly across the Chicago River from the Civic Opera Building. The manager expressed surprise that Mitchell had not been retained as WENR manager adding, "You can start any day as chief announcer at WMAQ."

The other important call was from Morgan Eastman. The newly-named station manager said he would come to WENR the next morning to discuss the transition.

The meeting was difficult for both men. Eastman, a slight man in his fifties who seemed determined to assert his authority, began by announcing that Mitchell and everyone else should continue to do their jobs until he could "arrange for their replacement." Eastman explained that he did not plan to retain anyone on the present staff. Mitchell was surprised. He could not help but wonder if this was really the man who was going to manage Station WENR, but he maintained an outward calm. Eastman advised Mitchell that he would be back in touch with him shortly. It was not a good start.

Everett was still shocked by the abrupt turn of events when he talked the matter over with Mildred the next morning. What disturbed him most was the indication that the Insull group had little understanding of what was required to operate a radio station in the highly competitive environment of Chicago broadcasting. In their discussion, the Mitchells agreed that Everett would probably not be at WENR for long. They decided that before making any move, he should talk to Rauland.

But before he had a chance to arrange a talk with his former employer, Mitchell received one of the most memorable phone calls of his life. Samuel Insull's secretary called to ask when it would be convenient for Mitchell to come to Insull's office in the Continental Bank Building (Insull maintained several offices) for a conference. The appointment was set for one o'clock on an afternoon early the following week. The secretary asked that Mitchell report to her not later than twelve forty-five, fifteen minutes before the appointment.

As he always did in approaching momentous events, Mitchell made a point of being well informed. He learned all he could about Insull's background and how he had managed to achieve such immense power.

Insull was born in London, England, in 1859 into a family of modest circumstances. His mother was brilliant, and for a time his father had political connections that enabled Samuel to attend historic Oxford. At nineteen young Insull took a job at the Edison Telephone Company in London where his assistant was George Bernard Shaw, who would later become as famous in letters as Insull would be in the field of energy and electric power.[1]

Insull's study at Oxford and his two years of association with young Shaw imparted to him a firm resolve to help the poor and encourage young people and a disdain for the idle rich. This personal philosophy contributed much to his achievement in business but isolated him socially from the wealthy society leaders. (When Insull built the Chicago Civic Opera building there were no traditional boxes in which the wealthy might be seen and display their latest finery. The Chicago Gold Coast set never forgave him.)

His energy and brilliance of mind earned him an opportunity to come to America as the private secretary of Thomas Alva Edison in 1881. Edison had invented his electric light only two years before. When Insull arrived, Edison was in the process of closing his famous Menlo Park laboratory and workshop in New Jersey and moving to New York City to be close to the building of the world's first large scale electrical generating plant.

Bankers and financiers behind Edison were so skeptical of the high cost involved in building the first large electrical generator that Edison was having to liquidate his own holdings elsewhere to complete the big Manhattan power station.[2] Insull arrived on the scene at a time when Edison's finances were in dangerous disarray, and he skillfully brought order out of financial chaos. As a result, the young Insull quickly became Edison's most trusted and useful aide. His salary rose in the first year from $1,200 to $13,000. Insull saved most of it.

The Edison Manhattan generating plant was an immediate success. It became the pattern for quick electrification programs in the populous northeastern quarter of the nation. Other plants developed after the success of the Manhattan facility included the Boston Edison utility, Detroit Edison, where Henry Ford[3] was employed while he built his famous "quadricycle," and Chicago Edison. But that was as far west as Edison's direct guidance extended. This western "hinterland," with Chicago Edison as its base, would later become the hub of the Insull operations.

Meanwhile Insull married, had a family and began taking an intense interest in American economics and politics. In 1896 he received his United States citizenship, primarily so he could work with the political campaigns of William McKinley, who later be-

From the beginning of Everett Mitchell's career in radio, mail from his listeners at home and abroad rolled into the studios. The many letters shown here were in answer to a crowing contest held on the *Farm and Home Hour*.

came President of the United States.

In 1892, eleven years after he had arrived from England, Insull owned Chicago Edison. He lowered the cost of electricity, bought out his competitors and in 1907 merged his Edison company with Commonwealth Electric, which operated Chicago's streetcars, to create the giant Commonwealth Edison Company. Gradually this mammoth concern spread across Illinois to the Mississippi River, becoming one of the largest utilities in the nation.

Meanwhile Insull was founding associated companies which produced not only electricity but manufactured gas for heating and lighting, operated coal mines and established railroads to move the coal for generating plants. At the time Everett met him, Insull owned companies providing electricity, gas and transportation in five thousand communities in thirty-two states.

If anything, his check into Insull's background made Mitchell even more apprehensive about meeting this man who collected thriving businesses the way some people collect rare books. He recalled how nervous he had been as a boy the morning Alvin McDonald took him to meet the famous evangelist Billy Sunday and how Sunday had been immediately friendly and reassuring, even calling him "son." He had since been told that most truly great people are friendly and courteous. Now he would have a chance to see.

Although being appropriately dressed had always been his practice, before the appointment with Insull Mitchell went to a Loop clothing store and bought a $35 suit (good suits could be bought for $15 to $20 in the spring of 1928) and the matching shirt and tie the haberdasher recommended.

Mitchell arrived at Insull's office about twelve-forty. He found that Insull had two secretaries, and an "outer" secretary in the waiting room and an "inner" secretary in an office situated in such a way that she could monitor Insull's wishes constantly. In the next two years Mitchell was to learn the system for meeting with Insull in every detail.

Exactly at twelve forty-five the outer secretary went in to report to the inner secretary that the person with whom Mr. Insull was scheduled to meet at one o'clock had arrived. At twelve fifty-nine Mitchell was escorted inside to meet the inner secretary. At thirty seconds before one o'clock, he was advised that he might go into Insull's office, where he should stand in front of the desk until he was invited to sit down.

At least fifteen seconds before one o'clock, Mitchell was stand-

Leonard K. Firestone, host of the *Firestone Champion Farmers*, watches as Margaret Speaks, distinguished soprano soloist, cuts a cake in honor of her sixth anniversary.

ing before the utility magnate's desk. Insull paid no attention to him but finished examining some papers on the desk before him. He seemed to devour an entire page at a glance. He might or might not make a notation on the page, then he would toss it onto the floor on one side or the other of his desk. Although Mitchell later saw many such accumulations of papers on Insull's floor, he was never able to determine what kind of order, if any, Insull tossed the papers.[4]

At what Everett Mitchell to this day believes was exactly one o'clock, the heretofore impassive Insull looked up, smiled graciously, and said, "Son, it is good of you to come. I have followed your work with great interest..."

For a little more than two years Mitchell would meet with Samuel Insull regularly, usually two or three times a month. On each of these occasions the routine was the same. There was always the personal greeting. And Insull always called him "son."

On this first occasion Insull explained that he needed Mitchell's assistance and added that he hoped they might work together closely in a number of ways. Insull said he would like Mitchell's help the following week, when he would be entertaining a group of engineering students from the University of Illinois who might become Insull company employees. He wanted Mitchell to lead some group singing before the luncheon was served. Then he would like Mitchell to handle his own introduction. It should be limited to a one-sentence identification phrased in whatever way Mitchell thought best.

Mitchell saw that he was not the only one who had been gathering background information. Insull knew enough about his career to be aware of his singing ability. Mitchell was later to realize that Insull had learned of all his contributions to WENR, including his solo work, before deciding to buy the station.

Pleased with the way Mitchell handled the student luncheon, at their next meeting Insull explained that he wanted to use the services of WENR to give the public more information about the corporate affairs of the Insull companies. The annual meetings of Commonwealth Edison would be broadcast. Insull would personally participate, and when he was to speak he wanted Mitchell to handle his introduction. Later Mitchell was called upon to introduce Insull many times, both on the air and at programs that were not broadcast. He appeared so frequently with Insull he came to be known as "Mr. Insull's personal announcer."

## FOOTNOTES

(1) Both Samuel Insull and George Bernard Shaw wrote briefly of having worked together in London. Insull described their work in his *Memoirs.* Shaw's reference to his association with Insull is found in the preface of his novel *The Irrational Knot*, published in 1905.

(2) From the moment Edison invented the electric light, he realized it would remain useless until electricity was widely available. Edison had to invent every gadget from the generator to the transformer to the fuse (for which he was granted more than one thousand United States patents) in his crash program to find a way to produce and distribute electricity to homes. Insull arrived in the midst of this historic effort. Edison realized that electricity had to be produced on a large scale in order to drive down the cost for widespread use. The reluctance of others to accept this fact opened the way for Samuel Insull to establish his utility empire, which by 1928 reached into most of the states in the union.

(3) Although he had the title of engineer for Detroit Edison in the 1890s, Henry Ford, then in his early thirties, was actually in charge of firing the furnaces producing steam to run the big generators. In 1896, the year he built his first gasoline-powered car, he attended the summer convention that Thomas Edison held annually for the management of his numerous companies. Ford sat next to Edison at one of the dinners, held in the Orient Hotel in Brooklyn, and explained his experiment with a gasoline-powered self-propelled vehicle. "Young man, that's the thing. Keep at it," Edison told Ford. It was the beginning of the long friendship and the later vacations they had together, sometimes joined by Harvey Firestone of the Firestone Rubber Company and naturalist John Burroughs.

(4) In an address before a group of retired people in Naperville, Illinois, in 1980, Mitchell described his meetings with Insull and the way Insull tossed his papers on the floor around his desk. Immediately a woman in the audience stood to be recognized. She said she had been a secretary for Insull late in the 1920s, serving both "inside" and "outside," and that Mitchell's account of Insull's method was correct in every detail.

# Chapter 16
# The Dream That Died As A Child

Almost immediately after Mitchell's conference with Samuel Insull, WENR manager Morgan Eastman asked to meet with him again. Eastman apologized for his "abruptness" at their first meeting on the grounds that it had been a hectic time for him. This remark left Mitchell with the impression that Eastman's appointment had been a last-minute development.

It was clear that Eastman now knew Mitchell was to have an important role in WENR's future. Still, he continued to take an assertive attitude. The station would make an immediate change in policy, he said. It would no longer use volunteer performers but would have "an ample budget for its operation," and those appearing before WENR microphones would now be paid.[1] Nor would it any longer be necessary for Mitchell to "do everything" as he had when Rauland owned the station.

At Rauland's station, Mitchell had been both "talent" and program director, Eastman added. Now, he decreed, Mitchell would have to give up one of these roles. At first Mitchell thought Eastman was proposing that he give up all work before the microphone, but he soon realized that Eastman meant only that he give up his singing role. The choice, Eastman explained, was for Mitchell to be either a performer or the program director. As program director he would continue to serve as master of ceremonies on many of the station's programs, and, Eastman's choice implied, continue to develop program ideas.

It was a ridiculous choice, a fact of which Eastman had to be aware. Because of the press of his other work, Mitchell had largely given up singing on WENR, except on special programs and at the 2 a.m. sign-off. He was sure Eastman knew exactly what choice he would make. But he decided to honor his father's advice and "sleep on the matter." He told Eastman that he would let him know the next day.

When Mitchell reported that he chose to accept the program director's role, Eastman was obviously pleased. He told Mitchell he would immediately receive a raise in pay. Mitchell could not help but believe Eastman had been ordered to name him program director. Mitchell also believed, although he could never confirm it, that Eastman forced his retirement as a soloist to make sure there would be no comparisons made between Mitchell and the relatively unknown soloists appearing with the Edison Symphony Orchestra, which Eastman continued to conduct and which now performed on Friday evenings on WENR.

As program director, Eastman said, Mitchell would be in charge of hiring staff to produce programs. He made no objection to Mitchell's keeping the present staff intact, evidently deciding to forget his earlier announcement that he would be replacing everyone. Mitchell was very pleased that he did not have the unhappy duty of telling his fellow workers they were no longer needed. But perhaps as a result of Eastman's first announcement, the orchestra leader had decided to leave WENR. This left Mitchell in need of a replacement. Remembering Frank Westphal, who had so capably directed the first WENR orchestra and who Mitchell had replaced as station manager, he called Westphal's mother. She said her son had mastered his drinking problem but was having trouble finding work. Mitchell interviewed Westphal and hired him to direct the WENR orchestra once again. It proved to be a pleasant and productive association for both of them.

Mitchell soon came to realize that a large part of Morgan Eastman's job was to be "front man" for Gilchrist. Eastman was to deal with the public, answer questions and pass requests on to Gilchrist and Mitchell. His job was time-consuming and tedious and did not involve much major decision-making, but it did take a large burden off Mitchell's shoulders. Mitchell soon saw that it was a difficult role for Eastman and one for which he had little taste or experience. He has always been sure that it was Samuel Insull himself who saw to it that he was not tied down to these administrative tasks.

With his direct channels to Insull and Gilchrist, Mitchell soon began to see the part WENR was meant to play in the Insull empire. Acquiring the station was the culmination of one of the grandest dreams in the entire realm of broadcasting. Like most great dreams, Insull's was not rooted in self-interest. It would make him no richer. Rather, it would require that he use his wealth and power to benefit the people of his adopted country.

Insull's interest in great music and the arts was sincere and deep. Before World War I he had become Chicago's leading supporter of the opera company and the symphony orchestra, not as a means of mixing with the social set, whom he despised, but because he and his wife wanted to see Chicago become a major cultural center. By the mid-1920s an idea was taking shape in Insull's mind, a conception of a building in which the world's great operas and symphonies as well as the classics of the theater could be presented. There seemed to be no reason why Insull himself should not create such a facility. His utility empire was thriving, the world was peaceful and the nation's future had the appearance of unlimited progress. It seemed the right sort of atmosphere to make a great dream come true.

By 1926 Insull had acquired a piece of land on the east side of the Chicago River, directly across from the property where Col. Frank Knox, publisher of the *Chicago Daily News*, would soon put down the foundation for the new Daily News building. Col. Knox's plan called for locating the newspaper's radio station, WMAQ, on the top floor. It was an idea Insull kept in mind.

By the middle of 1927 architects' sketches had been completed for the structure Insull had conceived, which would rise nearly six hundred feet into the Chicago sky. The new building would be fully as high as the recently-built Chicago Board of Trade building on LaSalle Street, recognized as the city's tallest structure. From its top floors there would be an almost unobstructed view of the lake.

The first ten floors on the south side of the building were to be given over to one of the world's great opera houses, large enough to seat an audience of four thousand. The lower floors on the north side would be allocated to a theater. There would be office space, rent free, for the headquarters of the Chicago Civic Opera, the Chicago Symphony and other groups committed to the city's cultural life.

Not only did Insull plan to pay for the building, he also had a plan to pay for its operation and maintenance. The Civic Opera Building would have enough extra office space so that its rental would maintain the entire structure. The Opera House and the theater would never be faced with rent bills.

The cost of maintaining the radio station on the top of the

Opera House would also be paid by the Insull companies. The radio station, too, was part of the grand dream. If Insull could complete his plans for a clear channel and 50,000-watt transmission, the cultural programs originating at the opera house could be broadcast to people all over America, in much of Canada and in some of Mexico.

There would be no reference on the cornerstone, or anywhere in the building, to Samuel Insull or the Insull companies. The building would be named simply the Civic Opera Building. Insull's dream, on which he would not even put his name, was a temple of culture rising in the greatest city in the American heartland.

By the time Mitchell became program director, Gilchrist and the staff of the Great Lakes Broadcasting Corporation were working feverishly to prepare WENR to take over its new role atop the Civic Opera Building. The 50,000-watt transmitter was on order and the station was seeking permission to use it and the assignment of a clear channel from the U.S. Department of Commerce. No one doubted that the arrangements could be made; the Insull utility companies maintained close ties with the Department of Commerce and in any case Insull and Secretary of Commerce Herbert Hoover were on good terms. Broadcasting hours of the new WENR, formerly eleven hours a day, were gradually being increased to eighteen hours, from 8 a.m. around the clock to 2 a.m.

There were big feature shows involving large costs. *The Smith Family*, written by Harry Lawrence, Chicago radio editor turned dramatist, and the WENR Minstrels, doing the weekly *Weener Minstrel Show* with Gene Arnold as the interlocutor, were two of the new entertainment anchors. Along with the Edison Symphony Orchestra, which performed weekly, was the fourteen-piece WENR Orchestra heard daily.

To back up its motto, "The Voice of Service," WENR presented a daily feature by a home economist, Anna J. Peterson, the first home economist to be heard in Chicago and perhaps the first to be heard on nationwide radio. To reach the station's increasing number of farm listeners, WENR installed a farm director, "Farmer" E. W. Rusk. Rusk and Phil Evans, well-known livestock authority for the Chicago stockyards, were heard daily.

One of the longest-lasting and most popular programs which Mitchell put on the air for Insull's station was the children's radio show, *Air Juniors*. Mitchell created the program in response to a request from the Commonwealth Edison Company in

Chicago, which wanted to sponsor a children's program that was educational and not simply entertaining. Mitchell was master of ceremonies for the program; WENR pianist and performer Irma Glen joined him as the show's regular hostess. The program was on the air each evening for one hour and for two hours each Saturday afternoon, when it featured child performers.

Children could enroll in the *Air Juniors Club* and receive membership cards and special WENR lapel pins. The membership cards were sent to most of the states in the union. Even today when Mitchell speaks in public it is not uncommon for someone in the audience to proudly show him an *Air Juniors Club* membership card.

Of the many programs Mitchell created and brought to the air in the years before network broadcasting in Chicago, none had so much impact or drew such a large audience so quickly as *Air Juniors*.[2] The *Chicago Times* reported that in the first six months 32,000 listeners (not all of them children) wrote for membership in the *Air Juniors Club*. "Irma and Everett are already known to children all over the country," the *Times* reported.

Evidence that the new WENR programming was also capturing a wide adult regional audience was found in the March 1929 issue of *Radio Digest*. "I think Everett Mitchell and Irma Glen have more personality than any artists I have heard on radio, and I will watch for any information regarding them with deep interest," wrote Mrs. C. D. Rector of Indianapolis, Indiana.

With the increase in broadcasting time, Mitchell's job of developing new programs and building the staff to support them was massive. Within three months there were twenty-five "before the microphone" specialists on Mitchell's staff. (Rauland's WENR at its peak had no more than twelve.) By the time the station moved to the top of the Civic Opera Building in the fall of 1929, there were nearly one hundred staff persons being heard each week—announcers, musicians, entertainers, educators and service specialists. No independent radio station in the nation could match the WENR staff or its variety of original programs.

The handling of advertising at WENR revealed the station's unusual goals. By now opposition to radio advertising was disappearing, and most Chicago stations were vigorously seeking advertising revenue. WENR was an exception. The station accepted "sponsors" only if they were willing to invest enough in talent and station time to produce a significant program.

This policy was not as high-handed as it appeared. Even in the

Rauland period, Mitchell had insisted that WENR programs have wide appeal. The new policy had the same goal. Only companies doing a regional or national business could afford to sponsor WENR programs. Insull did not intend that WENR would be merely a Chicago station.

Newspapers in other states took note of the unique advertising policy. A radio writer for the Akron, Ohio, *Beacon Journal* wrote a story headlined "WENR Creates Lofty Plane for Broadcasts" that was typical of these reports:

> WENR, Chicago, is setting a high standard for entertainment. In fact, it's set so purposefully high that most advertisers give the station a wide arc in passing. . . .
>
> Not wanting to step below the plane which it has created, the station demands that each advertiser spend at least $1,000 for entertainment during each hour broadcast. Many are called but few are willing.

While Samuel Insull was putting the foundation under his dream in Chicago, David Sarnoff and M. H. Aylesworth were moving the National Broadcasting Company's fortunes ahead rapidly in the east. NBC was launched at a grand opening in New York on November 15, 1926, only two months after it had come into existence. To emphasize the network's capacity to coordinate programs around the nation, there were "pickups" of comedian Will Rogers doing a spoof on President Coolidge from Kansas City, of opera star Mary Garden singing "Annie Laurie" from Chicago, and of famous bands like Ben Bernie's and Vincent Lopez' playing in cities across the United States.

In 1927 NBC launched its Red and Blue networks, fed by two New York stations, WEAF for the Red and WJZ for the Blue. By June 11, when Charles Lindbergh was being welcomed home to New York from his solo flight to Paris, there were fifty stations that had affiliated with NBC's new networks and were carrying the coverage of the ticker-tape parade live. On-the-spot radio coverage of such important events gave radio an excitement never before known in mass communications. That, and the many newer, better receiving sets on the market, meant a growing audience of radio listeners across the nation.[3] The new radio network grew, as well; with more stations joining monthly.

The first week of October, 1928, NBC introduced *The National Farm and Home Hour*, presented from the studios of KDKA in Pittsburgh over a thirteen-station network that extended from New England to Ohio. The new program was created by

162

This was the latest style microphone when Everett Mitchell became station manager for WENR in 1925.

Frank Mullen, former farm director of KDKA, who began broadcasting farm news over that station in 1923 while he was on the editorial staff of the *Stockman and Farmer* magazine, whose offices were in Pittsburgh. During 1923 his broadcasts were part of his work on the magazine staff, but in 1924 KDKA invited him to join its staff as the nation's first full-time farm director. Soon after its formation, NBC bought Station KDKA, and Mullen became a member of the NBC staff. He went to New York and proposed the network farm program to Aylesworth. The NBC president and Sarnoff not only liked Mullen's farm program idea, they were also greatly impressed with the clean-cut, pleasant and very knowledgeable young man from the Midwest. Since Mullen was already a member of the NBC family, it was a simple step to assign him other special duties, something Aylesworth began doing almost at once.

Everett Mitchell's interest in these important developments in the east was low key. None of them seemed to have significance for Chicago. The launching of the *The National Farm and Home Hour* was an example. Chicago was generally recognized as the agricultural hub of the nation, yet the new program did not even use a pickup from Chicago. In fact, the newly-organized Columbia Broadcasting System (CBS), taken over in the fall of 1928 by the Paley family, was making more stir in Chicago than NBC. Although its headquarters were also in New York, the new network, under President William S. Paley, had already established a Chicago affiliate, WBBM. The first serious NBC rival, CBS was quickly gathering member stations all across the country and for the moment being watched with more interest in Chicago than the giant NBC.

Also, there were other reasons, both personal and professional, for Mitchell's casual interest in the NBC developments. Now that WENR had more staff, it was possible for the Mitchells to take their first out-of-the-city vacation since Everett had become involved in radio five years before. In June they bought their first car and went to Colorado.

By the time Mitchell was back, a hearing on WENR's request to be allocated a clear channel had been scheduled before the Federal Radio Commission. Getting a clear channel had become increasingly complicated by recent events. A chaotic situation had prompted new legislation. Too many stations—by now about seven hundred—were broadcasting with too much power over too few frequencies. Often listeners trying to tune in a station could get nothing but static because of the interference. Prodded by Secretary of Commerce Hoover, Congress passed the Radio Act of 1927, which placed all radio channels under the control of the federal government. The act created the Federal Radio Commission (FCC), whose first job was to parcel out the limited number of broadcast frequencies to the many applicants.

All stations had to petition the Commission for licenses to broadcast. Both WENR and WLS, who had been using channels shared by small stations outside Chicago, asked for full-time clear channels.

At a hearing in November, 1928, the FCC made 870 kilocycles a clear channel and directed WENR and WLS to share it, with WLS having five-sevenths of the broadcast time. The split was unthinkable for WENR, but when the Great Lakes Broadcasting Corporation officials asked that the split be made fifty-fifty, the Commission turned them down.

WENR took its case to the Circuit Court of Appeals in the District of Columbia, which finally ruled that the clear channel must be shared equally by the two stations. WLS immediately appealed the ruling to the United States Supreme Court. Although the Supreme Court sustained the lower court's ruling, it was February 15, 1930, before WENR achieved its goal of being on a clear channel and using 50,000 watts of power.[4] In the meantime, WENR continued to use its old channel at 1050 kilocycles full time.

Before the end of 1928, while the station's studios were still in the Strauss Building, WENR had what in light of subsequent events was an important visitor, Frank Mullen of NBC. He called at the studio unannounced, asked to be given the "Cook's tour" of the studios and had a visit with Station Manager Eastman. In his brief visit, Mullen said that NBC had major plans for Chicago and that he was doing some scouting for President Aylesworth.

In the early fall of 1929 WENR moved to the top of the Civic Opera Building. The Chicago papers all ran glowing reports of the new WENR studios. The *Chicago Tribune* radio writer gave a detailed account:

> What is believed to be the most elegantly appointed radio studio in America, the $150,000 plant of Station WENR on the three top floors of the Civic Opera Building, will be formally opened at 8:30 tomorrow evening with a reception for invited guests and a special program.
>
> The series of studios, visitors' galleries, audience rooms,

operating rooms and offices occupy the three top floors of the skyscraper, forty-one to forty-three stories above Wacker Drive. The studios, etc., are on the forty-second floor. Studio No. 1, the main one, is approximately 30 feet wide, 52 feet six inches long and 19 feet three inches, or two stories high, and is a modern adaptation of a roof garden.

Operations at WENR changed with the move to the new studios. For the first time, Samuel Insull began taking a personal interest in the station, even visiting the studios while programs were in progress.

One afternoon, Mitchell remembers, Insull came unannounced by the back door into the large Studio One, attracted by the sounds of hilarity. The *Smile Club* program was in progress, a big production devoted to shut-ins, the first program of its kind in Chicago.

The afternoon Insull stopped in, the *Smile Club* was being dedicated to patients in a Chicago area veterans hospital. When the cast saw Mr. Insull come into the studio, the sight of the famous man, whom many had not seen in person before, all but collapsed the show. The surprise was so great that it took Mitchell several minutes of concentrated effort to restore the pace.

At the first opportunity, Mitchell went to speak to Insull. Insull asked what had stopped the show. Mitchell explained that Insull's unscheduled visit had given the staff a sudden case of stage fright. Insull said he had never intended to create a problem. Then he took a seat and not only stayed for the remainder of the program but entered into the hand-clapping and "amens." When the show was over and the studio off the air, Insull came to the microphone, gave Mitchell a hearty handshake, waved to the performers and then was gone.

Mitchell has another unforgetable experience during the fall of 1929, one that gave him the opportunity to meet many of the famous men and women of the time. The occasion was the celebration of the Golden Jubilee of Light in Dearborn, Michigan, arranged by Henry Ford to honor his old friend Thomas Alva Edison on the fiftieth anniversary of Edison's perfecting the incandescent light bulb.

Although cities, towns and villages all over America took part, the world headquarters for the great celebration was Henry Ford's Greenfield Village Museum. Ford had secured Edison's original Menlo Park, New Jersey, laboratory and had completely restored it to the smallest detail, using much of the original equipment. As the highlight of the celebration, Edison would repeat each important step of his historic experiment.

The experiment was scheduled on Monday, October 21, when President Herbert Hoover would come to deliver his Jubilee address. But the event was actually a three-day celebration that began with the arrival of Thomas Edison on Saturday. Mitchell was present both as a representative of WENR and, more important, the personal representative of Samuel Insull.

Henry Ford sent his private railroad car, Fair Lane, to East Orange, New Jersey, for Mr. and Mrs. Edison and their son, Edison's former secretary, William H. Meadcroft, and other former co-workers. Meeting the Edisons at Greenfield Village were Mr. and Mrs. Henry Ford, Mr. and Mrs. Edsel Ford and a small group of others, including Everett Mitchell.

Immediately Henry Ford took his guests to the restored Menlo Park laboratory, which Edison had not seen for almost fifty years. The eighty-two-year-old inventor stopped at a small mercury vacuum pump which was operating perfectly, took out a notebook and pencil and began making notes. "I've been having a little trouble with a job I am doing, and there right in front of me I see where I worked out the same problem fifty years ago," he explained. He watched the pump for a few moments and continued to take notes.

Before evening Harvey Firestone had arrived, and the old friends, Edison, Ford, and Firestone, who had often vacationed together, spent the evening visiting.

The Henry Fords had invited six hundred guests to help honor Thomas Edison. Many of them arrived on Sunday. In the afternoon and again in the evening there were receptions for the guest of honor. For Mitchell the day seemed like a dream even after it was over. He met Henry Ford and was introduced to Thomas Edison, with whom he had a short visit. Edison was keenly interested in news of his longtime friend, Samuel Insull, especially his having acquired a radio station. Before the day was over Mitchell had met Orville Wright, Dr. William Mayo, Harvey Firestone and many other famous Americans.

On Monday the President and Mrs. Hoover arrived. That evening the guests were served dinner in the Greenfield Village replica of Philadelphia's Independence Hall. They began their banquet by candlelight, as did the hundreds of groups and organizations throughout the country who were holding dinners as well as the people who were commemorating the event with family and friends. The candles and kerosene lamps were a reminder of how dining was before the coming of Edison's electric light.

At 7:30 Edison, in the restored laboratory, began to retrace the steps that fifty years earlier had led to the lighting of the first incandescent light bulb. There was no hitch in the re-enactment and at 8:09 the replica of the first light bulb came alive. Within seconds, thanks to the new NBC network, Americans from coast to coast, including those at Greenfield Village, switched on electric lights in a nationwide tribute to Thomas Edison. At 8:30 p.m. a special tribute direct from Germany, again through the magic of radio, was given to Edison by Albert Einstein. After the dinner, President Hoover gave the national tribute to the Wizard of Menlo Park.

By the fall of 1929 it was becoming evident that the National Broadcasting Company's interest in Chicago was intensifying. Frank Mullen was becoming a regular caller. On one of his visits, which came soon after WENR was moved to the Civic Opera Building, Mullen spent an evening looking over the new station headquarters and observing a number of programs. Mitchell was the announcer handling the programs on that particular evening. When Mullen realized that Mitchell was the program manager, he remained for more than two hours to talk between station breaks. Mullen seemed impressed with the station's new studios and with the number of service programs carried by WENR.

Others from NBC were seen in Chicago with increasing frequency. There were even reports that the NBC president, M. H. Aylesworth, and David Sarnoff of the Radio Corporation of America, the company that owned fifty percent of the stock of NBC, had been in Chicago separately and together.

Then came the announcement. At last everyone knew the extent to which Chicago figured in NBC's future plans. The Marshall Field estate was erecting the nation's largest office building, the Merchandise Mart, on the north side of the Chicago River facing Wacker Drive. When completed, the building would be two blocks long, a block deep and nineteen stories high. Aylesworth and Sarnoff wanted to establish headquarters in the new Mart with studios for originating programs, executive offices, and, most important, the technical facilities for dis seminating programs nationwide on both the Red and the Blue networks.

This would require more space than the builders could arrange

Everett Mitchell and the *National Farm and Home Hour* presided over the greatest farm sporting event ever held in October, 1940, when 140,000 people gathered on a farm near Davenport, Iowa, to witness the 1940 National Cornhusking Contest. Mitchell was reporting the Battle of the Bangboards begun in 1922 by Henry A. Wallace, editor and publisher of *Wallace's Farm Magazine.*

in the existing plan. Finally, the Marshall Field estate agreed to add two stories, the twentieth and twenty-first floors, to the top of the Merchandise Mart, and NBC agreed to take a fifty-year lease. The appointments for the new studios were built to NBC specifications. NBC also announced that it would soon acquire two Chicago radio stations to function as regional feeders for its two networks.

Everett Mitchell returned from the Golden Jubilee of Light on Tuesday, October 22. The year of 1929 had been the most demanding of his career, a stubborn pattern of days that began early and ended late. Besides his work at the microphone he had struggled to expand the WENR broadcasting day to eighteen hours and to implement Gilchrist's goal of presenting programs of special interest to every member of the family, from small children to grandparents. There had been the intense preparations necessary for the move to the Civic Opera House and the additional duties of assisting Samuel Insull at his radio and other public appearances.

Mitchell had had little time to see his family, much less take a vacation. He had promised Mildred weeks before that after the Golden Jubilee, they would take a long-planned auto trip (a major undertaking before roads were paved and one that had to be done in the dry fall season) to New England.

The Mitchells left Chicago late in the week and were in Maine by Tuesday, October 29. Being on vacation, they were hardly aware of news, but on this day the financial strength of many American businesses simply disappeared in the worst stock and bond collapse the nation has ever known. Even the strongest institutions were rocked to their foundation, and the shock left the American people from President Hoover on down to the most menial worker in a daze of disbelief.

Early in September the New York stock market had begun to show signs that the climb that had lasted more than four years was leveling off, if not coming to an end. On the Thursday before the crash, spoken of as "Black Thursday," there had been a $5 billion decline in the value of New York Stock Exchange stocks. Businesses had been wiped out in the rush of selling, and at least one business executive took his life in his office.

But all that had gone before paled against what took place on October 29. On this day events occurred never before witnessed in stock exchanges anywhere in the world. One wealthy New York business investor began the day with $17 million in cash. He attempted to protect his stock and ended that day owing a million dollars to each of three New York banks.

By 2 p.m. the entire world of American stocks was in disarray. Even veteran stockbrokers could not keep track of what was happening. The president of a successful old line cigar manufacturing company saw his stock selling at $115 a share at the beginning of trading that day. At 1 p.m. it had dropped to two dollars a share. This was more than he could stand. He went to the window and jumped to his death from his Wall Street office.

Even blue chip stocks experienced unimaginable losses. The largest businesses in the nation, including General Motors, General Electric and even AT&T recorded staggering losses in the value of their stock. On October 29 General Electric stock dropped forty-eight points from the day before and AT&T dropped thirty-four points as stockholders dumped even their most valuable holdings in the panic.

Leaders like Samuel Insull understood the realities triggered by the stock market disaster. Insull knew that unless some way could be found to restore the public interest in investing in stocks to permit business development, all his plans and dreams for the future would soon perish. This must have been in his thoughts three weeks later on November 19 when he was honored on opening night at his Civic Opera House before a capacity crowd of four thousand, the largest audience ever to see and hear an opera indoors in this country.

Everett and Mildred Mitchell continued their vacation trip through New England, not completely aware of the seriousness of the stock collapse. When they arrived in Chicago in mid-November, they were shocked to learn of the drastic changes the crash had already brought in their way of life. In an effort to redevelop stability in the operating utilities, such as Chicago's Commonwealth Edison Company and the Public Service Company of Northern Illinois, Insull executives had already cut wages of all employees of all Insull corporations by ten percent. The Great Lakes Broadcasting Corporation was, of course, an Insull company.

Even worse, the stock of the Insull companies concerned with investments and financing the huge utilities, like the Insull Utility Investments and Utility Securities Company, was no longer even listed on the stock exchange. These stocks were currently worthless, and within a month it began to appear that they might never recover. They never did. These were the stocks that before October 29 had been regarded as fully as sound as government bonds. These were the stocks in which tens of thousands of

Americans, including Everett and Mildred Mitchell, had invested their life savings, hoping to buy a home, educate their children and provide for their old age.[5]

"When I got home," Mitchell recalls, "I had already been given a ten percent cut in pay and it looked as though my savings might be gone too. Within a couple of weeks I knew they were. We had worked hard and lived frugally to accumulate those savings, which when we left on our vacation would have built two nice houses.

"While I didn't see it quite that clearly then, all I really had left was the seventy-five dollars in cash we had with us when we came back from New England. But I was lucky. I had a job."

As Mitchell returned to his duties at WENR, he found everyone in some degree changed by the new economic situation. Everyone was apprehensive about the future. There was less laughter in the corridors. Mitchell met with the producers of the station's comedy shows and emphasized that their programs were now more important than ever before, because laughter was the best way to raise people's spirits and restore their confidence.

At no time was Mitchell as much impressed with the change as the first time he met with Samuel Insull after the crash.

"Well, son, a lot has happened since the last time we met," was Insull's greeting.

Insull seemed older (he was then seventy). His manner was subtly different. He appeared to be more concerned about the present, whereas before he had generally focused on the future. He seemed more kindly and more concerned about the well-being of those around him. He made no direct reference to the crash.

Not every business was adversely affected by the economic crisis. The young radio industry was among those that defied the depression. The public continued to buy radio receivers in 1929 and through the rest of the Great Depression. Supported by profits rather than having to face losses, the industry was able to continue its expansion. This was nowhere demonstrated more convincingly than at NBC.

The National Broadcasting Company had earned a profit almost from the beginning. Since its stock was entirely held by the strongest corporations in America—RCA, General Electric and Westinghouse—NBC was immune to the crisis in the stock market. NBC made an offer to buy not only Station WMAQ but Station WENR as well. The offer was not withdrawn as the economic crisis deepened but was pressed even harder. Within months after the October catastrophe, Insull agreed to the sale, which was delayed only until a satisfactory arrangement could be worked out with the Federal Radio Commission and Station WLS for a shared time agreement on the 870 clear channel. Terms of the sale became effective in early 1931.

With the sale, Mitchell's association with Samuel Insull came to an end. In 1932, as the agony and terror of the depression demanded that there be scapegoats, Insull was charged with criminal intent to defraud in his handling of his investment companies in the years before the stock crash. Aware that at the time a fair hearing of the charges would be impossible, he resigned his eighty-five directorates and went to Europe, returning when the climate for settling matters seemed more favorable. The Chicago World's Fair was in progress when he came back to America to stand trial, in which he was ultimately vindicated on all counts.

Everett Mitchell was an established personality on the NBC network by 1934. He had the assignment of "putting on the network" the daily concert of the United States Marine Band at the World's Fair. On an afternoon late in June, 1934, Mitchell noted, from his position at the microphone, that Samuel Insull was sitting in the back row of the large crowd. As soon as the concert was over, Mitchell went to meet him.

Insull inquired about Mitchell's work at NBC during the time the former utility magnage had been in Europe. The men spoke of old times and how unnecessary the suffering of the depression was, since people wanted to work and the need for goods and services had never been greater. Always conscious of time, Insull soon made ready to leave. He had stood up to go when he turned once more to Mitchell.

"Son, you have a great career ahead of you. These business problems will get straightened out in time, perhaps more time than I have. I have only one piece of advice for you. Choose your friends carefully. Make sure the roots of friendship go down to bedrock. I made one important mistake. The roots of my friendships were in shifting sands."

Insull held out his hand. Then, with a gracious smile, he was gone. Everett Mitchell never saw him again.

### FOOTNOTES

(1) It was Mitchell's painful job to notify the amateur performers that they would no longer be needed at WENR. Few of them ever broadcast again. There were exceptions, however, such as Mitchell's friends Charles Correll

and Freeman P. Gosden. The two did Negro comedy skits and were at the time performing nightly on WEBH, the Edgewater Beach Hotel station, in exchange for meals. They were hired by WGN when WEBH let its amateurs go, and together were paid $50 a week. Later they moved to WMAQ and within months of the move had a $100,000 a year contract with NBC for their Amos 'n Andy show. The show established them among the nation's leading entertainers for a generation.

(2) The program maintained its popularity for many years. In the early 1930s, in the depth of the Great Depression, Commonwealth Edison was forced to withdraw its sponsorship. Announcements that the show was going off the air brought many letters to the station (by then part of the NBC network) and comment in the radio columns of the newspapers. NBC executives decided to continue the program at network expense until a new sponsor could be found. In all *Air Juniors* was broadcast live for fifteen years, with Mitchell presenting the show all of that time.

(3) As soon as the agreement on broadcasting's future had been reached between RCA, AT&T and the other firms, RCA, in an effort to beat back monopoly charges, offered to license a limited number of competitors to manufacture radio receivers under the package of patents controlled by them. There were some spectacular results. With Zenith leading the way, receivers operating on regular house current rather than on battery power were offered before Christmas in 1927. The same year Philco took the lead in introducing car radios. E. N. Rauland's All American Radio also got a share in the patent distribution and profited from the agreement.

(4) The time-sharing agreement between WENR and WLS made WENR primarily an afternoon and evening station and WLS (then owned by *Prairie Farmer* magazine and broadcasting to a farm audience) an early daytime station. WENR would begin broadcasting about 3 p.m. and continue through the evening hours, except for Saturday when WLS put is famous *National Barn Dance* on the air. The split time arrangement continued until the mid-1960s, when WLS bought WENR from NBC, took over the entire channel and cancelled the WENR call letters.

(5) Everett Mitchell's life savings were invested in the Insull Utility Investment Company bonds. They are today pretty pieces of paper. Yet Mitchell continued to hold Insull in high regard, convinced that the courage, judgment and energy with which he met the problems of the crash no doubt prevented the collapse of the operating companies, which would have increased the suffering many fold.

174

One of the first children's programs broadcast from Chicago was the *Air Scouts*, later renamed the *Air Juniors*, broadcast on WENR. The host and hostess for the program were Everett Mitchell and Irma Glen. Each child was offered a membership card and pin.

The dedication of the new 50,000 watt transmitter at Downers Grove for WENR occurred soon after Samuel Insull became its owner. On hand for the ceremonies were Ransom Sherman (left), an actor, and Everett Mitchell.

# Part 4
# It's A Beautiful Day in Chicago

Radio and television personalities, almost from the beginning of broadcasting, have used special opening or closing comments, repeated on each program. The intention has been to give a greater degree of individuality to the program and to establish a closer and more lasting audience relationship.

This has been a favorite practice of broadcasters presenting the news. Seeking to emphasize the authoritativeness of his newscasts, Walter Cronkite for years signed off with "And that's the way it is."

Stressing name linkage, friendliness and an invitation to listen to the next program, Lowell Thomas finished each newscast with, "This is Lowell Thomas saying 'So long until tomorrow.'" Calling attention to the wide area where his broadcasts were heard, the late columnist and broadcaster Walter Winchell began his news program with a crisp "Good evening Mr. and Mrs. America and all the ships at sea."

These special additions have been used on other types of programs as well. For years Ed Garner opened the classic humor program, *Duffy's Tavern*, with this remark: "Archie the manager speaking. Duffy ain't here. Oh, hello, Duffy." The immortal Jimmy Durante imparted a note of nostalgia and mystery to his radio programs and later his television specials with this closing: "Goodnight, Mrs. Calabash, wherever you are." Durante refused ever to explain the meaning of his memorable program signature.

With but one exception, these special openings and closings served only to identify the personalities and programs and to promote greater listener identification. The exception was Everett Mitchell's "Beautiful Day."

Even on that first day in 1932, the audience that heard him say "It's a beautiful day in Chicago. It's a great day to be alive, and

177

I hope it is even more beautiful wherever you are" knew there was something special in the message. They sensed that Mitchell was concerned about them and their day-to-day battle against the greatest depression this nation has ever known. What they could not know was that Mitchell's concern was so great he risked his job as moderator of the *National Farm and Home Hour* to bring them a message of hope and cheer.

As Mitchell left the studio that day, the NBC switchboard was swamped with calls for him. The first call was from a man speaking at his own expense from halfway across the nation. "How could you say something like that in times like these?" he asked. "But it made me feel so good. Please say it again tomorrow."

Everett Mitchell continued to say it to millions each week for more than thirty years.

# Chapter 17
# Haystack, Strawstack

By the fall of 1930, Chicago broadcasting facilities capable of sending radio programs to every state in the nation were in place. The two floors atop the new Merchandise Mart were in use by the National Broadcasting Company (NBC) with its two independent networks, the Red and the Blue. The growing Columbia Broadcasting System (CBS), located in the new Wrigley Building, was also using Chicago as its major program dissemination point. Col. Robert R. McCormick, owner of the Chicago Tribune, was organizing yet another radio network, the Mutual Broadcasting System based in Chicago.

Even though the Great Depression was swamping businesses right and left, the new radio industry's profits were going off the tops of the charts. NBC used its considerable resources to further entrench its position in Chicago and the nation's midsection. Not only was NBC producing and feeding programs across the nation from its headquarters in the Merchandise Mart, it was also originating programs in the almost-new studios of WENR at the Civic Opera Building, the station it was in the process of buying from the Insull interests.

Everett Mitchell moved quickly and securely through the transition from Insull to NBC ownership of WENR. He was saddened by the fact that less than half of his big WENR staff could be retained as the station's programs were meshed with the NBC operation. The business upturn that America hoped for had not materialized. There were few jobs to be found even in radio, although it was relatively unaffected by the deepening depression.

Niles Trammell, vice president in charge of the Chicago operations, sent a message to Mitchell as program director of WENR, asking him to prepare a memorandum giving the salary of every WENR employee and to bring it to him within two days.

When Mitchell went to report, Trammell was delightfully low key. He inquired about Mitchell's family and his experiences in radio. Within minutes a lifelong friendship had begun between the young Chicago announcer and Trammell, who was second in NBC management only to the president, M. H. Aylesworth. (Later, Trammell became NBC's second president upon Aylesworth's retirement.)

After reviewing all of the responsibilities that Mitchell had at the Insull station—program manager, producer of important programs, announcer and station promotion director—Trammell turned to Mitchell.

"You have been doing several important jobs, some of which we are already staffed to handle. We have adequate management and promotion people. You will be classified as an 'announcer' at NBC. We are paying our announcers $25 a week. How much are you being paid now, Everett?" he asked.

"My report provides that information," Mitchell answered, and Trammell began examining the report.

"You are getting $175 a week, and we don't have an announcer even in New York who is paid that much in these times. But I'll tell you what I will do. I will continue your $175 a week salary so long as you don't permit other announcers to know what we are paying you.

"It will be unusual, but I think we will make you the official producer of *Air Juniors*," Trammell continued. "You will be paid for that, but you will get just one check for $175. But you will be known as an NBC announcer."

At the time, Mitchell had no idea why Trammell was willing to pay him seven times the base pay for NBC announcers while insisting that he continue to be known as an announcer. Trammell, of course, knew that Mitchell brought a wide range of experience to the new Chicago NBC staff and that an announcer could be given a variety of assignments. The "announcer" title was merely a convenience.

Mitchell was soon to find this out. President Aylesworth decided to present a complete "live" opera performance from Chicago's new Civic Opera Building each Friday evening over the entire NBC network. Presenting the opera was a complicated broadcasting task, and Mitchell was chosen to handle the job. The assignment required him to be master-of-ceremonies without a script for at least three hours. Only Graham McNamee, NBC's ace announcer who broadcast on-the-spot events nationwide, had been given the authority to handle network programming without a script.

The most exacting part of the assignment was the twenty-minute intermission—twenty minutes of continuous description done mostly ad-lib by the announcer. Mitchell would begin the intermission by describing the new auditorium. He would then report on some of the famous persons present. Before the intermission was over he would recount what had already unfolded in the opera story and give comments on what was to come.

There was an unexpected pleasure for Mitchell in the opera assignment. Each Friday evening Samuel and Mrs. Insull would come to the opera and pass within a few feet of the NBC announcer's booth. Insull never failed to pause an instant, turn slightly and smile. Mitchell got the impression that the smile, interpreted, said, "Son, you are doing a fine job. I'm proud."

The opera broadcasts proved to Trammell, Aylesworth and Sarnoff that Mitchell could be counted on to put any special event "on the network" and give a performance that would reflect favorably on NBC with listeners from coast to coast.

In the fall of 1931, less than a year after Mitchell had joined NBC, he was appointed chief announcer in Chicago. He was now in charge of assigning the announcers for all NBC programs. In addition, he volunteered to organize and teach a class on the art of announcing for the studio page-boys. In the years that followed a number of topflight NBC announcers appeared who had gotten their start in Mitchell's announcers' school.

This friendly yet aggressive young radio personality seemed targeted for a career that would take him into more administrative work, such as his chief announcer's job. Before retirement he might hope to become the vice president in charge of the huge NBC broadcasting service in Chicago or even the network's national president.

But this was not to be. Instead, Mitchell was moving toward a life-long career before the NBC microphone. The incident that set him on this course occurred on an October morning in 1930 at the NBC offices in the Chicago Merchandise Mart.

The afternoon before, Frank Mullen, whose title now was Director of Agriculture for NBC, called Mitchell for an appointment. Mitchell knew that Mullen was devoting his entire time to guiding and improving radio's first network farm program, the *National Farm and Home Hour*, broadcast across the nation over both NBC networks from Chicago. Mullen gave no hint as to what their conference was to be about.

When Mitchell arrived for the appointment, Mullen, whose manner indicated that he was confronted with a serious problem came immediately to the point.

"Everett, do you know the difference between a haystack and a strawstack?"

Mitchell was surprised and for a moment thought it was the opening line of the latest office joke. "I've not heard the joke before, so what is the punch line?" he asked.

Mullen assured him this was no joke. He really did need to know if Mitchell understood the difference between a haystack and a strawstack.

Still thinking it might be a game, Mitchell answered in the most elementary terms. "Hay is livestock feed for winter use, grass or clover cut in the summer and dried. It is stored either in stacks in the field or in the barn.

"Straw is the stems and leaves of grain crops left after the threshing machine has removed the grain. The straw is blown from the threshing machine and put in stacks, usually right in the field where the crop is grown. Generally it is used later in the barn as bedding for farm animals. Straw is not feed. Hay is."

Mullen's face registered a mixture of surprise and disbelief. His first reaction was that Mitchell had been tipped off to his question in advance.

"Would you be offended if I asked you how you knew the answer to my question?" he asked.

"I know from experience," Mitchell answered. "Until I was six years old we lived on a small farm. My father raised vegetables for the Chicago market, but we had no pasture ground. In the summer I used to go with my father to the open prairie where he cut hay with a cradle to feed our two horses and the family cow in the winter," Mitchell reported.

"Father raised no grain so we had no straw. He would go to the neighbors, usually about three times each winter, to get some bedding for the animals," Mitchell added.

Mullen, who had grown up on a South Dakota grain farm and spent many a summer day on the threshing·run, saw that Mitchell knew what he was talking about.

"Well, Everett, there is no question but that you know the difference between a haystack and a strawstack."

Only then did Mullen reveal what had occasioned his question. Months before the program created by Mullen and now heard on some sixty Red and Blue stations had been moved from KDKA in Pittsburgh to Chicago. A New York announcer, Wallace Butterworth, had been brought to Chicago primarily to be the announcer for the farm show.

The shift to Chicago proved to be unfortunate for Butterworth. A handsome, articulate man in his mid-thirties, he had spent his entire life in New York. He had been a highly successful shoe store clerk when he decided to enter the radio business as an announcer. His shoe store job required that he dress well for his stylish Manhattan customers. He wore spats, a derby and in cool weather a velvet-collared overcoat.

When he came to Chicago, Butterworth continued to dress as he had in New York. Some of his colleagues on the Chicago announcing staff resented his unusual dress. They thought he stuck to his New York attire as a way of reminding them that he was from the "home office" and therefore a better announcer. On occasion, too, he had remarked that Chicago was a "hick town."

Though Butterworth's attitude did not endear him to the other announcers, it was handling the farm program that brought about a crisis. In the studio everything was done from a script, carefully reviewed in advance by Mullen, but the on-farm broadcasts involved Butterworth in difficulties which were to prove his undoing. When going to farms to do "pick-ups," Butterworth continued to wear his spats and derby and his velvet-collared coat. With his rural hosts, this instantly labeled him as a "city slicker." Also, when doing the on-farm broadcasts he was required to introduce the farmers taking part and to describe the farm scene without a script.

The week before Mitchell's interview Butterworth had handled a *Farm and Home Hour* on-the-scene broadcast of a corn husking contest on a northern Illinois dairy farm. The contest was broadcast from a nearby grain field and the makeshift studio was next to a strawstack. Butterworth several times during the program referred to the strawstack as a haystack.

"Our listeners realized Butterworth's error and the mail has been heavy and critical," Mullen told Mitchell.

"We are going to make a change," Mullen added. Then came the electrifying question. "Everett, would you like to be considered for the *National Farm and Home Hour* as announcer?"

Mitchell, finding it difficult to believe what he had heard, hesitated a moment. Then he assured Mullen that he would, indeed, like to be considered.

From that moment matters moved rapidly. Mullen asked Mitchell if he could arrange to clear his schedule for the following Tuesday so they might drive through the farm country near the Illinois-Wisconsin line. As they drove through this lush dairying area in Lake County, Illinois, Mitchell described the farms they saw as he might picture them to a radio audience—the crops, livestock and farming practices. Even as they drove, Mitchell was aware that Mullen was impressed.

At noon they listened to the *National Farm and Home Hour* on Mullen's new car radio. Then they stopped for lunch on Milwaukee Road as they headed back toward Chicago in the early afternoon. Even before the waitress took their order, Mullen spoke the words that changed so much for Mitchell.

"Everett, I think you can handle the announcing job for the *National Farm and Home Hour*. I'm only asking you to give special attention to two things. Be friendly with this great audience and be accurate in your reports."

The following Monday, November 3, 1930, almost seven years to the hour since Everett Mitchell's first broadcast on KYW, Mullen introduced him to the *National Farm and Home Hour* audience as the new announcer.

Wallace Butterworth, who had few allies at Chicago's NBC station, monitored Mitchell's handling of the program for a few weeks. Convinced that the appointment was permanent, he resigned and returned to New York.

Mr. and Mrs. Abner Sprague of Rocky Mountain National Park, Colorado, invited Everett and Mildred Mitchell to be their guests in 1928. They were listeners to Station WENR and Mitchell was their favorite radio personality.

On an overseas trip to visit with students in the International Farm Youth Exchange in Australia and Asia, Everett Mitchell and party stopped in Pakistan. He is shown here holding the tether for a camel pulling a wagon near Karachi.

Wallace Butterworth was brought from New York City, where prior to entering radio he had been a shoe salesman, to announce the *Farm and Home Hour.* He lost his assignment when he could not tell the difference between a haystack and a strawstack.

# Chapter 18
# Frank Mullen's Finest Hour

When Frank Mullen and Everett Mitchell began working together on the *National Farm and Home Hour* in the fall of 1930, they knew they were creating the first program of its kind—one with tremendous potential for the nation's farmers and homemakers. What they had to work with, securely in place, was the hour broadcast at noon six days a week on a forty-station NBC network which could be heard by most of the people of the nation. They had, also, the unprecedented fifteen-minute daily segment directly from the United States Department of Agriculture in Washington. The complicated technical arrangements had been worked out so the studio in Chicago and the studio in Washington were linked and moving from one to the other could be done quickly and smoothly. No similar technological arrangement existed in radio at that time.

The person primarily responsible for the farm program was Frank Mullen.[1] The National Broadcasting Company had its network premiere November 15, 1926, and one of the member stations was KDKA in Pittsburgh, where Mullen was farm service director. Months later, in the fall of 1927, Mullen made a trip to New York to see Merlin H. Aylesworth, NBC president, and David Sarnoff, head of the NBC parent corporation, Radio Corporation of America. At these meetings Mullen proposed that the nation's first radio network be used to conduct a farm program for the entire country.

"Aylesworth was born on a farm too, and we talked the same language," Mullen said later. "I really didn't talk much after the first few minutes, because he started telling me what he thought could be done to establish a national farm radio service. The man I was talking to made the program possible."[2]

Aylesworth and Mullen agreed on the program's format. It

would originate in Pittsburgh with Mullen in full charge. The show would be broadcast at the noon hour so farmers could hear it during their midday meal six days a week. Aylesworth especially liked Mullen's proposal that the United States Department of Agriculture be invited to present a fifteen-minute segment daily from its offices in Washington.

Mullen's first move was to take up the matter with his friend, Morse H. Salisbury, director of radio services for the Department of Agriculture, with whom he had worked closely as farm service director at Station KDKA. Salisbury was delighted with the prospect of having Department scientists and other specialists able to talk directly to farmers, homemakers and consumers over most of the nation. But he pointed out a possible roadblock.

Milton Eisenhower, younger brother of former President Dwight D. Eisenhower, had shortly before become director of information for the Department of Agriculture. Eisenhower had already made it clear that the informational programs provided by the Department could at no time be directly associated with commercially-sponsored radio programs. Salisbury doubted that Eisenhower would consider making an exception to his rule. But he urged Mullen to come to Washington, meet with Eisenhower and himself to see what might be worked out.

By the time Mullen, Salisbury and Eisenhower could meet to discuss the matter, Montgomery Ward in Chicago had indicated its interest in sponsoring the program. In a long conference in Washington that set policy for almost twenty years, Eisenhower prevailed. Appealing as the NBC proposal was, the Department, supported by taxpayer's funds, could not take part as a co-sponsor with a commercially sponsored program. To do so, Eisenhower contended, would imply that the United States Department of Agriculture was endorsing products in the market place.

But Mullen came away from the Washington conference with a compromise that left his dream intact. The unprecedented opportunity was so great that Eisenhower agreed to allow the Department to provide a service program immediately following a Montgomery Ward sponsored *Farm and Home Hour*, if NBC would make the time available. The sponsored daily program would last forty-five minutes, to be followed by a fifteen-minute service broadcast directly from the Department of Agriculture in Washington. Network officials agreed.

The first broadcast of the program, followed by the Department of Agriculture's unsponsored service segment, took place on

October 2, 1928, less than a year after Mullen's first meeting with Aylesworth and Sarnoff. A network of thirteen NBC stations, extending from Ohio to New England, carried the historic broadcast. Shortly after, Mullen was appointed agricultural director for the network, in recognition for his having originated radio's first national farm program.

Eisenhower, Salisbury and others at the Department of Agriculture found the results of their fifteen-minute daily program hard to believe. Talks by Department specialists often brought mail from a third of the states in the nation. Letters came from farm homes that did not have telephones and where no daily newspapers were taken. These farmers, who had always been the last to know of the new developments affecting the business of farming, now had information about crop and livestock production, family nutrition and health and farm markets instantly and directly from the nation's top authorities. In the first year, the Department in its segment presented nearly two hundred specialists on subjects of interest to farmers and homemakers.

By mid-1929 the *Farm and Home Hour* had been moved from Pittsburgh to Chicago, even though the new NBC midwest headquarters, the top two floors on the Merchandise Mart, had not yet been completed. New stations were being added monthly to the network, big regional stations like KYW in Chicago, WHO in Des Moines, Iowa, and WFAA in Dallas, Texas, each of which brought large blocks of new listeners.

All was going well with the program. Then came the paralyzing collapse of the stock market in October, 1929. Montgomery Ward did not renew its sponsorship at the end of the year, and it was doubtful whether another sponsor could be found for 1930.

Shortly before Thanksgiving Mullen was in New York for meetings with Aylesworth and Sarnoff. He was, no doubt, afraid of hearing that the farm program was to be dropped. But instead, Aylesworth had surprising news. The program was not going to be endangered by the country's deepening depression; instead, it was to be given a new and even more important place in the NBC broadcasting plan.

Sarnoff and Aylesworth had been greatly impressed with what had been accomplished on the *Farm and Home Hour*, handicapped as it was by having the Department of Agriculture segment actually outside of the program. What was needed, Aylesworth said, was to get the Department of Agriculture to become a full partner in an hour-long program.

If the problem of commercial sponsorship did not exist, he asked, did Mullen think he could interest the Department in becoming a full partner and helping to enrich the program with new features from its staff? If so, Aylesworth explained, NBC would be prepared to make the six-day-a-week hour-long noontime broadcast into an NBC sustaining service program without commercial sponsors and with the network paying the entire cost of production and transmission. Network stations would provide the broadcast time. The question was whether Milton Eisenhower would recommend that the Department of Agriculture join with a private business, NBC, in presenting the program as a public service.

Aylesworth explained further. As an NBC sustaining public service, the *Farm and Home Hour* would not be allowed to languish merely because it did not produce revenue. On the contrary, there would be an additional investment to make the program more interesting and useful to both rural and urban audiences. It would meet the same high standards that were maintained on the NBC evening network programs, with a full orchestra and a "name" announcer.

Aylesworth told Mullen there were several reasons for NBC to make this unusual move.

There was the potential number and variety of listeners a program like the *Farm and Home Hour* could reach. The new program format must devote more attention to homemakers. They constituted a general audience, and the program needed urban listeners, too. NBC wanted to have a daytime program that would give its two networks, the Red and Blue, an edge in the increasingly competitive broadcasting business.

Also there was the crucial problem of government regulation of radio. Based on his earlier experiences, Sarnoff knew the government would step in quickly if it believed the public interest was not being served. Since broadcasting used the public airways, the government expected radio to provide, at its own expense, a generous schedule of public service programs. NBC wanted its *Farm and Home Hour* to be an outstanding example of public service.

Mullen began conferences in Washington at once on the transformation of the program. Approval was not long in coming. Salisbury pointed out that the precedent already existed. The Department was regularly sending news releases to radio stations requesting that they be broadcast on station time rather than on time used by a sponsor. The NBC relationship would simply be a little more intimate, in that personalities of the Department would actually be heard rather than just being quoted. So it was a deal.

Mullen went back to Chicago, impressed by the responsibility of producing radio's "showcase" service program, one that network officials would be monitoring closely. He had his work cut out for him. Five days a week he would have the fifteen-minute Department of Agriculture pickup from Washington and the Homesteaders Orchestra in Chicago, but that still left at least thirty-five minutes to fill with special features that must provide variety from day to day. On Saturdays, he would have only the Homesteaders Orchestra as a regular feature.

Until Mitchell joined the *Farm and Home Hour* in the fall of 1930, Mullen had had to work out his programming without the help of an announcer who understood farm problems. Now he had someone who was not only experienced in creating new radio features, but who also had first-hand knowledge of life in the rural midwest. The two men quickly developed confidence in one another and a close working relationship.

By now the program was being presented in the big Number One NBC studio in the Chicago Merchandise Mart, which was capable of seating hundreds of guests. Even then, at times, especially during major agricultural events such as the National 4-H Club Congress, there were often more guests than seats.

Mitchell and Mullen quickly developed a working routine. Mullen would usually monitor the *Farm and Home Hour* from the studio production booth. Immediately after the sign-off, he and Mitchell would go to his office, review the broadcast just over and examine the next day's program for ways to make last-minute improvements.

Then came the most important part, when they turned their attention to creation of new features which would make future programs more interesting. Lunch would be sent in and the conferences would often last far into the afternoon, occasionally even into the evening. At times Mullen would reach for the telephone and they would be joined by script writers, production specialists, or Harry Kogen, conductor of the Homesteaders Orchestra.

Mullen established *Farm and Home Hour* guidelines. He set the final test for every feature: Is it interesting or useful to farm families or homemakers? At every opportunity, Mullen repeated, the program must emphasize the importance of agriculture, not just to farmers but to all the nation's citizens.

191

Mullen often started their discussion by making some interesting observation to Mitchell about farmers and agriculture. For example, he would point out that the United States is one of the few nations in history that has never experienced general hunger or famine.

Such challenging observations brought out the historian in Mitchell. He proposed to give the program a special dimension for both farmers and urbanites by saluting the historic developments in the nation's agriculture. Mullen liked the idea.

Mitchell presented many historical features over the years, usually short vignettes just before the close of the program. For example, President George Washington was honored for his recommendation, in his final message to the seven-year-old Congress, that an American Society of Agriculture be established with support from the federal government. President Abraham Lincoln was credited with having founded the United States Department of Agriculture in 1862, even though the nation was in the throes of the Civil War.

The inventions of individuals, often farmers, that effected sweeping changes in agriculture were also saluted: John Deere's invention of the steel plow in 1837; Cyrus McCormick's grain reaper in 1847; and Joseph F. Glidden's invention of barbed wire shortly after the Civil War.

The *Farm and Home Hour* paid tribute to the nationwide system of sixty-eight Land Grant Colleges which were made possible by the Morril Act of 1862 to assure that for the first time the teaching of agriculture was generally available.

There were salutes for the Hatch Act in 1887 that created the state agricultural experiment stations, the Smith-Lever Act of 1914 that established the Cooperative Agricultural Extension Service, and the Smith-Hughes Act of 1917 that provided agriculture teachers in the nation's high schools. Tributes were paid to the founders of the first 4-H Clubs and Future Farmers of America chapters for rural youth.

The Mullen-Mitchell planning conferences continued for more than three years, through 1933. Mitchell's role took on an importance not achieved by Butterworth or any of the earlier announcers. Mullen soon began using Mitchell as a sounding board and as a source of new programming ideas, many of which were quickly adopted. Mitchell's handling of the program, especially his on-farm interviews, were attracting favorable comments in the ever-increasing mail from listeners. Mitchell advanced from being just an announcer, reading from a script and putting the programs on the air, to becoming a moderator who worked with the writers, suggested new features, and found better ways to present the program.

In his planning sessions with Mullen, Mitchell always urged the inclusion of more humorous and inspirational elements to provide listeners with some relief from the worries caused by the continuing depression.

For example, he suggested that the *Farm and Home Hour* would attract greater audience loyalty, especially among urban listeners, if the same music was used to end each program and a closing inspirational or humorous message given by the announcer. He recalled his own standard closing for his WENR programs — "Goodbye, everyone, and lots of luck."

Mullen liked the idea. After some discussion, he urged that the Homesteaders be given a musical motif for the end of the program and that Mitchell use an inspirational "thought for the day" as a closing. Mitchell selected the quotations himself, and the thought for the day became a feature that brought in listener mail. Many reported they stayed tuned to the very end of the program just to hear Mitchell's closing, which began, "From your old friend, Everett Mitchell, a thought for the day. . ."

Typical thoughts were maxims such as these:

"The greatest ability is dependability."

"There are a lot of good ways to become a failure, but never taking a chance is the most successful."

"The dictionary is the only place where success comes before work."

"You learn a lot more by letting the other fellow tell you all he knows than you learn by telling him all you know."

"Luck is always against the man who depends on it."

"It is better to walk with God in the dark than to walk alone in the light."

Now that it was possible to present the Department of Agriculture's segment during any part of the program, Mullen concluded that the Washington segment should appear at the same time each day so that listeners could know when features important to them—the market for example—could be heard. Soon it was agreed in both Washington and Chicago that the segment was most effective in the second fifteen minutes of the hour program. At the beginning of this segment, Mitchell would send the program to Washington, saying, "Now we take you to Washington and Morse H. Salisbury of the United States Department of Agriculture." Later, Salisbury was followed by Wallace L. Kadderly, Ken Gapen and Layne Beaty.

Salisbury and his staff proposed a new feature, one which reveals something about the state of the broadcasting art early in the 1930s. Radio networks did not yet present news regularly, and local stations gave their attention, if any, to local events only; thus, rural people had little opportunity to learn of daily, national and international developments. Salisbury proposed the Washington segment add a three to five minute "tight" summary of the day's top world and national news events. H.R. Baukhage, a Washington, D.C. newsman with a pleasant voice, was the most remembered of the *Farm and Home Hour* newscasters; he always opened with "Baukhage Speaking." He soon became the first nationally known news personality in broadcasting.

The Department of Agriculture's segment of the program was built around three major features, two of them used daily. First was the summary of livestock and crop markets, providing vital price reports for farm commodities, often only minutes old, information that had not before reached most farmers. The second was the Baukhage newscast. The third important regular feature, used three times a week, was the homemaker news presented by Ruth Van Demen of the Department of Agriculture's Bureau of Home Economics. This feature, on the air for years, drew more mail than any other.

Music and humor were provided through special features, none of which appeared more than once or twice a week. A male quartet, The Four Cadets, was added. For greater appeal to the homemaker audience, humor was provided by two comediennes. One of them was especially popular in the characterization of Aunt Fanny, played by a young Chicago actress, Fran Allison, who starred on television in the *Kukla, Fran and Ollie Show*.

Another long-time feature, no doubt linked to Mullen's interest in forestry, was a dramatic series, *Uncle Sam's Forest Rangers*, based on the experiences of a kindly forest ranger, Jim Robbins, played by Chicago actor Harvey Hay. This was the one feature on the program done cooperatively by the Department of Agriculture and NBC. The scripts were written by C.E. Randall of the Forest Service informational staff in Washington and the dramas were produced by NBC in Chicago. Usually heard each Friday, the series extended from 1932 to 1944.

Although the farm program continued to attract larger and

larger audiences, Mullen did not let up. He was constantly suggesting new features. At one meeting, for example, he told Mitchell it was time for the *"National" Farm and Home Hour* to live up to its name. The whole nation was the program's "beat," he said, so it should broadcast on-the-scene reports of events of national significance wherever they took place, just as they had been doing with the National Corn Husking Contest. Mitchell should handle the coverage himself, Mullen continued, so the listeners would know that the program host was really there. In the list of important events he included the National 4-H Congress, the International Livestock Show in Chicago, the Kansas City Royal Livestock Show, the Western Livestock Show in Denver, the Cherry Festival in Michigan, tobacco auctions in the Carolinas, the Apple Fest in Virginia and cotton festivals in the various southern states.

Mullen also turned his attention to the private not-for-profit organizations whose objective was to help farmers. On the Saturday programs when there was no Washington segment, these organizations were given the chance to be heard regularly, some as often as once a month. The National 4-H Organization was assigned the second Saturday program of the month and the National Grange the third Saturday. Programs were also scheduled for the American Farm Bureau Federation and the National Farmers Union.

Among these special Saturday presentations, the monthly 4-H program gradually took on a special format that sometimes required it to be broadcast entirely away from Chicago. The Department of Agriculture was able to arrange for the United States Marine Band to provide the music for these 4-H programs. At times the Marine Band was presented as a pick-up from Washington, but as the series progressed, more often the entire 4-H program, features as well as music, was presented from the auditorium of the Marine Band in Washington. Mitchell opened the program in Chicago, moved it immediately to Washington, then received the program back for sign-off, much as he did for the weekly Washington segment. The mail indicated that the *Farm and Home Hour* audience enjoyed having the program travel.

The 4-H Organization brought many prominent persons to the program's audience, among them Mrs. Herbert Hoover, wife of the President. She appeared on November 7, 1931, at National 4-H Achievement Day. In her message honoring the 4-H clubs, she said:

> Greetings from Washington, boys and girls. I like the
> sound of Achievement Days. . . You are deliberately learning
> that you may achieve—to grow more corn, heavier beef, bet-
> ter pigs and chickens. . . But don't neglect to plan for your
> "super joy hours" as well as your achieving, working hours.
> Don't let amusement just happen.
>
> You have all read and heard so much of these times of de-
> pression, when crops and prices have been bad and unem-
> ployment has existed in the industrial sections of our coun-
> try. There is something for each one of you to do in this
> emergency, a special achievement awaiting you.[3]

Perhaps the experience with the 4-H program had something
to do with it, but soon Frank Mullen made a far-reaching proposal that would require the *Farm and Home Hour* to travel
back and forth across the United States for several years. The
program, Mullen said, should visit each state's Agricultural Experiment Station and report on what was being done to advance
the nation's agriculture. These research centers were almost always located on college campuses, often land grant colleges, so
there could be music from the college band, campus personalities
and area farmers involved. This was a bold advance in agricultural communication. No farm magazine or newspaper had ever
sent a representative to all the state experiment stations.

The format for the series would have to be different, Mullen
ruled. The entire broadcast would originate outside of the Chicago studios. Mitchell would need to go to the college campus in
advance to make sure of every detail, consult on scripts and arrange for the music group that would take the place of the
Homesteaders Orchestra.

By the early weeks of 1932 the day-by-day format for the six-
day-a-week *National Farm and Home Hour* was in place. It consisted of the regular segments from Washington, traveling programs that took the program the length and breadth of the land
and a variety of informative and interesting programs that kept
listeners wondering what the next day would bring.

But for all the hard work and planning that had gone into the
program so far, the feature that would be longest remembered
had not yet even been considered. It would come completely by
surprise and would become the *National Farm and Home Hour's*
chief calling card. Everett Mitchell would say that it was

"heaven sent" and the new element would confer upon him a particular stardom in radio not to be visited upon another.

## FOOTNOTES

(1) Frank Ernest Mullen was born August 10, 1896, on a farm near Clinton, Kansas, and spent his boyhood on a South Dakota farm. In 1916 he entered Iowa State College at Ames where he studied forestry. In May, 1917, he joined the Forestry Regiment of the American Expeditionary Force in France. The war over, he returned to Iowa State and in 1922 was graduated with a degree in farm journalism. Briefly he was farm editor of *The Sioux City*(Iowa) *Journal*, but before the end of 1922 joined the staff of *The Stockman and Farmer Magazine* published in Pittsburgh, where the nation's first radio station, KDKA, had been on the air just two years. As a joint venture between KDKA and the magazine, Mullen became the first full-time radio farm editor.

(2) Frank Mullen gave this report to the *National Farm and Home Hour* audience April 8, 1935, on the program's 2,000th broadcast. The recording of his remarks is preserved in the files of The Museum of Broadcasting in New York.

(3) Mrs. Hoover's complete *Farm and Home Hour* address to the National 4-H Achievement camp on November 7, 1931, is available as a recording in her voice at the Museum of Broadcasting in New York.

"It's a beautiful day in Chicago, it's a great day to be alive and I hope it's even more beautiful wherever you are. Oh, yes, it may be raining outdoors and a little damp but it is a great day to be alive." *Life* magazine used this photograph to highlight a story on *Radio's Beautiful Day*.

# Chapter 19
# "Beautiful Day" Is Born

"It's a beautiful day in Chicago. It's a great day to be alive, and I hope it is even more beautiful wherever you are."

Flashing over the nation's air waves from ocean to ocean, "It's a Beautiful Day. . ." was like a lighted candle in the smothering darkness of the Great Depression. Public response was immediate and overwhelming. To understand the impact of this short message, it is necessary to know the mood of the people of the United States on that spring day in 1932 when the words were first heard on the *National Farm and Home Hour*.

The United States was in the grip of the worst economic collapse the nation has known. One fourth of the nation's entire work force was without jobs. For many it had been two years and more since they had had work. There was no Social Security program to help older people. Farmers in Iowa sold their corn for as little as ten cents a bushel. Both rural and urban families were being evicted because they did not have the money for rent or mortgage payments.

The morale of Americans had reached perhaps the lowest point in the nation's history. Even well informed citizens found themselves wondering about the ability of the private enterprise system and our democratic form of government to survive. Against this background the Beautiful Day message was so unexpected, so unusual and so startling that it instantly attracted attention.

The events which led to the unscheduled and spontaneous use of "It's a beautiful day. . ." took place in less than two hours. On the morning of May 14, Everett Mitchell, as usual, was enroute from his home to the NBC studios in Chicago's new Merchandise Mart. He walked to the train in threatening weather and boarded the 9:30 North Western commuter train at the Ravenswood Station near the Chicago-Evanston border.

This train had for years been known as the "Bankers' Special" because it came through Evanston and other plush northern Chicago suburbs. The men who used this train were mostly middle aged and older executives, typical of the leaders who ran much of the business of the nation's second largest city.

As Mitchell entered the car, he saw that it was crowded. Near the middle of the car three men were sitting together in facing seats that could accomodate four. They motioned to Mitchell to join them for the twenty-five minute ride into Chicago's Loop. Mitchell had seen the men occasionally on the train, but although they addressed him as "Everett" he could not call them by name with certainty.

From the moment he sat down, Mitchell noted that his companions appeared to be unusually depressed, although there had been long silences before on the Bankers' Special as the Great Depression worsened. Certainly it was a discouraging time, not only generally but particularly so the past few days. The worst financial panic Chicago and the nation had ever known would soon enter its third year. Despite all that President Hoover and the federal government were doing to counter it, the economic mire appeared to be getting deeper with each passing month. Worst of all there was less and less talk of things getting better; hope was becoming as difficult to find as a job.

Mitchell and his companions knew every landmark along the corridor of wealth and misery through which their train passed. It was common knowledge that the Lake Shore Drive mansion of Edith Rockefeller McCormick (daughter of Cyrus McCormick, the inventor of the mechanical reaper) was patroled by Pinkerton guards. They carried the same kind of submachine guns that Al Capone's thugs used in Chicago's mob wars. They were on duty twenty-four hours a day to protect the estate from riots by the hungry, which Chicago's wealthy feared constantly.

Soon the Chicago skyscrapers came into view—most of them the same buildings that are there today. Everyone on the train knew that some of the city's most respected business leaders had plunged out of those buildings to their deaths in the past year, convinced that the end of America as they knew it was but a matter of time.

As the train moved through the heart of the city, passengers could see street corners where unemployed World War I veterans and former Chicago businessmen were selling apples for a five cent tip (the apples cost about a cent delivered all the way from

200

Oregon) just to keep body and some respect together. "Help a vet, buy an apple—5 cents!" the signs read. Some of them were even printed, indicating that depression selling of apples on the street had become an institution. It was a way of begging with dignity.

Mitchell and his companions knew that much of Grant Park, Chicago's renowned recreational and cultural center on Lake Michigan, had been taken over by a horde of unemployed men and women whose major concern was finding enough to eat. A few had packing boxes that provided some shelter, but many of these destitute people slept on the ground in the rain or snow with little more than newspapers for protection. What is now Chicago's lake front airport, Meigs Field, was one of the most popular havens for these desperate people. During the day they would cross Michigan Avenue to pick through the garbage they found behind Loop restaurants. At some of these restaurants there would be new garbage cans put out by understanding kitchen help who had taken up collections to provide depositories for the "best" garbage.

The men with Mitchell knew, as the train pulled into North Western Station and they made ready to cross the new Wacker Drive, that below on the Drive's lower level men had gouged out holes under the concrete. There they were secure from the rain and snow and by wrapping themselves in newspapers they could, after a fashion, keep warm. There were so many of these human burrows that even the police did not know where all of them were located. At intervals attention would be called to an unknown retreat by the stench which made it clear that for someone the burrow was no longer a haven but a tomb.

All these things had come to be accepted in Chicago during the years of the Great Depression, which was slowly draining life itself away from the poor, a class which expanded with each passing week. The poor included an increasing number of formerly successful professional people who had run away from their families to hide their shame. The men on the Bankers' Special also knew that things were pretty much the same in New York, San Francisco and the big cities in between.

While the prevailing atmosphere generated by the depression was the foundation for the general gloom among Mitchell's companions, there were more immediate matters that added to their distress that morning. Even the weather was depressing. It was a warm, humid and showery morning. Trains were not yet air-conditioned and the car was uncomfortable.

But it was the news of this particular week that had stunned these men into a trance-like silence. Perhaps no single week of the depression had the news from the morning *Chicago Tribune*, the bible of the Bankers' Special, been so numbing. Each morning during the last week its pages had reported some additional tragedy or disaster.

On Sunday three events claimed much of the *Tribune's* front page. The murder of President Paul Doumer of France was attributed to a communist plot. President Hoover and Secretary of the Treasury Ogden Mills, after a meeting with Republican leaders at the White House, announced that Congress would hold evening sessions in an effort to get the annual revenue bill passed. A paralysis of the federal government was threatened unless a way could be found to pass the big revenue bill before the June 1 deadline. Featured on page one was another item that was good news short term, but bad news long term. The price of milk was being reduced for the second time within a year, further evidence of the deepening economic crisis. The price now would be eleven cents a quart and eight cents a pint.

Only the day before the *Chicago Tribune* had carried the account of one of America's great family tragedies: "Lindy's Baby Slain," the twice-size headline read. Snatched from his crib on the second floor of the Lindbergh home at Hopewell, New Jersey, the night of March 1, Charles A. Lindbergh Jr. was the first child of the famed flier and Anne Morrow Lindbergh. The child had been found the evening before by a truck driver in a woods less than five miles from the Lindbergh home, obviously murdered shortly after the kidnapping and long before Col. Lindbergh had paid a $50,000 ransom for his son's return.

Lindbergh, the "Lone Eagle," was easily the best known and among the best loved persons in America when the kidnapping occurred. The nation perhaps has never grieved as it did when the news of the murder of his son broke.

The *Tribune* that Mitchell and his companions were carrying that morning was mostly devoted to the Lindbergh murder. But distressing as the murder was, the week had brought news of tragedy even more sobering for the men on the Bankers' Special. Donald P. Ryerson, 53, chairman of the board of Ryerson Steel Company, Chicago's leading steelman and civic leader since World War I, had been buried two days before, dead by his own hand on the grounds of his North Shore home.

On the previous Sunday morning, Ryerson had arisen before Mrs. Ryerson and their children, Joan, 16, and Anthony, 14. About 7 a.m. Ryerson passed through the basement of his spacious Lake Forest home, spoke pleasantly to his chauffeur, who was tending the furnace, walked across the long lawn to the Ryerson family beach on Lake Michigan, fashioned his coat as a pillow, lay down and using an automatic pistol ended his life.

Ryerson's death was not an isolated case. There had been an epidemic in the past year of business and civic leaders taking their lives, many by flinging themselves from the windows of skyscrapers in New York, Chicago, San Francisco and other American cities. The autumn before there had been one week when four prominent Chicago business leaders committed suicide by jumping from high Loop buildings. Within hours one of the three men riding with Mitchell this Saturday morning would meet death in the same way. The monstrous depression that was moving over the nation like a fog of despair was more than many men who had invested their lives in their businesses could stand.

Mitchell tried to listen sympathetically to the listless and infrequent comments of his companions. But actually, something of a rebellion was taking shape in his mind. Mitchell, who in a little more than an hour had an appointment to speak to several million people, found himself in sharp disagreement with his friends and their hopeless attitude toward the future.

The depression had already cost him all his savings. But he had been reared in a family of great religious faith that had endured seemingly insurmountable hardships. The family and he had come through. He was sure the nation, too, would somehow survive this crisis.

He thought of his father's short prayer, "Lord Jesus, we thank thee for all our blessings." No matter how great the hardship, there had never been, he thought, a day without blessings.

Now the Bankers Special was coming into the station. Even as it came to a stop, there was no conversation. The men got up from their seats and left in silence. A spring shower was falling outside as they left the train. Mitchell stood for a time in the train shelter, waiting for the shower to pass. He continued to struggle with the problem. The country would have to change its attitude or the depression would simply continue to get worse, Mitchell concluded. Someone had to start a different trend of thought across the country. But what could he do? What could one person do to bring people a measure of good cheer that could, perhaps, begin to cut through the thick clouds of despair?

A poem his mother used to recite suddenly came back to him. It was an old English nursemaid's verse. Over and over the words rang through his mind as though someone were talking to him.

"If any little word of mine can set a heart to singing;
If any little word of mine could set a bell to ringing;
God, let me say that word,
And set that heart to singing,
God, let me say that word,
And set that bell to ringing."[1]

The poem suggested an idea—perhaps a few words of encouragement to the large radio audience could lead to some change for the better in the national mood. Then another inspiration came to him, this time from the sky. The clouds broke apart for a moment as the shower passed, and suddenly there was a patch of brilliant blue. As Mitchell looked up he thought of another of his mother's sayings: "If in the morning there is enough blue in the sky to patch a Dutchman's britches, it will be a beautiful day." It would be a beautiful day in Chicago after the shower.

A beautiful day...Yes, it was a beautiful day everywhere if you could just see through those clouds.

Mitchell walked to the NBC studios in bright sunlight under a blue sky. By now he was wondering if he could open the *Farm and Home Hour* with a reference to his beautiful day in Chicago, his belief that it was a great day to be alive, and a wish that it be a beautiful day for all his listeners, wherever they might be.

Minutes before 11 a.m., a page boy responded to Mitchell's knock and opened the door to the NBC studios. The audience for the program was already gathering in the large auditorium.

During the period of the final rehearsal and the program alterations that preceded the 11:30 opening of the show, the beautiful day phrase was constantly in Mitchell's mind. So, also, was the NBC rule against deviating from the prepared script. Mitchell did not think he had time to explain the new program salutation to producer Bucky Harris, who had absolute authority over the broadcast, and obtain an official permission for the change. Besides, he was not sure Harris would understand.

Now, it was exactly 11:30. The band began playing the introduction, "The Stars and Stripes Forever." Then came the pause so that Mitchell could announce, as always, "This is the *National Farm and Home Hour...*"

But not on May 14, 1932.

Instead, in a clear and confident voice heard from coast to coast, he said, "It's a beautiful day in Chicago. It's a great day to be alive, and I hope it is even more beautiful wherever you are."

In the control room Producer Harris turned white. Then his face flushed with anger. Was Mitchell taking the program over? Was he sick? For an instant Harris considered taking the program off the network by "killing" Mitchell's microphone and directing the standby announcer to use the disclaimer, "Because of conditions beyond our control, this program will not be heard. . ."

Some members of the band raised their hands to their heads in gestures of despair. "Would they attempt to continue playing?" some later admitted thinking.

However, when Mitchell, after an instant's pause, returned to the script saying, "This is the *National Farm and Home Hour*," the orchestra leader raised his baton with his customary vigor and authority. The crisis subsided and Harris decided to allow the program to continue.

Everyone kept an eye on Mitchell for the rest of the hour. Mitchell was sure he would be called on to explain his defiance of the NBC rules. He even thought he might be fired, but he had no regrets. He had to do something. The listeners needed a few words of cheer in these difficult times. Yes, he would do the same thing again.

When the program ended, Mitchell was immediately summoned to the control room. Harris demanded that he explain why he had dared to depart from the approved script, something that had never before been done in the three years the *Farm and Home Hour* had been on the air.

"There is so much gloom everywhere, I just had to remind people that it was a beautiful day," Mitchell explained.

Harris said he would have to take such an infraction of the rules up directly with Niles Trammell, the vice-president in charge of NBC Chicago operations. He directed Mitchell to come at once with him to the vice-president's office.

Mitchell had just begun explaining to Trammell why he had departed from the script when a pageboy opened the door and reported that there were a number of telephone calls, some of them on long distance, for Everett Mitchell, the "Beautiful Day man." Trammell excused Mitchell to take the calls and said they would resume their discussion as soon as he was back.

When Mitchell got to his office, the operator reported that there were many calls on hold for him and that the first was a listener in Boston. "I don't know how you can be so cheerful at such a gloomy time. But say it again, keep saying it, because it makes me feel so good," the first caller said. For more than an hour Mitchell took calls, some of them local, but some from as far away as Utah, Minnesota and Louisiana. Many calls went unanswered because the listeners could not wait. The calls continued even after Mitchell returned to Trammell's office.

Harris was still angry. He urged the NBC vice-president to drop Mitchell from the program or at least remove him for a week without pay. Trammell also talked to Frank Mullen, who was in charge of the *Farm and Home Hour*, and asked him to be available for a conference as soon as Mitchell was finished with the telephone calls.

When Mitchell returned Trammell immediately called in Harris and Mullen to discuss Mitchell's violation of the script rule and to find out how the listeners had reacted. He reported on the call from the man in Boston, explaining that the call was typical. More than half of the callers had expressed the hope that Mitchell would continue to open the *Farm and Home Hour* program with his declaration, "It's a beautiful day in Chicago. . ."

When Mitchell finished his report and explained again why he had inserted the Beautiful Day message, Trammell suggested that Mitchell go to lunch while the three executives conferred. In the discussion that followed, Harris still insisted that Mitchell be given a reprimand and not be permitted to return to the *Farm and Home Hour* until he had provided assurance that he would do no more of "this beautiful day stuff."

Mullen, while not condoning Mitchell's departure from the script, was more concerned whether the greeting which had demonstrated such immediate appeal should be written into the script for future programs. He favored continuing the Beautiful Day greeting in the following week and letting listener response via letters and phone calls be the guide to further use.

In the end Trammell sided with Mullen. He said that this was a new experience for everyone, Mitchell included. From the telephone calls, it would seem that Mitchell's greeting had met with favor from listeners over a wide area. If this proved to be true, Trammell said, Mitchell should be encouraged to begin future programs with "It's a beautiful day in Chicago."

The next week's mail furnished final proof that Trammell had taken the right stand. Several thousand letters came to the NBC studios in response to the Beautiful Day greeting; the writers, like the callers, were overwhelmingly in favor of the new opening.

In time the greeting became better known even than Mitchell himself. Everywhere he went he was requested to adapt the Beautiful Day opening to the place where he was speaking. Even when he was invited to address the United States diplomatic staff in Russia, he was asked if he would begin with, "It's a beautiful day in Moscow." He did.

Nine months and two weeks later one of his listeners stood on the steps of the White House and expressed to the nation the same philosophy in different words. "The only thing we have to fear is fear itself," said Franklin D. Roosevelt.

### FOOTNOTE

(1) Everett Mitchell had been searching for years, but has never found in print the exact words that he heard from his mother. In *Poems That Touch The Heart*, published by Doubleday in 1965 on Page 61, there appear two verses that are very similar, but the author is unknown. These verses read:
"If any little help may ease
The burden of another,
God give us love and care and strength
To help along each other.

If any little thought of ours
Can make one life the stronger,
If any cheery smile of ours
Can make its brightness longer,
Then let us speak that thought today."

Many honors were bestowed upon the *National Farm and Home Hour* and its host, Everett Mitchell, over the forty years he was affiliated with the farm broadcasts on radio and television. In the top photograph, Mitchell (left) receives an award for his promotion of the Farm Safety program. Making the presentation is Ned Dearborn, head of the National Safety Council of Chicago. In the bottom photograph, Mitchell and the program became honorary members of the National 4-H Clubs. Making the presentation is Guy Noble, head of the 4-H in 1948.

# Part 5
# By Popular Demand

In the ten years between 1934 and 1944, for Everett Mitchell and others appearing regularly on *The National Farm and Home Hour* it was like putting in a long distance telephone call to two-thirds of the rural homes in America east of Denver. Listenership in some rural areas of the Midwest approached absolute saturation, and there was also a significant urban audience. There were *Farm and Home* listeners west of Denver, too, but the time zone difference in the Pacific Coast and Mountain states greatly reduced this audience.

There were special reasons why so many rural families arranged their daily schedules so they could tune in to hear Everett Mitchell and the *Farm and Home Hour*, and why such a thing is not likely ever to happen again. For many it was the best and fastest link to the outside world. Those isolated families who had always been the last to know could learn the latest national and international news, since the *Farm and Home Hour* presented the first and for years the only scheduled national newscasts. These were the years, too, when Secretary of Agriculture Henry A. Wallace was appearing regularly on the program to announce the sweeping new federal programs to combat the farm depression. Even the President, Franklin D. Roosevelt, spoke on the network program. Besides the news and market reports, there was helpful advice for farmers and homemakers, good humor, fine music, and a bit of Mitchell philosophy.

Threading each week's program together was the memorable opening line, "It's a beautiful day in Chicago. . ." whose universal appeal increased listenership among men, women and even children. For seven years comment remained favorable on the use of the Beautiful Day opening. Then in the first week in June, 1939, a Florida newspaper editorial took NBC to task for spreading an obvious promotion ploy for the city of Chicago. When copies of the editorial reached the New York headquarters of NBC, Mitchell was directed to drop the Beautiful Day salutation. Protest letters began to coming after the second day without the time-honored opening, and the Chicago *Times* reported that five thousand letters were received the first week.

Robert M. Yoder, Chicago *Daily News* writer, did a page one story on June 20. It said, in part:

> Mark Twain said (but maybe you've heard) that while everybody talks about the weather nobody does anything about it. This veteran nifty, however, doesn't cover the strange case of Everett Mitchell, radio announcer. Mr. Mitchell does something about the weather. He lies about it.
>
> His tussle with the truth started in 1932. Gloom was deep over the land, and Mitchell was racking his brain for a few cheerful words to give the listeners. About the only thing that ever turned good was the weather. Mitchell adopted that. He began putting in a phrase about it ringing with good cheer. "It's a beautiful day in Chicago," he would say.
>
> Two weeks ago he drew a complaint about this propaganda. The NBC bosses told Mitchell to quit. It was announced that he would drop the phrase and see who cared.
>
> Since then the radio system has been flooded with letters, demanding Mitchell continue his daily fib. "It make us feel better," said listeners.
>
> The little white lie will be resumed tomorrow, by popular demand.

That was the last time anyone at NBC or anywhere else suggested that Mitchell stop "telling lies" about the weather in Chicago.

# Chapter 20
# Wallace's Wireless Telephone

Good things happened to Everett Mitchell at NBC in the months after he introduced the Beautiful Day philosophy to the *National Farm and Home Hour*. Vice President Trammell appointed him chief announcer for the Central Division of NBC, an important responsibility that included assigning the announcers for all NBC radio programs produced in Chicago and the midwestern states. President Aylesworth awarded Mitchell a special year-end bonus for his outstanding work in 1932.

There was one important exception to the general appreciation of Beautiful Day. The Mullen and Mitchell relationship was never as close again. It was not that Mullen did not approve of the greeting; he had urged that it continue to be used until the wishes of listeners were known. With so many of Mitchell's suggestions being used on the program, Mullen understandably had some feeling that the control of the program was slipping away from him. Mullen also began to regard Mitchell, who was skilled in so many of the phases of the broadcasting business, as a potential competitor in the NBC hierarchy.

With its new Beautiful Day introduction in place, the format for the program was now complete. There would be new features added from time to time, but for more than a decade the program would begin with, "It's a beautiful day in Chicago...," present an hour of information, education and inspiration for the families of farmers and homemakers and end with Mitchell's thought for the day.

As the months of 1932 passed, marked by the political campaign between President Hoover and his challenger, Franklin D. Roosevelt, the fabric of the nation's social order showed unmistakable signs of pulling apart. More factories were closing. There were street disorders in many of the country's industrial centers.

The total unemployment in the nation's work force stood at twenty-five percent, and in many cities especially hard hit by factory closings a third or more of the families were without a jobholder or an income.

The plight of the nation's farmers was even more critical, especially in the Corn Belt and other grain-producing areas. Total farm income had dropped to less than half what it had been before the Great Depression struck; in 1932, the income of all United States farmers was just over five billion dollars, compared to twelve billion dollars in 1929. Farm prices were so low that farmers generally could not recover the cost of producing their grain, meat or dairy products. Corn had almost ceased to have any value in the fall of 1932. A courthouse in northwest Iowa was heated that winter by burning corn, which cost less than wood or coal. In places angry farmers attempted to take things into their own hands. At Sioux City, Iowa, dairy farmers organized and blockaded the city, seeking to get a least the cost of production for their milk. Some midwest farmers refused to bring their own products to market and even attempted to stop other farmers from selling theirs. They blockaded roads, stopped farm trucks and wagons and dumped perishables like cream and eggs. In some places farmers burned wooden railroad bridges to keep grain from moving to market.

Iowa became a focal point of the farmer rebellion. At farm foreclosure sales farmers would drive off prospective bidders, then gather about the auctioneer and bid in horses at twenty-five cents each, cows at ten cents and fat hogs for a nickel. Then the next day they would return them to the former owner. Judges handling farm foreclosures were threatened. In at least one case a mob of farmers dragged an Iowa bankruptcy judge from his chambers, put a noose around his neck and staged a mock hanging during which the judge fainted. Still the farm foreclosures continued at record levels.

During the presidential campaign both candidates urged generally conventional solutions, such as cutting government spending and lowering taxes. President Hoover launched several remedial programs, including the Reconstruction Finance Corporation through which the federal government could extend credit to prevent corporate bankruptcies. But there was too little time for these measures to become effective.

Aware that he was not well known to the American people outside of the northeast, Roosevelt, appearing confident and optimistic, conducted an aggressive campaign that took him to twenty-seven cities from coast to coast for major addresses promising a "New Deal" for America. He had no specific solutions but spoke in generalities on how to turn the country away from the depression that was in its third year and worsening. On November 8, 1932, the formerly unknown easterner was elected president, largely because of the desire of the American people to turn to new leaders for solutions to the grave problems confronting the nation.

Before his inauguration March 4, 1933, President Roosevelt appointed Henry A. Wallace of Iowa Secretary of Agriculture. The choice was fortunate. Iowa farmers were among the hardest hit by the Depression, and the new secretary was well informed on their problems. He was also acquainted in general with the United States Department of Agriculture, which would have to be the keystone in carrying out the Roosevelt mandate. His father, Henry C. Wallace, had served as Secretary of Agriculture from 1921 until 1924.

Henry A. Wallace was a brilliant man of many accomplishments, something that later became obscured by his political activities at the close of his public career.[1] He was at the time of his appointment editor of the Iowa farm magazine, *Wallace's Farmer*, founded by his grandfather, affectionately remembered by thousands in Iowa and the Midwest as Uncle Henry Wallace. The new secretary was one of the nation's outstanding hybrid corn breeders, practicing a new science in corn improvement that would revolutionize Corn Belt farming within a decade.

As an agricultural economist and editor of an important farm magazine, Wallace had a clear understanding of the causes of the farm surplus problem in the United States. The main cause was that after World War I war-shattered Europe could no longer buy American food as it had done for years before the war. Wallace had urged Presidents Harding and Coolidge to adopt programs to help American farmers reduce farm production and eliminate the surpluses so that normal prices for their products could be restored.

Roosevelt liked Wallace's ideas for creating new federal agricultural programs. On becoming Secretary of Agriculture, backed by a sympathetic President, Wallace was able to take the first remedial step only two months and a week after he took office.

Wallace was well acquainted with the *National Farm and Home Hour* and its close ties with the Department of Agriculture long before he became Secretary. Frank Mullen, who had come to Iowa State College as a student in 1917, had followed Wallace's career teaching mathematics at Iowa State and at *Wallace's Farmer*, and the two men had become personally acquainted even before Mullen joined NBC. Wallace was intensely interested from the first in radio's ability to reach farm people quickly with vital information.

Radio Station WHO, the powerful station in Des Moines, began carrying the *Farm and Home Hour* soon after its inception in 1928. Wallace, a frequent listener, was aware that the program offered the only opportunity to communicate daily with farmers in most of the nation's agricultural states.

No public official in this country or any other had ever faced the situation which confronted Wallace when he became Secretary of Agriculture. The farm depression was painful for all farmers in every state of the nation, but the section of the country where an explosive situation existed—the area where the National Guard had been called to maintain order—was in the nation's breadbasket, the Corn Belt.

In the Upper Mississippi Valley, Secretary Wallace was confronted with mountainous surpluses of both corn and wheat. Even the references to ten-cent corn, which had become part of the language in the farm country, were not always accurate. In many places in the Corn Belt there simply existed no market for corn at any price. Elevators in the big wheat states were filled and in many places surplus wheat was stacked in huge piles in the open. With corn and wheat worth so little, farmers fed as much of their grain as they could to hogs in hopes that there would be a market for the pork later. As a result hog numbers were at all time highs for peacetime. Pork, too, was in surplus.

The farm crisis was so serious in the heartland that the President and Congress were calling for quick action on remedial farm legislation. Wallace, who had been living with the farm depression month by month since it began, had his own carefully worked out ideas about meeting the crisis, most of which had been described in detail earlier in his columns in *Wallace's Farmer*. He talked to many of his most respected farm friends in Iowa and other states for their views. There was general agreement on two matters: there must be supplemental income available to farmers as quickly as possible to stop the farm bankruptcies and there could be no solid farm price recovery until the huge grain and hog surpluses had been brought under control.

Weeks before he was confirmed by the U.S. Senate, Wallace had assembled a special task force to write the emergency farm legislation that would be sent to Congress. The task force was headed by Clifford V. Gregory, agricultural economist and editor of *Prairie Farmer*, a magazine published in Chicago for Illinois and Indiana farmers. Gregory left his home in Wheaton, Illinois, took leave of his Chicago editorial job, moved to Washington to be in close touch with Wallace and wrote the emergency farm bill in a Washington hotel.

As a result of these special preparations, the United States Congress was able early in President Roosevelt's "first one hundred days" to pass the Agricultural Adjustment Act which went into effect May 12, 1933, just nine weeks after Wallace took office. The Act was designed to bolster Corn Belt farm prices by beginning immediately to reduce surpluses of corn and hogs through what became a highly controversial practice of destroying excess crops and pigs.

The program was voluntary, but cooperating farmers in return for government payments would plow under a part of their crops already planted and kill off a part of their spring hog crop already on feed. What Wallace and his Department of Agriculture had done was to estimate the actual demand for the crops in the coming year. This estimate became the national production quota. Then each individual corn and hog farmer was assigned his share of the quota, taking into consideration the size of the farm and past production. AAA offices were set up in each county to issue contracts to farmers joining the new program.

Farmers who joined the program and limited their corn and hog production to their quotas were assured of additional income that year. First, they would be indemnified for the excess crops and pigs they had destroyed. Then after harvest they would be able to secure a loan on their corn crop. When the loan came due, if the market price of corn was not equal to the loan rate, the farmer could satisfy the loan by turning the corn over to the government to become a part of the national reserve.

That first year, in the fall, the corn loan was set at forty-five cents a bushel; that was the beginning of the end of ten-cent corn. Farmers who did not elect to take part in the adjustment program were not eligible for the corn loan. Ultimately the same principle was applied to other crops. From the day that Secretary Wallace personally announced on the *National Farm and Home Hour* the forty-five cent per bushel loan for corn, the tide

215

of Corn Belt farm foreclosures began to subside.

The new AAA touched off a national furor. Wallace quickly became known to most non-farm Americans as "the man who killed little pigs." They looked upon the effort to reduce farm surpluses as a pretext to raise the cost of food at a time when many of the nation's poor were without enough to eat. The handlers of farm products saw the cutback in food production as costing them jobs. Even among farmers who had always made their own decisions on how much to produce there was consternation and opposition. The farmers who quietly joined the new program did not get publicity even though county AAA offices were often crowded, especially as the deadline for joining neared.

Wallace was surprised and alarmed by the public outcry. Much of the opposition, he was sure, was a failure to understand the new program and its importance to both farmers and consumers. Immediately the Department of Agriculture called into action all of its many public information channels to explain the goals and operation of the new marketing program. Background papers, talks by Wallace and other department officials, and other information went regularly to farm magazines, radio stations, newspapers, extension editors at the land grant colleges and others.

Wallace had a special assignment for the NBC radio network, whose radio stations could be heard by most of the people east of the Rocky Mountains. Through his friend, Frank Mullen, Wallace appealed to NBC to become a full partner in the struggle to get public acceptance of the government's new farm program. He wanted to make intensive use of the opportunity to speak on the *National Farm and Home Hour* but he also wanted even more help from the nation's most powerful radio network.

Wallace would be making a series of major addresses before farm and consumer groups across the country. In most cases, these addresses would be made at noon luncheons. Could arrangements be made, he asked Mullen, so his talks could be heard on the program? He could be sure his mid-day speech was timed so it would fit into the program's broadcasting schedule. However, other addresses would be given in the evening. For these speeches, Wallace asked, would NBC consider making evening prime time available so his talks could be heard over the network by both farmers and consumers?

Mullen conferred with Trammell and Aylesworth. Since the interests of both farmers and urban consumers were involved, the NBC officials agreed the network would do its best to carry

Wallace's major policy addresses. When the talks were held at noon, Mitchell would originate the *Farm and Home Hour* in the city where the address was being given. Wallace would have the first half hour of the program, then it would be switched back to Chicago and Washington for the final thirty minutes.

From 1933 to 1939 Wallace, either in person or through officials speaking for him, used the nation's foremost radio network to talk to farmers daily. Most of his major agricultural programs, many of which are still in effect, were introduced on the *National Farm and Home Hour*. He worked constantly to increase consumption of food through programs such as the School Lunch Program for elementary schools, the Food Stamp Plan for low-income families and the Surplus Products Plan under which food in government storage could be given to the nation's needy. All three are still part of the services offered by the Department of Agriculture.

In June of 1934 Wallace delivered what in the long range view was his most important address carred by the *Farm and Home Hour*. In this talk the Secretary proposed an "Ever-Normal Granary" plan for the United States. It was, he acknowledged, patterned after the Biblical program carried out in Egypt by Joseph, who stored grain in the "good years" to prevent famine in the "seven lean years." The Ever-Normal Granary was presented as an insurance program for taking advantage of bumper crops in the Corn Belt and storing them as a hedge against years of low production. It was a plan he had earlier advocated in his *Wallace's Farmer* columns.

With the huge surpluses of corn and wheat in 1934, the Ever-Normal Granary proposal had little appeal, but even as Wallace spoke nature was preparing to confirm its importance. For the first time in the century, during the winter of 1934 there was no substantial snowfall nor any spring rain of consequence in the Corn Belt or the wheat states. The 1934 corn crop was cut to 1.1 billion bushels, less than half a crop. The 1935 crop was also below average, and in 1936 there was almost a repeat of the record drouth of 1934. By then it was evident that not only could a major drouth still occur, but it could be a disaster on a national scale. In the Agricultural Adjustment Act of 1938 Wallace's Ever-Normal Granary program was made a permanent part of the nation's agricultural policy and remains so to this day.

If selling the nation on the new farm programs was the greatest of Wallace's many achievements, it also brought him some of his

217

most discouraging moments. His public efforts to secure under-standing and support for the new farm programs were often met with more silence than enthusiasm. Although farmers were becoming supportive, business leaders and consumers were often antagonistic and even rude to the Secretary personally. This was particularly true of the processors of farm products, the financial leaders and even the industries providing farm supplies, who saw reduced farm production as injurious to their interests.

The Twin City area of Minneapolis and St. Paul, one of the nation's greatest centers for both processing farm products and distributing agricultural supplies, was known to be antagonistic to the new programs. But Wallace believed that if he could meet the Twin City leaders person-to-person he could secure their support, and a major address was scheduled for St. Paul.

Mitchell, carrying out the NBC pledge of cooperation, went to St. Paul and arranged for the *National Farm and Home Hour* to originate in that city so the Secretary's full address could be heard over the entire network. Mitchell was within a few feet of the Secretary the entire time. There were few farmers in the audience. Wallace was given a polite but restrained reception, but on occasion there were taunts from extremists. The applause at the close was muffled. After the broadcast there were a few questions, some of them barbed. Then the Secretary shook hands warmly with those on the stage and left alone. No one wanted to be seen extending courtesy to him.

"I know this to be the case," Mitchell recalls. "I left the hall soon after to catch the same train. There a hundred yards or so ahead of me was Wallace, walking alone. His appearance was that of a man who was not only tired but discouraged. He had not been able to win over the Twin City leaders.

"We pretty well knew in advance," Mitchell remembers, "what the reception would be when we originated the program in a city where Wallace was making an important address. When the audience was predominantly farmers, the reception was friendly and even enthusiastic. When he was speaking on a college campus or addressing an audience interested in farm research, the interest would be intense.

"This was the case on the final occasion when NBC originated the *Farm and Home Hour* in another city in order to present one of Secretary Wallace's addresses. We were surrounded largely by scientists, agricultural extension specialists and university faculty. The date was October 18, 1939.[2] We were in Peoria, Illinois,

218

for the address at the laying of the cornerstone for the Northern Regional Research Laboratory, one of four regional centers Wallace had provided for in the AAA of 1938 to find new industrial uses for agricultural products.[3] On this occasion people came early in hopes of having a few words with the Secretary, there was much appreciation for his remarks, and personal conferences continued afterward until he was forced to leave," Mitchell remembers.

By the time Wallace left the Department of Agriculture in 1940 to become Vice President, farm income had risen to twice its 1933 level and the farm depression had been halted. Regardless of his political activities later, millions of farm families were to remember Henry A. Wallace with gratitude and affection.

One of these was Oscar Heline, whose corn and hog farm at Marcus, Iowa, near the South Dakota border, was in the center of the area where the farmer rebellion flared hottest. Heline had devoted a great deal of time to organizing and working for Iowa farm cooperatives even before Wallace became Secretary of Agriculture. The two men became acquainted during Wallace's years at *Wallace's Farmer.* In 1969, Heline gave his opinion of Wallace's work as Secretary of Agriculture for Chicago writer Studs Terkel:

> It was Wallace who saved us, put us back on our feet. He understood our problems. When we went to visit him, after he was appointed Secretary, he made it clear to us he didn't want to write the law. He wanted the farmers themselves to write it.[4]

Heline was one of those farmers who helped write the law, part of the farmer group that went to Washington to the National Corn-Hog Conference. There Heline made the suggestion that to end the hog glut the government should buy up surplus little pigs and slaughter them on the farm.

Heline's daughter, Halcyon Heline Botkin, remembers those difficult years. "We always listened to Everett Mitchell and the *Farm and Home Hour,*" she recalls, "in order to keep up with the rapidly unfolding developments at the Department of Agriculture, often explained by Wallace himself.

"At every opportunity my father would say that it was Wallace who put us back on our feet."

## FOOTNOTES

(1) After being Vice President of the United States during the war years from 1941 to 1945, Henry Wallace resigned in 1946 from the Truman cabinet in protest of the administration's firm stand toward the Soviet Union. In 1948 he became the presidential candidate of the new Progressive Party whose pro-Soviet platform opposed the Marshall Plan aid to Europe and called for disarmament. The party polled only a little more than a million votes and carried no states. In 1950 Wallace left the party after it repudiated his endorsement of the United States-United Nations police action in Korea. Always open and sincere, Wallace subsequently issued a widely published statement, "Why I Was Wrong," explaining his shift from sympathy for the aims of the Soviet Union to a deep distrust of the Russian objectives. After that Wallace retired to private life.

(2) Secretary Wallace was now in the last months of his direction of the Department of Agriculture. At the Democratic National Convention held in July 1940, Roosevelt invited Wallace to be his running mate for Vice President of the United States. Roosevelt and Wallace were elected in November, defeating the Republican candidates, Wendell L. Wilkie and Charles McNary.

(3) The laboratory was built in fourteen months and opened in December 1940, a month after Henry A. Wallace had been elected Vice President. A program begun immediately delivered a great dividend to the nation and the world. The Peoria laboratory scientists discovered a way to make penicillin available inexpensively and in quantity. Although penicillin had been discovered by Sir Arthur Fleming in England in 1927, no means had yet been found to produce it in more than test tube amounts.

(4) Studs Terkel, *Hard Times: An Oral History of the Great Depression* (New York: Pantheon, 1970), p. 219. Oscar Heline remained on the family farm until his death in 1978. His wife and one daughter still live there, on the farm that has been in the family more than one hundred years.

Everett Mitchell, chief announcer for Station WMAQ in Chicago is ready to give the signal for a station break. The photograph was taken in 1932 soon after the station moved into its new quarters in the Merchandise Mart, Chicago.

Everett Mitchell and two members of his staff are shown at the Equator while they were on the Central and South American tour in 1952. The man on the left is unidentified. The others are Floyd Mischke, export manager of the Tractor Division of Allis-Chalmers, a *Farm and Home Hour* sponsor; and Jerry Seaman, account executive.

# Chapter 21
# Beautiful Day Takes Charge

In 1934 many things changed on the *National Farm and Home Hour*. The transition was so pronounced that 1934 stands as a watershed in the more than fifteen years the program was broadcast six days a week. Six years had passed since Frank Mullen introduced the *Farm and Home Hour* to the nation. Everett Mitchell had been announcer and moderator for four years. Two years had passed since Mitchell, without consulting Mullen or anyone else, had introduced the "Beautiful Day" opening which was making him the best known personality on the program.

The man who triggered these changes was David Sarnoff, president of RCA, of which NBC was a wholly owned subsidiary. Sarnoff saw that despite the Great Depression which was stifling most businesses, the new radio industry was growing rapidly and becoming competitive. The Columbia Broadcasting System (CBS), which did not even exist when NBC was established less than ten years before, was now operating a nationwide radio network. The Mutual Broadcasting System, using WGN in Chicago as its flagship station and backed by wealthy publisher Robert R. McCormick of the *Chicago Tribune*, was forming a third coast-to-coast network. With an eye to the future management at both RCA and NBC, Sarnoff made a series of staff changes among the decision-making people in both organizations.

Sarnoff, who had not before had a direct connection with NBC, arranged to become its chairman of the board. Niles Trammell was given additional responsibilities that led to his soon becoming executive vice president of NBC and its Red and Blue radio networks. But the most unexpected change involved Frank Mullen. He left NBC, giving up his post as NBC's director of agriculture, to take charge of advertising and communications for RCA.[1]

With Mullen gone to New York and no longer a member of the

NBC staff, it was inevitable that Everett Mitchell would have a greater voice in determining the content of the *Farm and Home Hour.* This was especially the case in the selection of the important special features which Mitchell generally did as pickups outside the Chicago studios.

Even before Mullen left, listeners were drawing Mitchell more deeply into the program's management. More and more mail was coming to NBC addressed to "Everett Mitchell, Farm and Home Hour, Chicago." Many of the writers addressed Mitchell like a longtime friend, often beginning "Dear Everett. . ." This trend had been growing ever since Mitchell's "Beautiful Day" greeting was added. Many of the suggestions for special features came from listeners. The linkage between Mitchell and the *Farm and Home Hour* was becoming so close that for many they were inseparable.

Although there was little Mullen could do about it, he found it increasingly difficult to accept Mitchell's expanding role. The man he had brought to the program merely as an announcer was being consulted more and more often on program content by farm leaders and listeners, and his decisions had a larger and larger influence on what would appear on the program. But Mullen was not ready to relinquish his authority over the program he had created. When he went to New York to join RCA, he took steps to continue to have an important voice in its operation.

Understandably, Mullen was possessive about the *Farm and Home Hour.*[2] The thought of leaving it largely in Mitchell's hands troubled him for reasons both professional and personal. Mullen recognized that Mitchell was one of the most capable broadcasting craftsmen he knew. But he also knew Mitchell had not had an agricultural college education and that he had not worked directly in agriculture or in an industry connected with it. Mullen himself had all the credentials, a college degree and a background of work as an agricultural journalist. It was hard for him to believe that, without these assets, Mitchell should be entrusted with such a decision-making role.

Still another factor contributing to Mullen's attitude was the sharp difference in his and Mitchell's personal life and outlook. Mitchell did not smoke, drink or use profanity. Mullen enjoyed drinking and the company of drinking people. He smoked and his language was sometimes salty. At the end of a tense day, Mullen often went to one of the bars near the NBC studio; Mitchell went home to be with his wife, Mildred. Mitchell had close church ties;

Mullen did not. Mitchell did not object to being called a Christian. Mullen at times kidded Mitchell about his "Sunday School" ways. Though Mullen and Mitchell had both spent their early years in rural midwest communities and had both shifted into a big city environment during the "Roaring Twenties," each had reacted to the drastic change in his own way. Mitchell had elected to live as his Quaker father had urged: "Don't do anything that will make your mother ashamed."

Mullen used two procedures for continuing his direction of the *Farm and Home Hour.* One consisted of calling Mitchell regularly from New York, often just after he had heard that day's program to offer his comments.

"Never a week passed but Mullen called me, and sometimes there would be two or three calls," Mitchell remembers. "He would ask what we were doing on the current programs. At times he would make suggestions, but mostly he seemed just to be checking to see if we were following the format he had originally worked out."

Mullen's second means of guiding the program was through the man whom he hired to be the new NBC director of agriculture. William Drips was named to the position ostensibly to work under the direction of the president of NBC. Actually he reported to Mullen.

Drips came with good credentials, a background similar to Mullen's. Reared on a South Dakota farm, he was graduated as an agricultural journalist from the University of Wisconsin, served as a county agent and taught agricultural journalism at Iowa State College before coming to NBC. But he was thrust into a position which required giving leadership to a farm program broadcast nationwide without even having had experience in local radio.

Drips was overwhelmed from his first day in his new job. Soon it was apparent to Trammell that Drips would be unable to handle any important part of the program direction and planning. Trammell wanted to admit a mistake and make a settlement with Drips so that he could leave NBC, but Mullen held that all Drips needed was more time. Gradually Trammell and his managers in Chicago came to recognize that Drips could do little more than observe what took place on the *Farm and Home Hour* and the Central Division of NBC in Chicago and report it to Mullen in New York.

But one person was able to immediately step into this critical void. By the end of 1934 precisely what Mullen had wanted to avoid had happened. Mitchell had become the dominant management figure in both the planning and operational phases of the program. For the next ten years, the remaining years that the program would air daily, Drips held the title but Mitchell made the decisions and did the work. It was having to meet this additional responsibility that led to Mitchell's becoming "the voice of American agriculture."

Mullen recognized what was happening and made one more effort to regain control. He proposed that the program and Mitchell be transferred to New York where he could help Drips and give more of his personal attention to the program. Trammell thought the proposal unwise, but it was Mitchell who killed it. He said he would leave the program rather than help originate it from New York.

"Farmers would never accept a farm program originating in New York," Mitchell told NBC officials. "The Chicago area is the acknowledged center for pricing and marketing of farm products and the manufacturing of farm machinery."

Even Mullen recognized that without Mitchell, the program would have limited possibilities and might even die. The proposal did not come up again.

If Drips had been satisfied just to hold the title and let Mitchell make the decisions, a great deal of embarrassment for both Mitchell and NBC could have been avoided. Possibly acting on Mullen's suggestions, Drips would from time to time thrust himself into situations which were not even remotely of his concern. Not infrequently associates would caution Mitchell that Drips was "no friend of his." The Firestone incident was typical.

The Firestone organization, which already used the NBC network to broadcast *The Firestone Hour*, a weekly program of symphony music, had invited Mitchell to present a special daytime weekly farm program, *Firestone Farm Champions*. The program dramatized the introduction by Firestone of rubber tires for farm implements—tractors, wagons and other farm machines.

Although Drips had no responsibility in this project, he went to Harvey Firestone, the still active founder of the Firestone company, and advised him against increasing Mitchell's retainer too rapidly "for fear that it might go to his head." Firestone was infuriated. He asked Mitchell to meet with him, reported what Drips had said, and directed Mitchell to advise NBC management that under no circumstances was Drips to have any part in the preparation of the Firestone farm programs.

As the years passed Drips became a tragic figure. Perhaps because of his inability to make an important contribution to the *Farm and Home Hour* and the tension of shadowing Mitchell and other NBC executives for Mullen, he became an alcoholic. At times when accompanying Mitchell on trips to produce special programs, Drips literally "drank himself under the table." Mitchell would watch Drips slide out of his chair and under the table, then later help him back to his hotel room. His drinking led to other incidents that were embarrassing to Mitchell and NBC, some requiring apologies. Finally, such an incident in Texas resulted in Drips' immediate dismissal. More than fifteen years had passed since Mullen had hired him as agricultural director for the NBC network.

On April 8, 1935, a year after Mullen had gone to New York, the *National Farm and Home Hour* celebrated its two-thousandth broadcast. From Washington, Secretary of Agriculture Henry A. Wallace saluted the program and acknowledged the supreme importance of radio communication to farm families across the nation. A special New York broadcast followed, honoring Mullen and others at NBC who had made the first network farm program possible.

"Now we are going to switch you to New York where you are going to hear greetings from the daddy of all this, our friend and yours, Frank E. Mullen," said Mitchell in Chicago.

There was no return of Mitchell's personal and friendly greeting by Mullen. Although in his remarks Mullen thanked the members of the thirty-five piece Farm and Home Orchestra, even greeting the orchestra leaders by name, at no time was there any reference to the only personality known to listeners in every section of the nation, Everett Mitchell.[3]

In 1934 Mitchell originated the *Farm and Home Hour* the first time from the campus of a land grant college. This program took place at the University of Missouri in Columbia where landmark work in animal nutrition was being done by William A. Albrecht. This was one of the last projects developed by Frank Mullen before he went to New York. The plan called for originating the program at a land grant college campus and its agricultural experiment station in each of what was then the forty-eight states in the United States.

Unquestionably, Mullen planned these college campus programs with the knowledge that airplane transportation would

227

soon be available between most cities in the United States. It would hardly have been practical to tie Mitchell down with time-consuming train travel to arrange programs in distant states.

The first campus programs were done in the Midwest where the travel distances were short. It was not until the DC-3 (the Model T of airplane travel) was introduced in 1936 that it became practical to go to campus locations in states such as California, Maine or Florida.

Mitchell and a radio engineer would arrive at the campus on Friday to prepare and rehearse the program. At the very first program, a college official asked if Mitchell could use the college town rather than Chicago in his Beautiful Day greeting. Mitchell agreed. "It's a beautiful day in Columbia, Missouri, and I hope it is even more beautiful wherever you are," was his opening.

At the campus of Texas A & M University, Mitchell had a confrontation in which he felt compelled to stand his ground against an unreasonable demand from Elliott Roosevelt, son of the President. Young Roosevelt, who operated radio stations in Texas, was engaged in a running feud with the university head.

Elliott Roosevelt met with Mitchell as soon as he arrived on the campus for the final rehearsal of the next day's program. Roosevelt explained his differences with the university president and asked, in effect, that he be given "equal time" on the program after the head of the university had spoken. Mitchell said that he did not have the authority to make such an important change in a program script that had already been approved by both NBC and the university.

Roosevelt insisted that Mitchell could make the change if he wanted to. There was more fruitless dialogue. Mitchell saw that he must take a decisive stand even though he was dealing with the son of President Roosevelt.

"Mr. Roosevelt, we all have people to report to. I cannot and will not make the change in tomorrow's script which you want.

But Elliott Roosevelt was not through. He played a final card.

"Father won't like it, and you can lose your job," he said.

"So be it," said Mitchell as he walked away.

When Mitchell returned to NBC in Chicago, still disturbed by the unpleasant exchange with Roosevelt, he reported the incident to the vice president of NBC in charge of the Central Division, Harry Kopp. He was so pleased with the way in which Mitchell had handled the difficult matter that he placed a commendation in Mitchell's file and gave him an immediate raise.

Many of the great breakthroughs in American food production which would come after World War II were already in evidence in the experimental plots and laboratories: hybrid corn, which would revolutionize farming in the Midwest; anhydrous ammonia to provide inexpensive soil nitrogen, which would bring unprecedented crop yields; new generations of livestock which would produce more milk, meat and eggs than ever before; and new ways to fight livestock diseases. Probably no one could have devised a better plan to educate the *Farm and Home Hour* listener in the rapidly-expanding agricultural industry.

The largest audience ever to hear the broadcast tuned in on December 9, 1935. The speaker was President Franklin D. Roosevelt. He came to Chicago to address the farm leaders of the nation attending the annual conference of the American Farm Bureau Federation. Eighteen thousand people crowded into the International Amphitheater to hear President Roosevelt in person, and more than twenty million listened to the address on the *Farm and Home Hour*, more citizens than had ever heard an American president's voice before.

Roosevelt's address had a special significance at this time, especially for farm families. Although the presidential election was less than eleven months away, the President had not yet made a statement on seeking reelection, though most supporters and political adversaries considered it a foregone conclusion. The dramatic changes in the federal agricultural programs introduced by Secretary of Agriculture Wallace were lifting farm families out of the despair of the Great Depression, and Roosevelt's program audience would be friendly. His coming to speak to the nation's farmers was a strong indication that he would seek reelection.

Upon reaching Chicago the President went to the Saddle and Sirloin Club to meet the city's civic and political leaders. Awaiting him at the club were Wallace and other cabinet members, as well as Everett Mitchell.

At eleven the President prepared to leave for the International Amphitheater. Although many from the Saddle and Sirloin Club walked the short distance to the Amphitheater, because of his handicap Roosevelt rode in the chill December air in an open car. Mitchell walked beside the President's car as it moved slowly through the crowd.

On that short trip, the mood of the warm welcome which the President had found in Chicago was rudely, if temporarily, disrupted. Something happened which rarely occurred during Roo sevelt's presidency—he was heckled in public.

The route to the Amphitheater took the President past some of the Chicago stockyard's high-fenced cattle pens. Sitting on these fences were scores of men who handled the livestock, whose jobs depended on the volume of hogs, cattle and sheep moving through the stockyards. These livestock wranglers were incensed because of Wallace's program of killing little pigs so they would not come to market. They saw this program as taking away their jobs. For much of the way to the Amphitheater, the President's car traveled at close range to the wranglers, who chanted, "There goes the man who took away our jobs. There goes the man who took away our jobs." Mitchell observed that the President was visibly troubled by the heckling.

Once inside the Amphitheater, the President's confidence returned. The massive crowd buzzed with excitement when he appeared. Mitchell opened the program with his usual, "It's a beautiful day in Chicago. . ." but when, moments later, he said, "It is my great pleasure to introduce to you the President of the United States, Franklin D. Roosevelt," there was instantly a standing ovation. The crowd would not quit clapping and sit down until American Farm Bureau Federal President Edward A. O'Neal came to the rostrum to rap for order so the President might proceed.

Roosevelt impressed his audience with his understanding of the complex farm problems facing them. His talk was full of facts about how farm income had risen from depression lows, how farm bankruptcies had decreased and how little the wheat farmers received from the sale of a loaf of bread—figures and observations only possible from someone who had closely followed the crisis in the nation's agriculture.

While Roosevelt was careful not to speak directly of seeking a second term, his remarks left no doubt that he believed there was more that the federal government could and should do to help farmers. He all but assured his nationwide audience that he would continue the fight to relieve the distress the depression had brought to the nation's farmers.

The President closed on a note of confidence and hope, a variation of his famous "we have nothing to fear but fear itself" remark. "We now know the way," he said, "to an even better day for our farmers, and we have only to be concerned about those dispensers of discord and calamity howlers."

## FOOTNOTES

(1) Sarnoff's faith in Trammell and Mullen as managers was rewarded. Trammell became executive vice president, president and chairman of the board of NBC before ill health forced his retirement in 1953. After handling several management positions at RCA, Mullen teamed with Trammell from 1940 until 1948 to run NBC, Trammell as president and Mullen as executive vice president.

(2) Frank E. Mullen's biographic reports in *Who's Who in America* always included the reference, "organized the *National Farm and Home Hour*, 1927."

(3) From a recording of the April 8, 1935 *Farm and Home Hour* broadcast in the archives of the Museum of Broadcasting in New York City. On this historic program NBC executive vice president Richard C. Patterson, Jr., explained for the first and only time on the air why NBC was broadcasting the *National Farm and Home Hour* at its own expense. "Neither NBC nor any of its associated stations receive any pay for this service to agriculture," he said. "We are paid on your daily appreciation."

E.D. Larson, director of the Bureau of Reclamation (left), listens as Perry Slater, outstanding Future Farmer of America (right), is interviewed by Everett Mitchell for the *National Farm and Home Hour's* salute to the Utah irrigation program and the Days of '47.

# Chapter 22
# Mr. Firestone Made It Clear

In the spring of 1936 Everett Mitchell received an unexpected long-distance telephone call from Akron, Ohio. It was from the secretary of Harvey S. Firestone, founder of the tire company bearing his name and one of the nation's best-known and most successful industrialists. The secretary said Mr. Firestone would like to have Mitchell call on him in Akron as soon as it was convenient. A date was agreed on.

Everett and Mildred Mitchell were excited about the call and the opportunity for Everett to visit Harvey Firestone, even though they did not know what the nature of the visit would be. Everett thought it might have something to do with rubber tires for tractors and other farm implements.

His conjecture was not without foundation. Each year since 1933 at the National Corn Husking Contests, he had seen the improvements in the Firestone tires used on demonstration tractors. It was generally known that Harvey Firestone himself had in 1931 initiated his company's program to prove to the nation's farmers that putting their tractors on rubber tires would lower farming costs. Firestone had played a similar role thirty years earlier in helping to shift the fledgling automobile industry from solid tires to air filled rubber tires.

But in 1936 Firestone was still going it alone. Neither the engineers at the land grant colleges nor those of any of Firestone's competitors in the rubber tire business were advocating the use of pneumatic tires on tractors and other farm implements. There were several possible reasons. Tractors were still "on trial" with farmers in the mid-thirties, to whom it had not yet been proven that the new machines could do better than a team of horses. Also, farmers were in the middle of the greatest farm depression on record, and few had money to invest in new equipment.

At their meeting in Akron, Firestone greeted Mitchell warmly, recalling the talk they had had about radio at their first meeting seven years before at the Golden Jubilee of Light in Dearborn, Michigan. He commended Mitchell on his contribution to the *Farm and Home Hour*, adding that he often had lunch at his office so he might hear the program. Then he came to the point.

"Everett, we want you to handle a special farm radio program that Firestone will sponsor to explain to American farmers the advantages of using rubber tires."

Firestone explained the advantages of the tractors equipped with the big, new, low-pressure tires Firestone was producing. He said the tires being introduced that year had a specially-developed tread which was so superior it had been given the patented name "Ground Grip."

"These rubber tires enable the tractor to cover more ground in less time. They save fuel and they spare the operator the fatigue that comes from the vibration of tractors with steel wheels. Rubber tires even make a tractor into a new kind of farm implement, a heavy duty road-hauling machine. Steel wheels, especially those with lugs, are not suited to running on roads and highways. Rubber tires are," Firestone explained.

"I know these advantages to be real. I myself have driven tractors equipped with these rubber tires for hours," he continued.

Firestone then outlined the new farm radio program he was planning. The most important feature would be interviews with farmers. He wanted to give the most expert of the nation's farmers—those who had built the best dairy herds, raised the best corn and wheat or produced the best flocks of poultry—a chance to tell their own story in their own words. The name of the program would be *Firestone Voice of the Farm*, and those who were featured would be known as Firestone Champion Farmers.

"I want to make it very clear to you why we are inviting you to develop our farm radio program," Firestone went on. "You have really earned this opportunity to work with us.

"We conducted a detailed survey in several states among our dealers and their farm customers," Firestone continued, as he reached into his desk and took out a voluminous file book. "We sent them a list of broadcasters in the United States who conduct farm service radio programs. Then we asked how many of them they had heard or could identify.

"Seventy-two percent of those responding had heard Everett Mitchell. The next highest broadcaster had been heard by just under fifteen percent. Everett, that is why we want you to take charge of our radio program," Firestone explained.

Mitchell found the statistics overwhelming. Because the *Farm and Home Hour* was an NBC sustaining program, without sponsors, the network had never taken a survey to determine just what its listenership was, although they had surveyed audiences for other programs. Mitchell had always supposed that he had a substantial audience, but he had not really expected to find himself so far in the lead in the field of agricultural broadcasting.

Before they parted that day, Mitchell told Firestone that he would, indeed, be interested in handling the program, if arrangements could be worked out around his NBC schedule. Firestone assured him that such arrangements could be made.

"Everett, you and I will work together," he said. "I want you to be in touch with me. You will hear from me from time to time and I want you to feel free to call upon me at any time if you think it is necessary."

The *Firestone Voice of the Farm* program began on more than sixty radio stations in October, 1936. It was a twice-a-week noon feature heard on most stations after the *Farm and Home Hour*. There were the interviews, music by an orchestra and popular songs by a barbershop quartet. Besides handling the farm interviews, Mitchell was the announcer. He also presented the commercials, which usually stressed the advantages of rubber tires for farm machines.

The Firestone company appointed farm specialists from the land grant colleges or from farm magazines to select the farm champions to appear on the program. Most of these champions were family farmers unknown except in their home communities. But there were a few exceptions. J.C. Penney, a household name in retailing, appeared on the show. He was also a farmer and had developed one of the nation's outstanding dairy herds. Another guest was Milton S. Hershey, the chocolate king who not only founded Hershey, Pennsylvania, but who maintained a school at Hershey in which boys, many of them orphans, learned dairying or another trade.

True to his word, Harvey Firestone did take a day-to-day interest in the program, and Mitchell did hear from him with surprising regularity.

"After a Firestone program or a *Farm and Home Hour* feature of special interest to him, he would call and tell me how much he liked it," Mitchell recalls.

"Besides words of commendation, his calls would usually include something extra—a suggestion for some future radio program or some other proposal. "One of his calls was a real surprise. He asked if it would be possible for me to be the announcer on *The Voice of Firestone*, the classical music evening program that had been heard across the nation on the NBC network for nearly ten years. I was sorry that my schedule would not permit it and he appeared to be quite disappointed," Mitchell remembers.

"Another time, when the planning was underway for the New York World's Fair of 1939, he called to tell mè that Firestone would be having an exhibition there. He reported that he had been talking to Grover Whalen, the person in charge of the fair, and had suggested there be a Farm Week, probably in mid-August, when farm families from all over the nation would be invited to see exhibits and features of special interest to them. 'I also proposed to Mr. Whalen that during Farm Week at the fair Everett Mitchell be made the official host,' Mr. Firestone told me."

The Firestone farm program attracted listeners immediately, and the number of stations carrying it increased to nearly one hundred. It was also successful in convincing farmers that rubber tires would make their work easier. In 1935, the year before the program began, only about fifteen out of every hundred new farm tractors sold were equipped with rubber tires. In 1937, after the program had been on the air for a year, forty-two out of every hundred new tractors were delivered to farmers equipped with rubber tires. Listeners were invited to send inquiries about the use of the new tires on farm machines to the *Voice of the Farm* program; this brought so many letters that the Firestone Farm Service Bureau was set up to provide farmers with the latest information.

The opportunity to work with a national corporation like Firestone added an important new dimension to Mitchell's career. This was his first chance to work directly at all levels of a large organization, from the chief executive to the dealers. He especially liked working with the dealers. He saw that his efforts could help make their goals easier to achieve. And the dealers were delighted to be rubbing shoulders with a national figure, especially one who showed them so much personal interest. When Mitchell met them at company functions they greeted him with the welcome reserved for a friend.

The Firestone experience led to Mitchell's gradually giving more and more of his time to sponsored farm radio, and later television, programs. Throughout his career he worked with a long list of non-competing companies that included some of the best known names in American industry providing products and services for agriculture.

What Mitchell liked best about his sponsored programs was "seeing the chips fly." Each program had a definite goal to be achieved in a specific period of time, perhaps two or three years, and the results could be measured against the goal. Armour needed more cream and chickens delivered to its Midwest processing plants in wartime. Pillsbury wanted to expand its mixed feed business. Funk wanted to consolidate its leadership in the rapidly growing hybrid seed corn industry. Sears wanted to shift more wartime business to its catalogue division. Mitchell enjoyed seeing the results of the programs these companies sponsored, knowing that the company and the men who worked for it were meeting their goals.

Mitchell did not choose to do programs only for sponsors with large budgets. His American Dairy Association radio program during the war years showed that if he thought the sponsor's goal was important he would work just as hard for an organization with a limited budget as for a Firestone.

Mitchell's friend, Owen Richards, was manager of the struggling American Dairy Association, which before World War II was supported by dairy farmer groups in only five states. (Today the Association is one of the most powerful lobbying groups in the nation.) The war came, bringing disruptions of the marketing of dairy products, travel restrictions and markets that were for the moment taking everything the dairy farmers could produce. Richards, who had been working hard to expand the association, was discouraged, but Mitchell urged him to go ahead with his plans, using the NBC network to communicate with the dairy farm audience. Even a fifteen-minute program once a week, properly planned, could provide the support necessary for expanding the organization, he told Richards.

The *Voice of the Dairy Farmer* began broadcasting on the NBC Blue network over sixteen stations in 1942. Clifton Utley of NBC, one of the nation's foremost wartime commentators, teamed with Mitchell on the program. Except for Utley's commentary, Mitchell wrote the script. He also used his Beautiful Day salutation. In addition, Mitchell went with Richards to important dairy states where farmers had not come into the Association to address key farm groups. In three years the radio program was being heard on forty-four Blue Network stations, and the Association's support had expanded from five states to eighteen. The American Dairy Association was on its way.

What was baffling was how Mitchell could find time to do sponsored farm programs and still preside over the planning and announcing of the most demanding program in broadcasting, the *Farm and Home Hour*. Technical advances had made pre-recording programs possible by 1936 when Mitchell took on the assignment with Firestone, and the Voice of the Farm programs were recorded. But the *Farm and Home Hour* continued live, six days a week, as did the children's educational program Mitchell originated and continued to broadcast, *Air Juniors*.

Three things made it possible for Mitchell to keep up his demanding schedule. NBC was glad to have the star of the *Farm and Home Hour*, a sustaining non-revenue program, in demand by sponsors paying for their broadcast time, especially those with such prestigious names as Firestone, Standard Oil, Armour, and Sears. Most of the sponsored programs Mitchell produced were broadcast on NBC stations, thus adding to NBC revenue. This made it less difficult for him to be away from his network duties to handle the sponsored programs on occasion.

A second factor was the rapid advance in air travel. Less than ten years before, when he was in Washington, D.C., he had taken his first plane ride in an unsteady barnstorming aircraft safe to fly only in the daytime and in good weather. The Firestone program was produced in New York on Saturdays, the least difficult day for Mitchell to be away from Chicago. He could fly there in three hours on the new, fast, dependable Douglas DC-3, which would rapidly become the Model T of air travel and which had just been put on the Chicago-New York run. By the time the Firestone program had ended four years later, United Airlines had honored Mitchell for flying a million miles.

But by far the most important factor in Mitchell's work schedule was his remarkable energy and stamina. He could sleep as little as two hours a night and still be at his best the next day. His ability to work twenty hours a day for long periods had served him well in the early years of WENR and was still a major asset. All during the 1930s he was chief announcer in NBC's big Central Division and carried the heaviest load on the *Farm and Home Hour*, as well as handling the sponsored programs. In the early days of World War II, he was broadcasting live programs on the NBC network seven days a week.

238

A typical schedule during those years was the Everett Mitchell Day in Marshall, Minnesota, on March 28, 1952. Marshall is the county seat of Lyon County and the farm supply center for a rich agricultural area deep in the southwestern part of the state. The Everett Mitchell Day had been arranged months in advance by the Funk Brothers Seed Company, for whom Mitchell was doing a special program, *Today's Farm Story*, broadcast in the Corn Belt states of the Midwest.

Mitchell had approved a schedule that would have incapacitated an ordinary person. He was constantly before the public from eight o'clock that morning until ten that evening and gave the appearance of loving every minute of the time. At an eight o'clock breakfast, escorted by an executive of the Funk organization, as he was all day, he visited with the Department of Agriculture specialists—members of the Lyon County agricultural extension office, soil conservation corps people and others.

At ten o'clock Mitchell spoke before several hundred students at the Holy Redeemer Catholic school. At eleven o'clock he spoke to students of the public junior and senior high schools of Marshall. In both school talks he reported on his visits to farm exchange students overseas.

At noon Mitchell was guest of honor at a luncheon given by the Funk dealers of southwestern Minnesota. The afternoon was spent doing interviews on Lyon County farms that would be broadcast on Marshall's radio station, KMHL.

A private dinner was given for Mitchell by the marketing executives of the Funk organization; its main purpose was to give him two hours when he did not need to make a speech. At eight o'clock came the banner event of the day, a dinner for Mitchell given by the Civic and Commerce Association of Marshall to which two hundred and fifty southwestern Minnesota 4-H club members who had won high honors in their projects that year, 4-H leaders and leaders of the Marshall business community had been invited as special guests.

Mitchell's address was broadcast to thousands of listeners in western Minnesota and eastern South Dakota. He had spoken in public four times since morning, speaking to fifteen hundred people in person and shaking hands with all his rapid schedule would permit, and he had talked to thousands more by radio. But he took the midnight train from Marshall and was in Chicago refreshed and ready for his *Farm and Home Hour* broadcast on the next morning.

Still Mitchell found time to do more. He met weekly with his NBC Page Boys Announcers School which he had organized as a volunteer effort to help bright teenagers find their way into permanent positions in broadcasting. In September, 1936, Harry Lawrence reported in his Chicago *Evening Post* radio column:

> Ralph Maddox, formerly production manager and announcer at Station WJDX in Jackson, Mississippi, has been added to the NBC Chicago production staff. Jack Simpson, a page at the NBC Chicago studios for four years and the sixth graduate of the NBC Announcers School, conducted by Senior Announcer Everett Mitchell, to graduate to an announcer's post has replaced Maddox at WJDX. Jack sold himself by sending a voice recording to the station manager.

As is the case with any well known and successful professional, Mitchell was regularly being given proposals for sponsored radio programs and even full-time jobs. For example, in 1947 Philip Pillsbury of the milling dynasty in Minneapolis proposed that Mitchell become an executive in the Pillsbury organization and direct not only the company's radio efforts but all other communications as well. In 1953 Mitchell's longtime friend and benefactor at NBC, Niles Trammell, acquired television stations in Florida and made Mitchell a most attractive proposal, including a share in ownership, if he would come to Florida.

In each instance, Everett and Mildred Mitchell weighed the new job offers thoughtfully, and in each instance decided to remain with NBC and the *Farm and Home Hour*. The merits of the job were not the only considerations. Shortly before World War II the Mitchells had built a comfortable house in Park Ridge, a Chicago suburb northwest of the city, which was close to their church, family and longtime friends, and fast transportation to the NBC offices in the Merchandise Mart. The Mitchells were reluctant to leave their new home.

There were other important reasons for Mitchell's recurring decision to remain with NBC in Chicago. He was now in the mature years of a career which even he recognized was unusual — or "fortunate" as he told his friends. He believed that being moderator of the *Farm and Home Hour*, which had the widest geographical listenership of any radio program in America, was the key to making him a national figure in broadcasting. So long as he was recognized as broadcasting's foremost spokesman on agricultural matters, he would continue to have good jobs offered to him elsewhere, jobs that might become very appealing toward the close of his career.

Nor was he blind to the hazards of keeping on top in broadcasting. Twenty years had passed since the orchestra leader and the piano player at WENR had tried to get him fired so they might have his job. During those years a lengthening list of other associates had schemed to oust him. He had to live with the Mullen-Drips clumsy and at times embarrassing efforts to control the *Farm and Home Hour*. But these problems at NBC were in large measure offset by the unbroken support he had always received from the NBC vice presidents in Chicago—first Niles Trammell, then Harry Kopp and then I.E. Showerman. This kind of support kept his position in the main a pleasant and rewarding one for the veteran broadcaster.

But though Mitchell chose to remain with NBC and valued the support of the NBC executives, he found that the men who became his best friends were the executives he worked with in private industry. Men like Owen Richards of the Dairy Association, Edward Wentworth of Armour, William A. Roberts, head of Allis-Chalmers, Eddie Condon of Sears and of course Harvey Firestone were people with whom Mitchell had much in common. All of them were men of deep religious convictions, all were devoted family men and most of them shared with Mitchell the memories of a rural childhood in which hard work played a large and formative part. In turn, these hard-working business executives sensed immediately that Mitchell was not the stereotype associated with "show business" but a man who shared their own values and who could be trusted.

Late in 1937, Everett Mitchell said his last goodbye to the first of these valued sponsors and friends, although he did not know it at the time. In mid-December, Harvey Firestone and his sons, Leonard and Raymond, left Akron to go south for the winter by way of Memphis. Firestone wanted to see the new line of large farm tractor tires for use in the cane and rice fields that were being produced in the Firestone Memphis factory. He had talked to Mitchell just before leaving and invited him and Mildred to come to Harbel Villa in Florida sometime during the winter. "Stay as long as you can," was his invitation.

Always looking toward the future, Firestone presided over a Memphis marketing meeting for Firestone sales executives. He discussed production and marketing for 1938 and also a brief projection of 1939 plans. There would be a Firestone Center at the New York World's Fair to open in the spring of 1939. There would also be, he thought, a special Farm Day at the fair and he was in hopes that Firestone's Everett Mitchell would be the official host to welcome the farm families. He closed the conference with the flat prediction that it would only be a matter of time until all American farm machines would be on rubber.

Firestone reached Miami on December 20, his sixty-ninth birthday. He quickly settled into his Florida routine. Sunday, February 6, 1938, was an especially pleasant day for Harvey Firestone. With his family he attended services at the Community Church. There were guests for Sunday dinner. Feeling unusually fatigued after an active day, he retired early. He fell quickly into a sleep from which he did not waken.[1]

Many of the dreams which Harvey Firestone had worked to create became realities. At the end of 1938, the manufacturers of farm implements in the United States reported that eighty-five percent of the new tractors bought by American farmers were equipped with rubber tires. There was no more fitting tribute.

The next year, the New York World's Fair did hold a Farm Week in mid-August and Everett Mitchell was there to greet the farm families as the official host. Another event which Firestone planned, and one that he unquestionably hoped to attend, took place during Farm Week. The Farm Champions who had appeared on the *Firestone Voice of the Farm* with Everett Mitchell held a reunion in New York and attended the special Farm Week festivities. Mitchell enjoyed the reunion but he felt keenly the absence of his old friend.

### FOOTNOTE

(1) Alfred Lief gives an interesting account of the last days of Harvey S. Firestone's life in his book, *The Fireside Story*, published by McGraw Hill Book Company, 1951, on pages 230 and 233.

A fishing trip off the coast of Clearwater, Florida was one of the few opportunities Everett Mitchell had to relax.

Vice President John Nance Garner broke with President Franklin D. Roosevelt over running for a third term in 1940 and went home to Uvalde, Texas. NBC sent Everett Mitchell to Uvalde to "put the vice president on the network" to give his side of the break during the latter weeks of the fall campaign.

# Chapter 23
# No Watergate In Uvalde

Everett Mitchell was on a special NBC mission, without question it was to be the most politically sensitive of his career, in Uvalde, Texas, the Friday evening before the 1940 presidential election. The instructions in his pocket from NBC Vice President Harry Kopp read, "to put the Vice President of the United States on the full NBC network at 9:00 p.m. Central Standard Time November 4, 1940."[1]

With war raging in Europe, Africa and Asia, Franklin D. Roosevelt, who had already been elected twice to the presidency, was seeking to break the two-term tradition begun by George Washington and unchallenged for one hundred and fifty years. Roosevelt was opposed by Republican Wendell L. Willkie.

John Nance Garner of Texas, who had served in Congress for thirty years and had been Speaker of the House, was the Democratic leader in the South. He had served as vice president during Roosevelt's first two terms. Had Roosevelt not sought a third term, Garner would undoubtedly have been the Democratic candidate for President in 1940. Long before the summer convention, Garner had made known his opposition to for a third term. When Roosevelt decided to run, Garner declined to continue as vice president and did not take part in the President's reelection campaign. He had, in fact, left Washington early in October and returned to his ranch at Uvalde.

As the presidental campaign heated up after Labor Day in 1940 and Wendell Willkie was proving to be a highly vocal and aggressive candidate, the President became concerned about Vice President Garner's silence. Roosevelt appealed to Jesse Jones, head of the Reconstruction Finance Corporation, a powerful figure in Texas politics and a close friend of the Vice President. Jones was asked to intercede with Garner and get him to break his political silence in a nationwide broadcast the week before the election. Roosevelt wanted Garner to endorse his election term and urge the election of Democrats running for Congress.

Jones called Uvalde immediately and in the next forty-eight hours held a series of phone conferences with the Vice President and Mrs. Garner. In the end, Garner made it clear that while he was unalterably opposed to any president having a third term, he did not wish to embarrass his many friends in Washington and across the country by a silence which might indicate that he would favor the election of Willkie.

He would consent to a fifteen-minute network radio program, but there were two conditions. The broadcast must take the form of an interview done by a well-known radio personality rather than be a formal statement by the Vice President. Further, the program must originate at his ranch in Uvalde.

Aides to President Roosevelt were immediately in contact with NBC asking if the network could be cleared for a 9 p.m. broadcast on the Friday evening before the election. They also wanted to know if the best-known and most respected radio announcer of the day—Everett Mitchell of Chicago—could be available to handle the interview.

Mitchell had not met Vice President Garner. From his own observations of the Washington scene and from the briefings for the Uvalde assignment, he knew that Garner had publicly differed with Roosevelt on major issues before, including the President's effort to pack the Supreme Court. The Vice President was his own man.

One of Garner's greatest political assets was his wife, Ettie. He had married the former Marietta Rheiner in 1895 and from the time he entered Congress in 1903 she had been his personal secretary. She still managed his Washington office. Perhaps even more important, she had during all this time been his closest adviser in what was generally acknowledged to be the most effective political partnership Washington had known in this century. Had it not been for Roosevelt's decision to attempt an overturn of the third term tradition, she might well have guided John Nance Garner to the presidency.

Mitchell arrived at the Garner ranch home just outside Uvalde at seven o'clock, exactly two hours before the broadcast. He and his engineer were met by Mrs. Garner, who took them to the library where they found the Vice President reading Homer's *Odyssey*, the classic poem about the ancient Trojan Wars. They discussed the interview and Mitchell reported on the questions he planned to ask. Garner expressed only one concern. He was an early-to-bed and early-to-rise man. The broadcast was scheduled for 9 p.m., which was his regular time for retiring, and he wondered if he would be alert enough to do justice to these important matters in a speech before the entire nation. All this time the engineer was monitoring Garner's voice and testing various microphone placements for the best sound reproduction.

Mrs. Garner apparently overheard snatches of the Vice President's comments about the broadcast interfering with his regular bedtime. The red velvet portieres that curtained the library off from the living room parted and Mrs. Garner came in. "Are you having trouble with Father?" she asked.

"No, not at all," Mitchell answered.

As though there had been serious discussion between them earlier regarding the broadcast, Mrs. Garner turned to the Vice President and directed, "Father, you do what Mr. Mitchell wants. He knows his business." With that she started to leave the room, but at the doorway she turned and said to Mitchell, "Mr. Mitchell, if you have any more trouble with Father, let me know and I will take care of it."

The Vice President continued to read the *Odyssey*, apparently undisturbed by Mrs. Garner's comments.

The preparations for the broadcast completed, the NBC men attempted to excuse themselves and leave Garner to his reading. But as they started to leave, the Vice President said, "The Old Lady doesn't permit any spirits in the house, but I know you fellows might get thirsty. If you will raise the window shade in the guest bathroom you will find some libation."

Then Garner for the first time spoke directly to Mitchell.

"Everett, come over and sit down. I have some questions for you." After Mitchell was seated, Garner asked, "Could you begin the broadcast with 'It's a beautiful day in Uvalde, Texas?' I have always thought that you have the best opening line in radio."

As the time drew near for the broadcast, the Vice President had another question for Mitchell: "Everett, have you ever hunted wild turkey? It can be great fun. We have a lot of turkeys on the ranch."

Mitchell said that he had not hunted wild turkey but that sometime he would like to.

"Take the later plane tomorrow, and I'll arrange for you to hunt wild turkey on the ranch in the morning. This isn't the turkey season, but I will call the game warden, and he will take you out. There is only one word of caution. Don't drop the empty shells on the ground or in the car. Just put them in your pocket." Mitchell did go wild turkey hunting the next day. The game warden made sure that he did not go home empty handed.

Just before the broadcast began, Mrs. Garner announced that she would go to the yard and hear the interview on their car radio. She wanted to hear it just as it would be heard all over the United States.

"It's a beautiful day in Uvalde, Texas, on the ranch of Vice President and Mrs. Garner where this evening Vice President Garner has consented to give me an interview this last week before the national election. This will be the first time that he has given an interview during the 1940 election campaign."

Mitchell confirmed that Vice President Garner had made it known months before that he was opposed to any move to draft President Roosevelt for a third term. For this reason Garner did not seek another term as vice president and did not take part in the fall campaign.

He opened the interview by asking Garner what he had been doing since leaving Washington nearly a month ago. Garner said that he had been mostly just relaxing—reading and visiting with old friends who had called at the ranch. After some discussion of the Uvalde ranch operations, Mitchell asked the question both friend and foe of the Vice President were waiting for. "In light of your break with the President over a third term, the rapid spread of the war and other issues, what are your thoughts about the national election that takes place next week?"

Though his words were carefully measured and Mitchell could tell he was speaking under tension, Garner came quickly and calmly to grips with the question. While he regretted that the third term issue had been injected into the campaign, it was clear that there were a number of issues, most of them related to the war overseas, that were of greater immediate importance.

Then his conclusion. There could be no doubt, Garner said, for the good of the nation the Roosevelt administration and the Democratic Party should remain in charge. He refrained from mentioning the President by name, but Garner said that it was this Democratic administration that had led the nation out of the Great Depression and had experience dealing with the tragic war that now involved important nations on three continents. He was convinced, Garner said, that the nation would next week call upon the President and his Democratic administration to continue their effort to keep the United States out of the war.[2]

The broadcast over, Mitchell congratulated the Vice President on his interview and predicted that there would be messages of commendation from both political friends and adversaries. Garner did not reply but went to a drawer, took out one of his official portraits as vice president and wrote across one corner the inscription, "To my friend Everett Mitchell, John N. Garner," and added the date. Mitchell still has the picture.

A moment later Mrs. Garner entered the library and commended both the Vice President and Mitchell for doing an excellent interview.

Then she added, "Just before the program began, there was an NBC flash which reported that earlier today Father's office in Washington had been entered, his desk broken open and the contents ransacked."

She turned to Mitchell.

"But they didn't find anything of importance in that desk. Father never wrote of his dealings in letters. All of Father's deals were made mouth to ear."

If Richard Nixon had only known.

#### FOOTNOTES

(1) Other than brief press references at the time, there is no published reference to Everett Mitchell's trip to Uvalde, Texas on November 4, 1940. There is no record of the broadcast in the Congressional Library in Washington, D.C., NBC records of the event long since been discarded and there is no known transcript of the interview.

(2) Vice President Garner did not vote for President Roosevelt in 1940. *U.S. News and World Report* on Page 72 in the issue of March 8, 1957, questioned Garner and gave his reply: "Q. Do you still vote Democratic? A. I never voted anything else in my life — only one time that I ever failed to vote. That was when Roosevelt ran for a third term. I didn't go to the polls. I was just that strong against the third term."

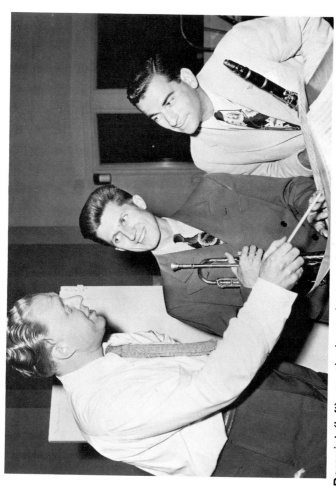

Whitey Berquist (left), musical conductor of the *National Farm and Home Hour*, discusses ideas for an arrangement with two of his musicians. They are trumpeter Dee Palmer (center) and clarinetist Freddie Aune (right).

# Part 6
# The Voice of American Agriculture

Time changes everything. For Everett Mitchell the 1940s, the years which took him from his early forties to his early fifties, brought the greatest period of uncertainty and change in both his professional and his personal life. Although these were the years American was fighting World War II, the war had little to do with the transitions in Mitchell's life.

In the middle of the decade, the *National Farm and Home Hour*, the broadcasting industry's show piece of public service, came to an abrupt end. The termination occurred because of developments precipitated by changes in government policy and the private radio industry rather than any decline of public interest in the program, which was at an all-time peak.

In the melee Mitchell was separated from NBC when its Blue Network and the *Farm and Home Hour* were sold in a deal that created the American Broadcasting Company (ABC). Mitchell gave up his work with the original *Farm and Home Hour* and returned to NBC shortly after. There he put down the foundation for a climactic twenty more years at NBC and the reestablishing of an NBC *Farm and Home Hour* program. He continued to broadcast farm service programs until his retirement in 1968.

The tragedies in his personal life occurred at the beginning and the end of the critical decade of the 1940s. In 1941 his mother, Lucilla Mitchell, died. He had visited with her either in person or by telephone every week in the twenty years since he had married and established his own home.

Since giving up her home in Chicago, Lucilla and her oldest daughter, Eva, who was confined to a wheelchair, had lived with another daughter, Edith, in LaGrange, Illinois. After Lucilla's death, Eva continued to live with Edith until her sister could no longer care for her. After a light stroke, she went to a nursing home in nearby Des Plaines. For as long as she lived, Everett maintained a close touch with Eva, his first singing teacher who helped prepare him for his career in broadcasting.

In the last years of the 1940s, Everett's beloved Mildred was stricken with cancer. Everett watched over her day and night, cancelling appointments and turning programs over to substitutes as her needs required. On the morning of February 9, 1950, he found himself alone with only his faith to sustain him in the darkness that followed. Director Whitey Berquist and the *Farm and Home Hour* orchestra asked to provide the music at Mildred's funeral service.

To fill some of the void, Mitchell absorbed himself deeply into his work. He began a schedule of overseas travel that ultimately took him to sixty-seven countries around the world to study agriculture. The informtion he gathered while on four continents added a new dimension to his radio and television programs.

On July 26, 1952, Clara Christensen of Park Ridge and Everett Mitchell were married. Clara, an executive in the Illinois Bell Telephone Company, was a specialist in communication and dealing with people. She quickly became an aide to her husband, especially in his tours overseas. In the spring of 1953, the Mitchells made a trip around the world to observe farming methods and rural youth exchange programs from the South Pacific to Europe.

Shortly after they returned to the United States, Everett and Clara established their Beautiful Day Farm near Wheaton. Their son, Peter, was born in December of 1954. Now an advertising agency account specialist, Peter grew up on Beautiful Day Farm where he could watch his father conduct a wide range of agricultural experiments. Clara and Everett lived at the farm until 1974, when they moved to their present home in Wheaton.

# Chapter 24
# "Don't Let Him Get Away"

In 1940 Everett Mitchell was forty-two years old, and to most observers his future would have seemed very secure. He was one of the best-known and most admired broadcasters in America, moderator of a program heard across the country and announcer for many other programs. Also, he was at last building a home of his own in the Chicago suburb of Park Ridge.

But Mitchell did not want to take his future for granted. It was the beginning of a new decade, and he was measuring what had happened during his years in radio and what was likely to happen next, in the period just ahead. The broadcasting business had been good to him almost beyond belief. He enjoyed his work so much it was difficult to make plans for a vacation. But his one overriding concern was for stability in a business that could rearrange the future in minutes and often did.

All of Mitchell's jobs in radio so far had come to him, that is, they had been offered to him by a station owner, a network or a sponsor. That meant that the jobs could and did end without his being able to do much about it. This was true even of the *Farm and Home Hour*, which was beginning its twelfth year and was universally recognized as the finest service radio program in all broadcasting. Mitchell never let himself forget that the show was a sustaining program, which meant that it cost NBC and its affiliated stations a million dollars and more a year. Even more unsettling in terms of his future was the developing attitude of the federal government, whose Federal Radio Commission had just concluded a study which held that the NBC ownership of two radio networks, the Red and the Blue, constituted a monopoly.

From the beginning Mitchell had observed that the people whose careers in radio were the most stable and rewarding were those who owned or controlled programs. He had twice survived

253

the sale of Station WENR and managed to keep his broadcasting career intact largely because he had originated and controlled sponsored service programs with a demonstrated listener following. When NBC bought WENR and retained very few members of the large staff, Mitchell's $175 a week depression salary (roughly today's equivalent of $1,000 a week) remained as it was largely because he was indispensable to the lucrative sponsored children's program, *Air Juniors.*

By mid-1940 Mitchell had reached the conclusion that he must develop his own morning farm program for NBC's Chicago station WMAQ, one of those which also carried the *Farm and Home Hour* at 11:30 a.m. He had talked to Vice President Harry Kopp, who encouraged him to make a proposal and welcomed the idea of WMAQ's seeking a farm audience in the early morning.

Although Kopp liked the idea, there were others who thought it was foolhardy. Such a program would be in head-to-head competition with Chicago's top farm service station, WLS. It was owned by the widely-read farm magazine, *Prairie Farmer*, and was recognized as having the most and some of the best farm and rural service programs of any Midwest station. Several blocks of farm programs, the first starting at 5:30 a.m. and another centering around the noon hour, were broadcast daily. The station covered all the important farm events in Illinois and Indiana, where the *Prairie Farmer* circulation was the greatest. In addition, WLS owned the popular *National Barn Dance*, broadcast nationwide on Saturday night from Chicago's Eighth Street Theater. Headliners such as Lulu Belle and Scotty and Bob Atcher were paid Hollywood salaries for their Saturday night's work.

In contrast, Station WMAQ did not even begin its broadcast day until just before 7 a.m. and was generally recognized for its urban listenership.

The difficulty of the task notwithstanding, Mitchell was sure he could develop an important audience for a WMAQ farm and homemaker program, somewhat along the lines of the *Farm and Home Hour* formula.

On the first week in November of 1940, when Mitchell was marking the seventeenth anniversary of his first broadcast and WMAQ was observing the twentieth anniversary of scheduled radio broadcasting in the United States, NBC's Central Division sent an announcement to all newspapers in that part of the WMAQ service area that extended from Iowa to Ohio and from Missouri to Michigan. The announcement said that on Monday,

November 18, Station WMAQ would begin broadcasting at 6:15 a.m., adding one-half hour to its schedule in order to present a new farm and homemaker service program by Everett Mitchell, the NBC announcer for the *Farm and Home Hour*. The new program would be called *Town and Farm* and would be heard Monday through Friday from 6:15 to 6:45 a.m.

*Town and Farm* began as a WMAQ sustaining feature. The sales department anticipated difficulty in finding a sponsor for a farm program competing with Station WLS. The marketing men proposed that *Town and Farm* be aired for six months; then, they felt, they would have a better chance to find a sponsor, perhaps one selling both to farmers and to the yard and garden market. Even then, they said, they would need Mitchell's personal help in signing a sponsor.

Unaware that Mitchell had earlier managed Station WENR and supervised its marketing, the WMAQ sales staff was in for a major awakening. Within ninety days, Mitchell brought Vice President Kopp a contract for sponsorship of the Monday through Friday broadcasts of *Town and Farm* for an entire year from one of the nation's best known retailers. In addition to providing the station with one of its largest sales contracts, the new agreement paid Mitchell nearly twice the amount he received for handling the prestigious *Farm and Home Hour* on the one-hundred-station network.

The singular success in finding *Town and Farm's* first sponsor came about because of what Mitchell describes as a "hunch." These hunches are not infrequent with Mitchell, and at this time in his life he was learning to pay attention to them. "If I paid attention to my hunches, it always worked out, and if I didn't pay attention later on I was sorry," Mitchell says today. "So I learned that when I got a hunch, the thing for me to do was to follow it through."

On this occasion, Mitchell had learned from reading the trade papers that the Sears Roebuck organization was pinched for merchandise for its new retail stores because of the number of suppliers who had government contracts for war materials and who were no longer producing consumer goods. Sears wanted to shift its emphasis from these stores, whose overhead could not be met without a full stock of merchandise, to its catalog division.

Mitchell's hunch was that this was the kind of assignment that could be most effectively handled by radio promotion. The Midwest rural market had made the Sears Roebuck Company successful originally and was still the backbone of the Sears business. Over only one station, WMAQ, *Town and Farm* would be heard across the Midwest; hence this was a job Sears could accomplish inexpensively with a single station.

Mitchell was aware that radio had already been suggested to the Sears advertising agency by Station WLS, the NBC network and, unquestionably, other broadcasters. After consulting with Sears marketing people, the Sears advertising agency had turned them all down. But Mitchell's proposal was different than any of the others and could be attractive to Sears in two important respects. Because of the wide coverage of WMAQ (in the dark morning hours of fall and winter the WMAQ 50,000-watt clear channel signal could be heard from the Gulf of Mexico to central Canada and from New England to Colorado), the cost would be more modest than anything which had yet been proposed to Sears. Further, Sears could be represented by one of the best-known figures on radio, one who already had a wide listening audience in the Midwest.

The problem, Mitchell reasoned, was how to get Sears and its advertising agency to change their minds and accept a proposition they had already turned down not once but several times. To overcome this formidable barrier, Mitchell knew he must have help from inside the Sears organization. He had a friend with a responsible job in the big catalog department. The friendship dated back to 1933 and the Chicago World's Fair, The Century of Progress. His friend was then manager of Sally Rand, the fan dancing sensation at the fair. Mitchell had helped him get personal appearances for Sally Rand in major Chicago hotels.

Mitchell and his Sears friend met at lunch and Mitchell explained his plan, saying he was sure it would be of interest to the company's catalog department. But how, he asked, could he get an appointment with the right person in the department when similar proposals had already been turned down? His friend assured him there would be no problem, and Mitchell would have an appointment with the head of the catalog department whenever he was ready.

Now, Mitchell had to get the Sears advertising agency to approve his going to see the Sears catalog department. Unless he had that permission, the agency would be in a position to squelch the proposal even after Sears had shown interest. The Sears account executive was not hostile, but like any good agency man he did not want to reverse his previous position to a client nor did he want new ideas being taken to a client by someone else. At first, he said it would be useless, but Mitchell was persistent. For a long while the two men continued to talk but were at an impasse. The agency man refused to give Mitchell his permission to go directly to Sears and Mitchell refused to leave until he did.

As the end of the day drew near, the agency man suddenly gave in. "It won't do you any good," he said, "but go ahead. Tell them you talked to me and I thought there was enough that is different about your proposal to warrant their hearing it directly from you rather than from me."

Matters moved quickly in the conference with the head of the catalog department. The meeting was set for 2 p.m., but Mitchell was there at 1:50. When he entered the department head's office, he could see immediately that the man was obviously intending to do no more than go through the motions of meeting with Mitchell, as he had promised his assistant.

"Mr. Mitchell, I am glad to meet you. I don't think we are interested in radio, but I will give you ten minutes to convince me that we should take another look."

Two hours and ten minutes later, Mitchell left. The Sears executive walked to the door with him and thanked him for coming. In Mitchell's pocket was a signed contract. *Town and Farm* had its first sponsor.

As Mitchell explained it that evening to his wife, Mildred, he had really done very little but outline the proposal. He knew the Sears executive was one of the country's foremost authorities on the cost of doing business by direct mail (catalog) and other print media, such as newspapers and magazines. Mitchell said he thought he could lay out a plan by which Sears could get the job done for half or less the cost that would be required in other media. The conference started immediately after that statement, and other executives were summoned to join in.

After going through his proposal carefully, Mitchell had invited questions. How good is WMAQ coverage outside Chicago the Sears men wanted to know. How good is it outside Illinois? Can radio really get listeners to write requests for the Sears catalog, using their own stationery and postage? And then the clincher. Would Mitchell be available to make some personal appearances for Sears?

When the questions had been answered, the head of the catalog department said he was convinced Mitchell's proposal should be given a try. There was, however, one more step he must take. He

257

could not consider making such a departure from previous practice without talking to the Sears director of information, Eddie Condon. He asked his secretary to see if Condon was in his office.

No, came the reply, he was in New York, but he could be reached by telephone. The catalog department manager went to his private office to make the call. He was gone such a short time that Mitchell thought Condon must not have been available after all. "Well, that didn't take long," said the catalog chief. "Condon said that if we had an opportunity to get Everett Mitchell to personally do a program for Sears, don't let him get away. Issue a contract at once."

Mitchell reported on his conference the next morning to NBC's Vice President Kopp, who then called in his sales manager. Kopp explained that Mitchell had come in with a year's contract with Sears Roebuck and Company.

"What must we do now? What's the next step?" the sales manager asked Mitchell.

"Just thank them when you acknowledge the order," Mitchell replied with a twinkle.

The *Town and Farm* program was successful for Sears almost from the beginning. After an initial sixty-day period which the Sears catalog managers thought satisfactory but which was below Mitchell's expectations, the volume of requests for the catalogs climbed steadily month by month. Sears renewed the contract four times as World War II continued and the consumer goods Sears sold became less and less available. As the availability of consumer goods went down, the requests for the catalogs increased, and so did orders. Finally, late in 1944, Sears found it was having to spend so much time and money returning orders that could not be filled that the management felt compelled to terminate the *Town and Farm* sponsorship. But the experience had been productive for everyone. Sears had accomplished its goal, and Mitchell had proved that WMAQ did have an important rural audience over a wide area of the Midwest. *Town and Farm* had no trouble finding other sponsors in 1944 or for that matter any time during its twenty-eight years of broadcasting.

During those years, hundreds of farmers, homemakers, land grant college specialists, agricultural leaders, private industry researchers, church leaders, teachers, 4-H members, Boy and Girl Scouts and others came to the *Town and Farm* studios to appear in interviews and demonstrations.

Almost exactly midway in its run, *Town and Farm* became

both a radio and a television program. Mitchell did the radio program at 6:15 a.m. over WMAQ and the television show at 7 a.m. over WNBQ (Channel Five). After about a year the radio time was taken over for other programs and *Town and Farm* continued exclusively on television until Mitchell's retirement in 1968.

As soon as *Town and Farm* went on television, Mitchell began featuring live demonstrations. Always determined to have features unique to Chicago television, Mitchell took live animals up the nineteen floors of the Merchandise Mart to appear in the demonstrations, including dairy and beef cattle, hogs and sheep.

The demonstration that attracted the most attention nationwide reached its climax on the Good Friday program in 1962. Twenty-one days before, Mitchell had brought in a portable incubator and, during the program, filled it with fertilized eggs and turned it on at the moment he calculated most likely to produce baby chicks on the Good Friday program. Each day viewers watched Mitchell turn the eggs and check the temperature and humidity in the incubator.

On Good Friday when Mitchell arrived at the studio, he knew that all had gone well. He heard chirps. When he opened the incubator door for the audience three chicks were already out of their shells, two others were working their way out and most of the rest of the eggs were in some stage of the hatching process.

*Town and Farm* won Chicago and national awards for NBC and Mitchell. None was more appreciated that the Billboard Award from the national advertising trade magazine, *Billboard*, which declared *Town and Farm* to be the outstanding farm, homemaker and community program on a single independent tation in the United States in 1948.

With *Town and Farm*, Mitchell had achieved his goal to own his own program and find stability in the fluctuating world of broadcasting. It remained on the air until Mitchell himself retired and was a fixture in the last half of his forty-five years of broadcasting.

Everett Mitchell traveled more than a million miles visiting the forty-eight states prior to 1951. One of his stops with the crew from the *National Farm and Home Hour* was at Dwight, Illinois where he observed a dairy project for a group of Future Farmers of America (FFA).

# Chapter 25
# Winds of Change

With his own daily morning radio program firmly established on Station WMAQ, Everett Mitchell turned his attention to the problems of the *National Farm and Home Hour*. The first week in August, 1941, the program celebrated its four thousandth broadcast. Mitchell had presented nearly thirty-three hundred of these programs, and the last twenty-five hundred had opened with "It's a beautiful day in Chicago..."

However, there were increasing uncertainties about the future of the program, which by now had been broadcast longer than any other daily network radio show in America. Three months before the four thousandth broadcast, the Federal Communications Commission had issued an order directing NBC to divest itself of one of its two radio networks, the Red or the Blue. For financial reasons, the *Farm and Home Hour* had earlier been assigned to the Blue Network. Rumors were that the Blue Network was the one to go.

Ironically, the program had never been more popular. Its listenership was growing and its audience was both discriminating and loyal. Volumes of letters showed that listeners kept close tabs on the program, a situation *Time* magazine noted in its August 4, 1941, story.

> This week with the shadow of dissolution hovering over it, the Blue Network celebrated the four thousandth performance of its farm show...The four thousand broadcasts of the *Farm and Home Hour* have held the national air for thirteen years. Six days a week, the program goes over one hundred stations, is heard by some six million listeners. The Hour finds a front seat for the U.S. farmer at all big agricultural events, keeps him posted about the weather and current markets, provides him with tips from the Department of

Agriculture and half a hundred other farm organizations. . .

Listeners are pretty crotchety about any fiddling with the *Farm and Home Hour.* When NBC, in response to a few quibbles, ordered Announcer Mitchell to abandon his sally about Chicago weather, the kickback was prompt and potent. Mitchell continues doggedly to begin the *Farm and Home Hour* with "It's a beautiful day in Chicago!"

As early as 1934, when the *Farm and Home Hour,* at a non-recoverable cost of millions a year to NBC and its affiliated radio stations, was helping Secretary of Agriculture Wallace and the federal government raise the nation's farmers out of the mire of the Great Depression, the Federal Radio Commission first posed the question of NBC's having a broadcasting monopoly. In 1936 Niles Trammell had urged NBC to permit him to buy the Blue Network, but David Sarnoff and the parent company, RCA, refused to consider the proposal.

By 1940 the Federal Communications Commission, successor to the Federal Radio Commission, had completed a long study of the monopoly issue and formally charged that NBC was in restraint of trade. Trammell was president of NBC, and Frank Mullen, his training with Sarnoff at RCA over, was executive vice president. In hopes of heading off an order to give up one of its networks, Trammell and Mullen immediately separated the managements of the Red and Blue, allowing them for the first time to begin developing complete individuality. But the government was not impressed and only months later, in the spring of 1941, directed NBC to sell one network.

Then came an important decision which had to be made public promptly. Which of the networks should NBC give up? Sarnoff, who was by now chairman of the NBC board of directors, huddled with Trammell and Mullen, adjourned and met again. They were free to rearrange the stations between the Red and the Blue in any way they wished. But Sarnoff and RCA were anxious to recover some of the millions previously invested to develop the networks. This meant that some good programs and good stations would have to go with the network to be sold to justify a multi-million dollar price tag.

The final decision was to sell the Blue and to include in it a number of radio stations in big cities where impressive advertising revenue could be offered the new owner. NBC would keep the Red Network and the regional radio stations such as WMAQ in Chicago and WHO in Des Moines, Iowa, but would put WENR in Chicago in the Blue Network. To make the Blue Network more attractive a number of major programs were consigned to it, including the *Farm and Home Hour* with its wide listenership.

Because Mitchell now had the *Town and Farm* program on WMAQ, Mullen could not be sure the popular announcer would elect to stay with the *Farm and Home Hour* when it became a feature of the new Blue Network, with its predominantly big city stations. To encourage Mitchell to go with the Blue, Mullen assigned Mitchell's *American Dairy Show*, an important revenue producer, to the Blue Network. Mitchell agreed to handle the two programs for the Blue Network but only on condition that he would also continue his six-mornings-a-week *Town and Farm* program over WMAQ on the Red Network. Mullen did not like the arrangement, but he recognized that he had to accept it. Not only would Mitchell's leaving the *Farm and Home Hour* impair the program's attractiveness to a possible Blue Network buyer, but Vice President Harry Kopp, in charge of NBC's Central division, had made it clear that Mitchell would continue with his *Town and Farm* program on WMAQ no matter what Mullen wanted to do.

The new plans were awkward for Mullen and his continued sponsorship of William Drips as NBC's director of agriculture. Drips would go to the Blue Network as part of the *Farm and Home* package, since all except those working directly with the program believed him to be indispensable. So when the transfer of the Blue Network to RCA was made, NBC lost its director of agriculture and the Blue Network acquired one.

Meanwhile, Sarnoff had transferred the Blue Network from NBC to RCA and then filed an appeal of the FCC's ruling with the United States Supreme Court. The move would buy more time to prepare the Blue Network for sale, and there was always the outside chance that the court would reverse the commission's order to dispose of the network.

This transfer was completed in January, 1942, a month after the United States entered World War II. The final Blue Network package included three company-owned stations, one each in New York, Chicago and San Francisco, and an impressive list of more than one hundred affiliated stations situated across the country from the Atlantic to the Pacific. Edgar Kobak was named president of RCA's Blue Network.

A few weeks after the network's transfer, the annual ratings for the top radio programs for the winter of 1941-42 were announced.

The *Farm and Home Hour* moved up to the top ten and was the Blue Network's highest-ranking program. The rural listenership could not improve much, it was already so high, but the Department of Agriculture portion of the program had been reporting the latest wartime programs for gardening and food preservation, and the urban audience was increasing.

President Kobak of the Blue was operating the network as though RCA would own it permanently. In September of 1942 he wrote the United States Department of Agriculture a revealing communication. He recognized that shifting the *Farm and Home Hour* to the new Blue Network had decreased rural listenership because the program no longer was broadcast on the large regional stations such as WHO in Des Moines.

Instead the *Farm and Home Hour* was heard in Iowa over smaller stations catering largely to urban communities and leaving the farm audience without an opportunity to hear "It's a beautiful day in Chicago. . ." Hostile letters were arriving with each mail, letters that could not be answered effectively because the change had been made to comply with government directives rather than with the interests of rural listeners.. The situation must either be improved or another way must be found to handle the program, Kobak said.

Another major factor was also working against an indefinite continuation of the *Farm and Home Hour* as a daily feature. When the show began in 1928, local radio stations were not staffed to provide their own homemaker and farm programs. But by 1942, things had changed. Many stations now had the staff to originate their own service programs which could be made more interesting by adding local features and news. Moreover, these local programs could have local sponsors and be providing operating revenue for the stations, while the *Farm and Home Hour* was a sustaining non-revenue-producing feature. From an economic point of view, these changes in the broadcasting business forecast an end in the not-too-distant future to the *Farm and Home Hour.*

Late in 1942 the Supreme Court ruled the FCC's order was valid. NBC-RCA must sell one of their radio networks. There was, however, no fixed date set by the court for compliance.

Sarnoff knew that he had something to sell that was the only product of its kind. No one in broadcasting's short history had ever had a network to sell. He also knew that there was definite corporate interest in moving into broadcasting. Radio was here to stay, and every person who took the trouble to be informed knew that television would emerge quickly when the war was over; it was already being billed in advance as the greatest communications explosion in history. Sarnoff priced the Blue Network accordingly, at eight million dollars, a figure so high in the early 1940s that there was no immediate rush of prospective buyers for the radio system.

When the financial report for 1942, the first full year of the Blue Network operation under RCA, was published early in 1943, it revealed that the network had earned a surprising one and one-half million dollars. Sarnoff and Kobak had pulled out all the stops to make sure the Blue had a good year, but it was a remarkable earning for a network that actually owned outright only three radio stations. A few weeks later came the announcement of the Top Ten most-listened-to radio programs.

The surprise in the Top Ten was the *Farm and Home Hour*. An informational and service program, it ranked number three. Only the *Grand Ole Opry* and *The Aldrich Family* had more listeners. The magnitude of the achievement was even more evident when the other programs in the Top Ten were listed—*Major Bowes' Amateur Hour, Jack Benny, Lum and Abner, Dr. IQ, Fibber McGee and Molly* and *Amos and Andy.*

With the financial report and the story of the Top Ten before them, forty-two organizations decided to take a closer look at the Blue Network. Many of them had a special interest in communications—Time-Life, McGraw Hill, Paramount Pictures, Marshall Field Enterprises, Columbia Broadcasting System, American Type Founders Corporation and others.

Now it was clear that the Blue Network was going to be sold sooner or later. It was also more and more evident that a new owner would not long pay the heavy costs of maintaining the *Farm and Home Hour* as a public service or that the affiliated radio stations would donate the broadcasting time. Everyone directly concerned with the program was prepared to accept that an epic of early network radio broadcasting would soon disappear forever. Everyone, that is, but Mitchell. Again, acting on another of his hunches, Mitchell had developed a plan for bringing at least a modified *Farm and Home Hour* back to NBC. He took his plan to Vice President Kopp in the spring of 1943.

The men agreed that a new owner of the Blue Network would be unable to carry the daily program as a sustaining feature for long. It would surely be terminated soon. When that happened,

265

Mitchell explained, it would be possible to convert the *Farm and Home Hour* to an NBC weekend feature, used probably at noon on Saturday. The new show would have to be broadcast on the NBC network's big regional stations that blanketed the rural areas. Kopp concurred, but told Mitchell that it seemed highly improbable that a *Farm and Home Hour* could ever be returned to the NBC network, much as he would like to see it done.

While that might appear to be true, Mitchell explained, actually there were only three moves that needed to be made. These moves would have to be undertaken with care but they could, in Mitchell's judgment, be made successfully. Immediately upon termination of the present daily program, the United States Department of Agriculture should ask the Blue Network to make the Department the legal owner of the name, the *National Farm and Home Hour*, with the understanding that the name could be used later on any network providing a service to agriculture.

Next, it would be necessary to get the Department of Agriculture to agree to participate in a sponsored *Farm and Home Hour*. Mitchell thought this too could be achieved though there was no precedent for it. Finally, it would be necessary to secure a sponsor who was willing to use a significant block of NBC stations.

Kopp immediately had several questions. Had Mitchell discussed his plan with Wallace Kadderly, director of radio services for the Department of Agriculture? Not specifically, Mitchell said, but he and Kadderly had talked about the future of farm broadcasting, and he thought Kadderly would be interested in having the program continue in some form. Did Mitchell have any organization in mind which might become a sponsor of a weekly *National Farm and Home Hour*? Yes, Mitchell acknowledged, he did have a good prospect in mind for at least a midwestern NBC network. It was the Allis Chalmers Manufacturing Company of West Allis, Wisconsin, where William A. Roberts had just become president. Roberts was determined to see his company join the exclusive billion dollar club of the farm machinery industry. Only two companies had made it so far: International Harvester and John Deere.

Mitchell also reported that the America Dairy Council, whose weekly program he and Clifton Utley presented on the Blue Network on Sunday, was unhappy and wanted to come back to NBC when the contract at Blue expired in the fall. Mitchell told Kopp that he, too, was anxious to return to NBC and concentrate all of his network broadcasting there as soon as possible.

More talks followed and within a month, Mitchell and Kopp had worked out a detailed understanding with a number of specific provisions. Three weeks after the Blue Network was sold, Mitchell would return to NBC's Central Division. Since William Drips was now at the Blue Network and NBC had no agricultural director, Kopp would name Mitchell, upon his return, NBC's agricultural director for the Central Division. Also, Kopp would see that no long term commitments were made for the noon to 1 p.m. hour on Saturday and be ready on short notice to have a weekly *Farm and Home Hour* broadcast over the NBC network at that time.

In the next twenty-six months every move projected in the Mitchell-Kopp talks during the spring of 1943 was carried out. Some of the moves took place earlier than expected. In the fall of 1943, when the American Dairy Council moved its Sunday network program to NBC, President Kobak attempted to keep Mitchell with the *Farm and Home Hour* at least temporarily by issuing him an ultimatum. If Mitchell took the Dairy Council program to NBC he would be fired. Mitchell and the American Dairy Council program went to NBC in September. The following week there was no "It's a beautiful day in Chicago. . ." opening on the *Farm and Home Hour*.

Being dismissed from the show was by then a matter of little significance for Mitchell. In October Edward Noble bought the Blue Network. (Noble had, in 1913, bought the Life Saver Candy Company for $1,900 and sold it in 1928 for $22 million.) Then under the agreement with Kopp, Mitchell would have returned to NBC in three weeks anyway. Noble chose Mark Woods, a capable NBC-trained administrator, to be the new president of the network, which would soon be renamed the American Broadcasting Company (ABC).

Without Mitchell, the *Farm and Home Hour* was immediately in trouble with its listeners. Six months later, in May, 1944, Woods announced the daily *National Farm and Home Hour* would end on June 19, and, after more than forty-seven hundred broadcasts, the final curtain came down. General Eisenhower's troops had just smashed the German defenses on the coast of France, the Second Front was going well for the Allies and the end of the long war was in sight.

At the appropriate time Wallace Kadderly of the Department of Agriculture wrote Mark Woods, asking that the ownership of the famous name be transferred to the Department of Agriculture for further possible use in a radio service to the nation's farmers. Woods, who had not been a party to the bitterness of the program's final months, sent a telegram immediately giving the necessary approval. Shortly after, Secretary of Agriculture Clinton P. Anderson approved his department's participation in a weekly *Farm and Home Hour* program with Allis Chalmers Company as the sponsor.

On the first Saturday in September, 1945, just days after Japan's surrender ended World War II, the new *Farm and Home Hour* was broadcast over one hundred and two stations of the NBC network. Everett Mitchell was back as the moderator, opening the program with "It's a beautiful day in Chicago. . ." The Homesteaders Orchestra, now with twenty-four pieces, played the music the program's audiences had enjoyed for years. Ruth Van Deman provided a feature for homemakers. Ken Gapen of the Department of Agriculture reported on the agricultural highlights of the coming week. There was an analysis of the markets for the past week and comments on what might be expected in the days to come.

There would be a similar program every Saturday for the next fifteen years.

The NBC-affiliated radio stations paid the *National Farm and Home Hour* a surprising tribute. Allis Chalmers included forty-four stations in its first year in the NBC network. Another fifty-eight network stations carried the program as a sustaining feature with special Department of Agriculture messages taking the place of the Allis Chalmers commercials. Each year Allis Chalmers added more stations to its network, and in 1953 it included the entire one hundred and ninety-nine stations owned by and affiliated with NBC.

Beauty queens were frequent guests on the *National Farm and Home Hour*. Everett Mitchell introduces the 1954 Yam Queen to his audience.

The late Miss Ruth Van Deman, former head of information for the Bureau of Human Nutrition and Home Economics, was a featured performer on the U.S. Department of Agriculture portions of the *National Farm and Home Hour* for a decade from the mid-1930s to the mid-1940s.

# Chapter 26
# Ambassadors from the Farms

By 1945, when the *National Farm and Home Hour* returned to the air in a weekly format, Everett Mitchell was forty-seven years old. Most of the other pioneers of radio broadcasting had by now disappeared, replaced by newcomers eager and able to cope with the accelerated pace of the rapidly-expanding industry. By ordinary standards Mitchell too should have been on his way out. But he not only kept up with the changes, he continued to bring broadcasting "firsts" to his audience. He was one of the first announcers to move into television broadcasting and was one of the first to take advantage of the opportunities for overseas travel to expand the horizons of his American listeners.

In 1945, broadcasting in the United States meant radio and nothing more. But by 1948 television had become a reality, and few people enjoyed its coming more than Mitchell. For twenty years he had been flatly predicting that "radio will have pictures in my lifetime." Although even good friends thought his prediction too far-fetched to be taken seriously, Mitchell was confident that after World War II engineers would find a way to make television workable.

As early as 1947 Mitchell began taking part in telecasting experiments at NBC. The Chicago television station, WNBQ-TV (Channel Five) began limited broadcasts in 1949. NBC network television between Chicago, New York and Washington began soon after.

On November 27, 1951, Mitchell scored another of his major "firsts" in Chicago broadcasting. He presented the first telecast to be fed to the NBC television network, an hour-long feature program from Chicago's International Livestock Exposition. For the first time, viewers across the nation were able to see the grand champion animals, and the farmers who had raised them.

By the mid-1950s, Mitchell was a television "regular" with his weekday morning *Town and Farm* program on Channel Five.

The end of World War II brought another major development, the rapid growth of overseas airplane travel. Mitchell was quick to make use of the opportunity to add a new dimension to his NBC broadcasts and also to help promote a cause in which he was vitally interested.

William A. Roberts, Allis Chalmers president, liked the idea of Mitchell's taking the *Farm and Home Hour* microphone overseas. The farm machinery company was interested in doing business in many foreign countries, but Roberts did not limit Mitchell's tours to only those nations. The choice of places to be visited would be left entirely up to Mitchell and the NBC staff, Roberts announced. He would be interested in having programs originate in Russia and other Communist countries, he said, even though Allis Chalmers had little hopes of doing business there.

So by the middle of the 1950s, memorable *Farm and Home Hour* broadcasts had originated in Europe, including Russia, the Near East, Asia, South America, New Zealand and Australia. The trips abroad, however, served more than one purpose.

Always interested in helping and encouraging young people, Mitchell had become an enthusiastic supporter of the American 4-H Club's new international youth exchange program and a key member of the foundations abroad.

The youth exchange program began shortly after the war ended, when personal travel was again possible. Its purpose was to bring about better understanding between nations by an exchange of farm young people. Outstanding older 4-H Club members, both boys and girls, would go to live and work with farm families overseas. At the same time, rural young people from the cooperating countries would come to the United States to visit and work with American farm families.

Known as the International Farm Youth Exchange (IFYE), the program, now in its thirty-fifth year, is conducted by the National 4-H Club Foundation and the Cooperative Agricultural Extension Service, with assistance from the Department of Agriculture and the State Department. Mitchell announced the formation of the IFYE program on the *Farm and Home Hour* early in 1948 and assisted the founders in many ways. The first small exchanges of young people took place in 1948 and 1949. By 1950 the operational procedures had been established and 4-H leaders were ready to expand the program to include more countries and more young people.

However, expansion of the program required more funding. Mitchell was asked to organize and serve as chairman of a new Builders Council, a fund-raising group. He was from the first an enthusiastic supporter. To raise the money, he brought together a group of thirty national leaders in banking, industry, retailing and entertainment, including such well-known figures as Fred Waring, director of the famous Pennsylvanians music group; Jesse Stapp, president of the Bank of America; philanthropist Nelson Rockefeller and bandleader Paul Whiteman. Mitchell said as part of his personal contribution he would visit half or more of the young Americans during their stay abroad in 1951 and bring back a report to the Council.

The funding goal was quickly met and sixty 4-H youths were able to go to Europe, the Near East, Brazil and New Zealand. Mitchell spent most of July and August visiting the students in Europe and the Near East.

The visits to the exchange students gave Mitchell an even better view of European farming methods to bring to his listeners back home. The contrasts were dramatic. Nowhere did he find so much diversification or farming done on such a large scale as is typical in the United States.

Mitchell found that agriculture in the British Isles had the most in common with that of the United States. There was wide use of tractors and other modern farm machines. The Angus, Hereford and Shorthorn beef animals were equal to the best of the animals of the same breed raised in America.

In France, the Low Countries and Germany, the farms, although highly productive, were small. Humans and animals provided most of the energy. Farmers did not live on the farms, as in the United States, but in nearby villages. In Germany Mitchell found the most intensive use of dairy animals. Often dairy cows would be milked in the morning, used during the day to pull plows or other farm implements and then returned to the barn for milking at the end of the day.

Mitchell was greatly impressed with farming in Sweden and Scandinavia generally. Farms were tended like gardens. There were no weeds. Everything that was produced was put to some use. In the forests and wood lots, even the twigs and small branches which fell from the trees were gathered and tied into bundles for use as fuel.

In Israel, the new Jewish state which was but three years old in 1951, Mitchell reported that an agricultural revolution was in progress. New settlers were arriving each week and were immediately given work on new farms. The newcomers, including the young Americans coming under the youth exchange, often began by building farm roads and ditches for use in irrigation systems. The land that for centuries had been used for grazing sheep, if used at all, was being made to yield bumper harvests of garden and grain crops. Olive and nut trees were being planted on a large scale in the new nation.

In Finland, where Mitchell observed farming near the Arctic Circle, there was an unscheduled incident. At a dinner for Mitchell in Helsinki, given by Finland's Minister of Agriculture, the conversation turned to Finland's relations with Russia. Mitchell's Finnish hosts explained that it was a fifteen-minute drive to the"seventh bridge" and the river which was the border between Russia and Finland. Here the Soviets maintained a twenty-four hour guard to keep anyone from escaping into Finland and its freedom.

Michell expressed astonishment that such measures were taken to keep Russians from leaving their country. Could he see the Russian guards at the border? Probably not, the minister of agriculture said, because of the danger in getting that close to the border, which could only be approached safely in the darkness. But the minister would see if Mitchell could be escorted to the border during the night, which in the latitude of Helsinki in August ends about 3 a.m.

Mitchell had returned to his hotel and was in bed when his phone rang. A man with a heavy accent said in English, "Mr. Mitchell, I am a Finnish patriot, which means that I survived service in the Finnish underground during the war. I understand that you would like to see the Russian guard at the border. If you will be in the hotel lobby at 2 a.m., about two hours from now, we will take you to the border."

Mitchell was in the lobby about five minutes before two. Three men were waiting for him. The patriot stepped forward and introduced himself and his companions. One was the head of the Department of Finnish Security and the other a Finnish soldier. The patriot explained.

"At the hotel we are but a short distance from the highway that leads to the Russian border. There are seven bridges on this highway. The first six are in Finland but the seventh is in Russia.

"The soldier will drive us without lights over the sixth bridge and to a point about half a mile from the border. We will walk until we are about three hundred yards from the river where we will see the Russian border boats pass every twelve to fifteen minutes. The last three hundred yards we will crawl through the underbrush on hands and knees." The patriot then handed Mitchell a pair of coveralls large enough to be used over his street clothing and a pair of heavy gloves to protect his hands on the trip through the underbrush.

The driver did not turn on the car lights even in Helsinki. After they crossed over the sixth bridge, the driver pulled the car off the highway. Mitchell and his two companions got out and walked until the patriot said, "We must crawl from here." They crawled to about one hundred feet of the river, where they could see the seventh bridge a hundred yards to the right. The patriot directed his companions to lie down flat on the ground, whispering, "The border guards will shoot anything they see moving where we are now."

In a few minutes the border patrol boat appeared out of the darkness. As it came past directly in front of him in the Finnish summer night, a kind of twilight, Mitchell could plainly see a Russian soldier at the prow of the boat, rifle in hand, standing rigidly at attention, looking and listening as the boat slipped silently past. Mitchell and his companions waited prone on the ground until the next patrol boat came about twelve minutes later. Again there was the soldier at the prow, rifle in hand.

As this boat slipped under the seventh bridge and out of sight, the Finnish patriot stood up and spoke words to Mitchell which revealed, as had so many other coversations on the trip in Europe, how greatly many countries were looking to the United States for support. With tears streaming down his cheeks the patriot said, "In the name of Jesus Christ when you go home ask your people to help us. We are a nation with a lost cause. We have no future at all unless the people of America help us. We are depending on your people. Please ask them to remember us in your prayers."

Then the patriot, not sure they could be away before the next patrol, got down on his hands and knees and the three men crawled back to the freedom of Finland.[1]

Mitchell also retains vivid memories of his visit to Israel. In his *Farm and Home Hour* report, he described Israel as a nation in which everyone worked almost from the hour he or she arrived.

New groups of Jews were arriving almost daily. A surprising number were from the United States, including a young teacher from Milwaukee, Golda Meir, who would become one of the nation's greatest prime ministers.

There were two American exchange students working on Israeli kibbutzim (community farms) near Jerusalem. Both were working alongside new settlers ten to twelve hours a day. Mitchell visited them and was compelled to extend his visit to the kibbutz because of the chaotic transportation. The delay led to one of the greatest acts of brotherhood he ever encountered anywhere.

Leaders at the kibbutz insisted that Mitchell remain as their guest until he could secure a plane reservation to continue his trip. Finally, the reservation was secured and on his last day at the kibbutz a special dinner was served in Mitchell's honor.

Since he had arrived in Israel, nothing but fish had been served, fish being the only unrationed meat available. Jewish practice did not permit the eating of pork. Beef was not yet produced in the new country and the only beef available was imported from the United States. Under the strict food rationing only a few ounces per person per month were allowed and the meat had to be paid for in American money. At the dinner, attended by all members of the kibbutz, everyone ate fish again, everyone except Mitchell. He was served American beef. The members of the kibbutz had taken up a collection—scarce beef coupons and equally scarce American money—in order that their guest might have meat at his last dinner.

The European trip of 1951 held one great surprise for Mitchell. While en route, he received an invitation to meet with Pope Pius XII to discuss the latest developments in American agriculture. Mitchell had not sought a meeting with the Pope.

The invitation was suggested by the Pope's staff. Upon learning that the "Voice of American Agriculture" was to be in Rome the Pope's agricultural advisor suggested to the Pontiff that he might wish to invite Mitchell for a conference. The meeting was scheduled at the Pope's farm and summer home, Castel Gandolfo, just outside of Rome.

Pope Pius XII, a member of a wealthy Roman family, had been elected in 1939 after the shortest formal papal conclave of record. He had served his church in many capacities and had been Papal Secretary of State from 1929 until 1939. In 1936 he had made an extended trip to the United States and had spent several days in

Chicago, and Mitchell's name was familiar to him.

During World War II Pope Pius was criticized for not speaking out more boldly against the atrocities being perpetrated by the Germans. However, when the facts were better known after the war, the Pontiff was seen in a different light.

By the time Mitchell met with him in 1951, Pope Pius was acknowledged to have worked hard, fearlessly and effectively to soften the impact of the war for many persons in many lands. He was the central figure in getting the warring powers to recognize Rome as an open city, sparing it the horrors of all-out war. As the Germans were retreating there was some bombing in the city. When the bombs fell, Pope Pius was among the first to reach the devastated area and personally administer to the needs of those injured and those made homeless.

He turned over his rural estate, Castel Gandolfo, for the duration of the war to be used as a home for war victims of many countries—Jews as well as Gentiles. Fifteen thousand persons were given sanctuary there.

Mitchell's conference with the Pope took place the morning of August 9. Before the meeting, Mitchell was given a quick tour of the Castel Gandolfo estate.

After the tour, Mitchell was shown into the Pope's complex of offices. The meeting was informal, but Mitchell found the Pontiff to be an impressive figure. He was tall and slim, graceful in his movements with penetrating dark eyes.

Like a good host, the Pope first inquired about the International Farm Youth Exchange. Knowing that Mitchell was a Lutheran, he inquired if the exchange program was open to Catholic youth. He seemed pleased when Mitchell assured him that the American youths were chosen entirely on the basis of achievement and leadership qualities without regard to race or religion.

"Pius was reported to be a very rich man, and some people felt that he was uppish, but I didn't find that to be the case at all. He was very gracious to me. At the close he even thanked me for coming to see him. Although he was an older man, there was an eager youthfulness and alertness about him that was even reflected in his voice.

"Pope Pius was well informed on farming matters and agricultural production. He asked me many questions. As soon as he was satisfied with my answer, he would ask another. There were a few questions that I could not answer and I said so. But thanks to the opportunities I had had through the *National Farm and Home Hour*, I was able to refer him to the state experiment station, business or even individual farmer who might have the answer he was searching for," Mitchell said.

"Our entire conference was taken down in shorthand," Mitchell added. "I had thought that if the discussion with the Pope lasted twenty minutes to half an hour it would be worthwhile, but I was with him for nearly an hour and a half. For a man with his responsibilities, that was a considerable amount of time."

Before leaving Italy, Mitchell visited an Italian farm and met with an exchange student who had overcome an unusual obstacle. On the farm where William Pressly of Stony Point, North Carolina, was working there were fourteen union farm laborers, men who were both fearful and jealous of the hard working young American. They were baling hay, and the Italians again and again increased their pace, hoping to embarrass Pressly, but he kept up with them. Then the baler broke down and the Italians, who belonged to the farm laborers' union and thus were not allowed to fix machines, were helpless, but the IFYE student went to work and repaired the machine. After that everything went smoothly.

Everett Mitchell's tour of Europe and the Middle East was but the first of a series of trips he would make around the world to visit American farm youths taking part in the exchange program. But those trips would have to wait until after his special assignment for the United States Army in South Korea, Japan and the Pacific Islands.

### FOOTNOTE

(1) The names of Mitchell's hosts in Finland have been withheld for fear that members of their families might even after thirty years be placed in jeopardy. Within a year from the time of his visit in Finland the patriot lost his life in what was officially described as "an incident on the Finnish-Russian border."

The late Nelson Rockefeller, financier, oil magnate, philanthropist and politician, was one of the original members of the International Farm Youth Exchange committee. He attended a
meeting at the NBC studios in Chicago where Everett Mitchell
presided over an IFYE board meeting. Rockefeller listened for
a short time and them wrote out a check for a quarter of a million dollars to begin the IFYE finance drive.

Everett Mitchell helped sell bonds during World War I while he was a vocalist singing part time with Evangelist Billy Sunday. During World War II, he took the *National Farm and Home Hour* to various defense industries for formal presentation of awards such as the Army-Navy E Award. This scene was taken at the Mall Tool Company in Chicago.

# Chapter 27
# Korean War Correspondent

On November 2, 1951, Everett Mitchell began the most difficult of his assignments overseas. His destination was Korea, and an unprecedented mission awaited him.

Mitchell had not asked to go to Korea, nor had NBC sought the opportunity for him. The request had come directly from the U.S. Army. And, over the strong objections of the NBC news department, Mitchell was traveling, at the flat insistence of the Army, as an NBC war correspondent.

The Army's assignment, however, had much more to do with peace than with war. Although the status as a war correspondent would open many doors for him, Mitchell was not in Korea to report on the combat. The Army wanted his help in another kind of battle, against the famine which was rampant in South Korea. Top officials had taken note of Mitchell's long and close association with the work of rural young people, especially the 4-H Clubs and the Future Farmers of America, and they wanted him to meet with Korean and also Japanese youth leaders to see if ways could be found for the young people in these countries to help increase food production, just as young people were doing in the United States.

Mitchell had traveled overseas before and had faced some tense moments, but this trip would be different. It would be his first journey into an active war zone where the battle lines shifted daily, sometimes hourly, and where the list of dead and wounded, including Americans, had reached numbing proportions.

There was another, more pleasant, aspect to the mission. U.S. Senator Elbert Thomas of Utah, trustee in charge of the United Nations Pacific Trust, was supervising a group of islands in the South Pacific which had been turned over to the United States at the end of World War II. These included the Marianas, the

Marshalls, the Carolines and Guam. It was Senator Thomas who had originally proposed the Korean mission and suggested Mitchell as the advisor. He had also asked that, on his way back to the United States, Mitchell stop off at his headquarters in Honolulu, Hawaii, to discuss establishing a 4-H type organization for young people in the South Pacific and to set up a return tour when Thomas and Mitchell might visit all the islands in the Pacific Trust.

This was the first time the United States government had ever asked him to undertake a direct service, and Mitchell agreed unhesitatingly. Also, the mission, with its excitement and its possibility for new achievement, would be a welcome interruption during a lonely period in his life. He had just lost his beloved wife, Mildred, and his grief was still overwhelming.

The extent of his loneliness was brought home to him when the Army directed him to write down instructions for returning his body to the United States in case there was an "accident" on the mission. Who should he list as the "next of kin?" His wife and his parents were gone, and he had no children. For the present, he was very much alone.

To get to the Korean war zone, Mitchell flew to Anchorage, Alaska, on an Army Transport Command DC-6. At Anchorage, he boarded another propeller-driven DC-6 for the two-day flight across the Pacific, landing at last in Tokyo on November 6. As he got off the Anchorage plane, he was met by Col. Charles A. Anderson, his Korean aide, and rushed to the plane used by the United States ambassador to Korea for immediate take-off for Pusan, South Korea.

The ambassador's plane proved to be the military version of the DC-3, known in World War II and now in Korea as the C-47. Mitchell noted that the modifications in the DC-3, in which he had traveled more than a million miles, were to the layman's eye so slight as to amount to little more than a name change. He felt comforted to learn that his Korean travel would be done in a close relative of his old friend the DC-3.

Anderson explained that they would fly to Pusan, almost two hundred miles directly west of Tokyo, where they would stay for the night. In the morning, they would leave for Seoul, capitol of South Korea, which would be their base for the rest of Mitchell's stay. They would use the plane as much as possible, but on occasion it would be necessary to leave it and travel by jeep in order to get to some of the agricultural areas.

Though this was not the growing season, officials wanted Mitchell to see the farms and meet the people who worked the land. A few would speak English, but most of the conferences would be handled through an Army interpreter.

The C-47 was soon in Pusan. Mitchell's first impression of Korea was that he was glad he had been warned to dress warmly. In contrast to the mild temperatures at the Tokyo airport, the wind at Pusan was cold and cutting. Mitchell was taken immediately to his quarters in a military barracks and a short time later had the opportunity to go to bed for the first time since leaving Chicago five days before.

On arriving at Seoul the next morning, Mitchell learned that it had been arranged for him to begin his mission with a trip north to a place just beginning to break into the news, Panmunjon. Truce talks had begun there during the summer. Keyes Beech, whose reporting career in the Orient spanned both the Korean and Vietnam conflicts, would write on the day the armistice was signed there: "Panmunjon is more a name than a place. It is merely a wide place in the road."

Mitchell went east from Panmunjon along the 38th parallel to a military base near the edge of the bloody Iron Triangle. Some of the most vicious fighting of the Korean conflict had taken place recently along the southern base of this mountainous retreat of the Chinese and North Koreans.

Mitchell learned immediately that word of his coming had preceded him and that he was well-known to many of the soldiers he met near the Korean battlefields.

"In war areas word spreads mysteriously by the grapevine," Mitchell observed later. "I was amazed at how many of the troops in the Panmunjon area knew I was coming. Almost from the moment we arrived, soldiers would call out, 'It's a beautiful day in Chicago' and wave to me."

Mitchell talked to officers and soldiers who were just back from the fighting in the Triangle. He went to the mess hall and visited the wounded at the base hospital near the fighting, exchanging views with the men who were bearing the brunt of the war.

The visits went on until evening. Col. Anderson was pressing Mitchell to get to the plane for the return flight to Seoul when word came from a young soldier who had just returned from the Triangle critically wounded. He had heard that Mitchell was in camp and asked to talk to him.

The medical officer explained that the young soldier was from Iowa, that he had sustained serious wounds in both the hip and the back and that just as quickly as possible he would be flown to an American military hospital in Tokyo.

Mitchell still speaks of the experience with emotion.

"When I got to his bedside, he looked up at me and smiled and said, 'Thank you for coming. I heard that "Beautiful day in Chicago" was here and I did want so much to talk with you. I wanted you to know that I am an Iowa farm boy and that I used to hear you at home. I certainly wish I was back in Iowa now where I could smell a fresh-turned furrow and look again at the beautiful skies.'

"Then his eyes turned away for a moment and he seemed to be assessing his own critical condition. He looked back to me and said, 'I wouldn't have to be here. None of us would have to be here if it weren't for the jealousy and malice in the world. This is the root of all evil. All this comes about because of man's disregard for the rights of fellow men.'

"Again his thoughts seemed to turn back to his plight. There was a pause. When he continued he made a petition, the first thing he had asked for himself. 'Speak to me of this Christ of ours,' he asked me.

"I said to him, 'How did you know that I am a Christian?'

" 'By some of the things you have said the tone of your voice,' the farm boy said. 'There is one thing I would like to have you do for me,' he continued, indicating a full awareness of the seriousness of his condition. 'When you go back home please tell my mother that I have kept the faith.'

"As we talked," said Mitchell, "he revealed his deep faith in Jesus Christ and the hope that his parents and friends were praying for him. Then I prayed with him and for him before the medical aide signaled that they were ready to prepare him for the flight to a Tokyo hospital."

The young soldier died shortly after his arrival at the Tokyo hospital. When he returned to America, Mitchell went to Iowa to report to the young man's parents of his visit with their son.

The next day, Col. Anderson took Mitchell to the United Nations military base at Inchon, the port city of Seoul. Mitchell's day at Inchon was perhaps the most important and productive of the entire mission. All morning was devoted to conferences with farm and rural youth leaders. Mitchell had begun the youth leader conferences at Panmunjon the day before, but the Korean participants there were so close to the war zone and the military situation was so fluid that it was difficult for the Koreans to project definite plans for the next farming season.

At Inchon, with its back to the Yellow Sea, which was firmly controlled by the U.S. Navy, there was an atmosphere of confidence that the Communists would not be back, and farmers could make plans for the next year feeling relatively sure they could be carried through.

Mitchell conferred with the farm and youth leaders during the morning, but it was not until lunch time that he was able to fully comprehend the urgency of the need for more food. The conferences had extended through much of the noon hour, and by the time Col. Anderson got Mitchell to the mess hall it was near the end of the lunch period. Mitchell, like the soldiers, ate and then carried his plate out to the disposal cans, not knowing that a wrenching experience awaited him.

"The garbage cans were surrounded by Korean children waiting to pick up the leftovers the GIs dumped into them. The boys and girls, standing close to the cans sometimes two or three deep, would watch intently as the GIs scraped their plates to see what food was going into the containers. A little arm would dart into the can and come up with a handful of food, and that child would quickly fade back to make room for another seeking to get to the garbage can," Mitchell remembers.

He was struck by the gaunt look of many of the children. It was evident, too, that this practice was a way of life for these children. The raiding of the garbage cans was orderly, and it was obvious the children had developed a system for "harvesting" the food discarded by the soldiers. The GIs also made it clear that the practice was regular and expected.

In his conferences that day, Mitchell made his first proposal that youngsters be given the opportunity to begin producing eggs and chickens to help solve the critical protein shortage problem. Drawing on his first-hand experience with 4-H poultry projects in the American Midwest, Mitchell pointed out that it takes only three or four months to turn an egg into a chicken big enough to eat, and only five or six months to turn it into a laying hen which can then produce more eggs. The Korean leaders were interested, but the idea of putting farm children in charge of small flocks seemed to them far-fetched. Anyway, they concluded, it could not be done because the tide of war had swept away all breeding stock and there was no chance of getting any eggs.

285

But they underestimated the man who conducted the *National Farm and Home Hour*. On the spot it occurred to Mitchell that if he appealed to his farm listeners in the great poultry and egg-producing Midwest, he could quickly get enough fertilized eggs to start poultry projects throughout South Korea.

But before saying anything to the Koreans, he interrupted the conference to talk with Col. Anderson. He needed to know if it would be possible for the Army Transport Command to airlift the eggs from the United States to Korea and for the Army to deliver them to the South Korean farmers. In minutes Anderson reported that it could be done.

Mitchell went back to his conference. Would the leaders be interested if they could get the fertilized eggs? he asked. The Koreans said that they would. Mitchell then promised them that the first shipment of eggs would be in Inchon as early as March 1. There would be no cost to the people of South Korea. The eggs would come from the people of the American heartland as a gift.

Mitchell soon expanded on his airlift project. In subsequent conferences he promised to deliver hogs, dairy and even beef cattle. And everything he promised was delivered, sometimes ahead of time. The first eggs arrived in mid-February. Planeloads of hogs were sent. A farmer in Wisconsin donated two young Holstein bulls. All together, half a million fertilized eggs were airlifted to Korea between February and June of 1952.

Mitchell's *Farm and Home Hour* audience was generous, as he had predicted, but he did not confine his efforts to broadcasting alone. His friends Dr. James Holbert, chief executive of Funk Hybrid Seed Corn organization, and Charles Carr, sales manager of Allis Chalmers, opened the way for Mitchell's personal appearances at farm meetings in several states. These meetings also brought more help for the hungry South Koreans. From one trip to Iowa, alone, Mitchell was able to send eighty thousand eggs.[1]

Mitchell's entire stay in South Korea was a period of intense work, made possible only by the meticulous planning and the transportation provided by the United States Army. His day began at times before daybreak and lasted far into the dark hours, sometimes until after midnight.

"Everything we did had its own priority, and sleep was close to the bottom of the list," he recalls.

The schedule was even more crowded than it might have been. At Inchon, Mitchell had an idea that brought still another dimension to his mission. He had made a few taped interviews in

Panmunjon with soldiers from the United States for use on his NBC programs. At Inchon it suddenly occurred to him that he could record Christmas greetings from soldiers in Korea and send them to wives, mothers and family members. Some of them could be used in his Christmas season broadcasts, but all of them would be transferred to records that would play on ordinary phonographs and then sent to the soldiers' families as a Christmas gift.

When Mitchell announced the plan, many of the GIs were enthusiastic. For some, the thought of being able to speak directly to their loved ones was a highly emotional experience. Although it meant tightening his already difficult schedule, Mitchell made the special Christmas recordings at each of his stops at Korean military bases for the rest of the trip.

Near Pyongyang, Mitchell had another disturbing confrontation with the plight of Korean children. He was taken by jeep to see a special camp for orphan boys being established near the military base. The camp was set up for five to thirteen-year-olds whose families and homes had been destroyed by the war machines that swept through the area, not once but several times. (The region was one of the principal north-south corridors of troop movements.) The orphans would be fed, clothed and given medical attention by the United States military forces until some member of their families could be found or they could be placed in orphanages.

Mitchell was shown a group of about thirty boys who were just arriving in the camp. Security police had been combing the countryside for these children, the remnant that had managed to survive in the open without food, shelter or care. Many were too frightened or feeble to speak. They were a pitiful sight, most of them just skin stretched over bones, some with distended abdomens and festering sores.

Mitchell talked to a few who were able to answer questions. Most did not know where their parents were or whether they were still living. One or two had seen their parents die. Mitchell asked what they had been eating., He could only get four answers —grains of rice they could gather up on the ground, blades of grass still green in the fall, angleworms and dirt.

The scene affected Mitchell deeply. "It left me with an even stronger resolution to do everything I could to help these youngsters in Korea, or anywhere else in the world where children are starving," he says.

When Mitchell returned to Seoul that evening, he discovered

that Gen. Matthew B. Ridgway was there. Both the Mitchell party and Ridgway's guests were eating in the officers' dining room that evening. Mitchell had been hoping to get an interview with Ridgway for the *National Farm and Home Hour*, asked Col. Anderson if he might be able to meet the commander of the United Nation's forces. Anderson said he would see what he could do, and later in the evening he was able to arrange for Mitchell to meet the General.

"I made my request for the interview, and hè was most gracious," Mitchell recalls. "He explained that at the moment he could not leave his guests. Then he asked if I would be coming back through Tokyo. He said he would be going back immediately to his headquarters there, and if I would come to his office in Tokyo he would be happy to give me an interview.

"While he was talking he reached into his pocket, took out a little card and wrote a few words on the back. As he handed it to me he said, 'When you get to the Allied headquarters in Tokyo, present this card to an aide.'"

When Mitchell arrived in Tokyo, he did go to the office of the United Nations Command to see if he could interview Ridgway. He was not only successful, the incident had a humorous side.

"When I went to Ridgway's headquarters and got into the appointment room, who should I see sitting on the bench with the other war correspondents but Edward R. Murrow. He looked at me and said, 'What the heck are you doing here, Mitch?' I told him I had come for an interview with Gen. Ridgway... He said, 'So did we, but it could be two or three days before we get in. Why don't you just keep on going?'

"I didn't say anything, but I did go on to see the aide and handed him the little card. In a few minutes I was called and went in and got the interview. I explained to Gen. Ridgway that I would not only use it on the *National Farm and Home Hour* but also at the annual dinner for delegates to the National 4-H Club Congress soon to meet in Chicago.

"As I left I had to go back through the appointment office. Ed Murrow was still sitting there. I didn't say anything to him, I just looked over and winked."

Mitchell's final field trip in Korea ended at Taegu in the south, not far from Pusan. The agenda at Taegu was the same, conferences with youth leaders, more pledges to send eggs, meetings with GIs who wanted to meet "It's a beautiful day in Chicago" and more recordings of Christmas messages for parents back home in America.

Col. Anderson and the ambassador's plane took Mitchell back to Tokyo, where Mitchell said a heartfelt thanks and farewell to Anderson and his men.

Arrangements had been made for Mitchell to spend the rest of the week in Japan, continuing his meetings with youth leaders who had already started organizing 4-H type clubs. He spent three days in the Tokyo area and in other cities meeting youth leaders who wanted to learn more about America's youth work with Boy and Girl Scouts, 4-H Clubs and other groups.

A day and à half later, Mitchell landed at Wake Island, where the Army had thoughtfully arranged à brief stop so he could get some much-needed rest and begin making the time zone adjustment before returning home.

Another long flight, and Mitchell was at the Honolulu airport. It was mid-morning, November 19, and the temperature was eighty degrees. It was a pleasant contrast to the Korean weather. Mitchell went directly to see Senator Thomas to discuss the planning of another mission when he could tour the South Pacific islands for which Thomas was the chief administrator.

Senator Thomas listened with interest to Mitchell's report of his mission. Then the two men began to plan an extended trip to many of the islands in the South Pacific. Mitchell learned that Thomas had visited the South Pacific long before he assumed his role as Pacific Trust administrator as an official of his church, The Church of the Latter Day Saints.[2]

Mitchell spent the rest of that day and all of the next with Senator Thomas. The following day, November 21, he returned to the United States. Two days after Thanksgiving, he was once again at the microphone of the *National Farm and Home Hour*, reporting on his Korean mission.

There were many satisfying postscripts to Mitchell's Korean mission, but none so rewarding as an experience he had five years later in Pittsburgh. On a tight schedule, he had come to Pittsburgh after an extended trip and had stepped out of his hotel to get a taxi to take him to the airport.

"The biggest black man I had seen in a long time brought his taxi to the curb," Mitchell recalls.

By this time in his life, Mitchell was once again a happy family man, with a wife and a small son. He explained to the driver that he would like to catch a plane that would get him to Chicago on time to have dinner with his family, which he very much wanted to do since he had been away from home for a week.

The driver was non-committal, but Mitchell noticed he kept looking at him in the rear-view mirror. Finally, he turned his head and said, "Korea? Korea?"

Mitchell studied him for a moment, then answered, "Yes."

"Aren't you 'Beautiful day in Chicago?' "

Again Mitchell answered, "Yes."

"Well, man," the big taxi driver said, "I'll tell you I will never forget the kindness you showed me when you made the interview in Inchon for my mother.

"You wouldn't remember, but we got to the place where I was talking to her about being home at Christmas and it brought back such vivid memories that I began to break up.

"I'll never forget what happened then. You put your arm around me to comfort me, and that was the first time a white man had ever done that, or had ever shown me any kindness or any love. I braced up then and got through the interview. I do want to tell you how much my mother enjoyed it. She must have played it over a hundred times. Believe me, you will make this plane."

Mitchell got to the airport with a chance to still get his plane. When he reached into his pocket to pay the fare, the driver interrupted. "No. The ride is just a some appreciation of what you did for me and my mother."

Mitchell did get back to Beautiful Day Farm in time for dinner with his family.

### FOOTNOTES

(1) Mitchell's Food for South Korea program nearly swamped the Army Transport Command. All the air space they could make available was utilized in the program's first six months. A version of the program continues today; in 1980, for example, Texas ranchers were still shipping breeding cattle to Korea. "Today protein in the diet of the South Koreans is among the highest in the Orient," Mitchell says. "I like to think some of this is because of our mission during the war."

(2) The Mormon Church (The Church of the Latter Day Saints) has a long record of service to the people of the South Pacific. It includes establishment of a fully-accredited four-year college in Hawaii where children of families on many South Pacific islands may receive a college education and return to their homes as skilled craftsmen, teachers, doctors, lawyer or ministers.

Korean War correspondent Everett Mitchell was given Army uniforms to wear for the brief period when he was at or near the front lines of fighting Korea in November 1951. It was the second of several overseas visits he would make. The trip was undertaken as a means of exploring ways to help the Koreans produce more food.

Gen. and Mrs. Matthew B. Ridgway are shown as they toured Japanese farming communities. The general is autographing programs for children of the school they visited. It was while on this portion of his tour that Everett Mitchell met the general and his wife. Later, this brief encounter would result in the farm program host obtaining an exclusive Christmas interview while other reporters waited several days.

# Chapter 28
# Beautiful Day Around The World

With his International Farm Youth Exchange tour to Europe and the Near East in the summer of 1951 and his special government assignment to Korea in November of the same year, Mitchell was becoming a seasoned traveler abroad as well as in the United States.

His travel accomplished several purposes during this time in his life. His interest in agriculture was world-wide, and he believed the more he could learn the more help he could give to his *National Farm and Home Hour* audience and the people he visited abroad. Also, he continued to have a vital interest in the International Farm Youth Exchange, and he took it upon himself to keep in close touch with these young people. He interviewed them before they left the United States, visited many of them during their stay abroad and then interviewed them again when they returned home. Finally, his travel helped ease the loneliness he still felt since the death of his wife, Mildred, in February 1950.

So in March of 1952, Mitchell agreed to make a tour of Latin America. He would visit with agricultural leaders and with the Farm Exchange students in the eleven countries that had adopted the program.

Although his Latin American visit was eye-opening in many ways, it was the least satisfactory of all his agricultural tours. This was due mainly to the attitude which Mitchell encountered in most of the countries he visited. Compared with the openness of the European farmers, who were eager to learn more about agriculture, Mitchell found the attitude of the Latin Americans suspicious almost to the point of hostility.

"I never once felt that I wasn't under surveillance while I was in Latin America," Mitchell says. "I did not feel free and accepted as I did in Europe. I always had the feeling that in the backs of their minds the Latin Americans were wondering what I was there for. What did I think I was going to get for coming and making a little contribution?"

His suspicion that he was being watched was confirmed during his stay in Buenos Aires, capital of Argentina. One day he inadvertently left a camera on the seat of a taxicab while on his way to a conference. He did not expect to see the camera again, but to his surprise found it was waiting for him when he returned to his hotel. When he asked the hotel clerk how the camera had been identified and returned to him, he was told, "the police."

Mitchell was also struck by the poverty he saw in Latin America and by the discrepancy between the social classes. "I found the people to be either very rich or very poor—there were few we could call middle class. The peasants who had nothing would wait until the farmers were just ready to harvest, then they would move in and steal the crops. They were so poor that was the only way they could survive."

Part of Mitchell's assignment was to try to interest other countries in South and Central America in the International Farm Youth Exchange program. Argentina was not a participant, so Mitchell had asked to meet with Eva Peron, wife of dictator Juan Peron, to discuss the program. She agreed to the conference, but by the time Mitchell arrived in Argentina she was too ill to see him personally and had to talk to him on the telephone.

"She told me she would give a permit for my *Farm and Home Hour* sponsor, Allis Chalmers, to bring fifty tractors a month to Argentina if they would give her five of them. Then they could sell the other forty-five. If she got the tractors, she would support the Farm Youth Exchange program. It was an outright bribe she was asking for. Of course, I would not agree. I told her we did not do business that way in our country. She said she would not support my program, and of course Argentina did not join it. Her word was law. She died just a few weeks after our Latin America tour ended."

This kind of graft, Mitchell noted, was not at all unusual in Latin America. The prevalence of graft in high official circles was in large part responsible for the attitude people had toward him, Mitchell believes. They thought he, too, wanted something "under the table" for his efforts.

The most satisfactory stop on Mitchell's Latin American tour was Mexico. Here he was genuinely welcomed by most of the people, as well as by the officials of the government and the agricultural organizations, although at times suspicion as to his real motives was still noticeable.

As Mitchell toured Mexican farms, he saw much farm machinery sitting idle because it needed repair. Obviously, no one on the farms knew how to fix it. When Mitchell had an opportunity to talk to Mexican President Miguel Aleman Valdes, he told Valdes of the problem. Then he suggested that the Mexican rural youth organization, the equivalent of the 4-H Clubs in the United States, would be an appropriate agency to set up a vocational school to which young people could go to learn how to repair machinery right on the farm. President Valdes was so pleased with the idea that he immediately said he would donate twenty-five acres of land from his own estate for the school. He did as he promised and the school was founded on the site, about twenty miles outside of Mexico City. It is still in operation today.

By the end of 1952, Mitchell's way of life had changed. He was no longer alone. In July of that year he had married Clara Christiansen, a Park Ridge resident who was a member of the Lutheran church he and Mildred had joined. So, when Mitchell made plans for his return to Hawaii for the long-delayed conference with Senator Elbert Thomas, the man in charge of the islands in the Pacific Trust, Clara was included. The trip would be a round-the-world tour, including stops at the Pacific islands, New Zealand and Australia, the Malay Peninsula, India and Pakistan, and end in London, England.

The Mitchells left Chicago on March 15, 1953, Everett's fifty-fifth birthday. Accompanying them for part of the tour was an old friend and member of the agency that handled the Allis-Chalmers account, Vern Lausten. An excellent photographer, Lausten kept a photographic record of the trip and also made written reports of its highlights.

When he arrived in Honolulu the next day, Mitchell immediately went to Senator Thomas' office. There he was shocked to learn that the Senator from Utah had died of a heart attack just the night before the Mitchell party arrived.

"We will never know what changes might have occurred in our lives if he had lived and we had undertaken the 4-H program which he wanted to established in the islands of the Pacific Trust," Mitchell says.

In spite of a great sense of loss at not being able to carry out his mission in the Pacific Trust, Mitchell knew he must continue the tour. So after several days in the Hawaiian Islands and a brief stop in the Fiji Islands, the Mitchell party went on to New Zealand where a busy six-day schedule awaited them. The Mitchells visited both the North and South Islands, where Everett interviewed Farm Youth Exchange students and their host families, visited with agricultural leaders and made some short-wave radio broadcasts to the *Farm and Home Hour* listeners.

A highlight of the New Zealand tour was a chance to see the Grasslands Project. New Zealand, along with Australia, is a major sheep-raising country and also raises large herds of dairy cattle. Grasslands for pasture are the major crop. Mitchell was able to see many of the various kinds of grasses raised in New Zealand and the different ways of using them.

Mitchell was impressed with the efficiency of New Zealand's farming operations, which he thought in many ways comparable to those in the United States. The farmers took full advantage of their eleven-month crop year and of all their soil resources, even those on a forty-five degree slope, he noted. Mountainsides were planted with grasses and also fertilized by light planes.

"It's some of the finest grassland I've ever visited, even though the cows have legs longer on one side than on the other from standing on those steep slopes," Mitchell quipped.

His reception in New Zealand, in sharp contrast to that in Latin America, was open and welcoming. New Zealanders had not forgotten that it was American armed forces, under Gen. Douglas MacArthur, that had turned the tide of the war in the South Pacific in 1942, at the Battle of the Coral Sea. It was American troops, too, that had held on in New Guinea and, with great loss of life, begun pushing the Japanese back, thus almost certainly preventing the invasion of Australia and New Zealand.

On March 26, Mitchell's party boarded a Pan American Clipper for the fifteen hundred-mile flight from Wellington, New Zealand, to Sydney, Australia. The propeller-driven Clipper was the plane that had opened the way for international air travel. Built by Boeing in the United States before civilian airports existed in many other countries, the Clippers were equipped with pontoons so they could take off and land on water as well as land. Regular trans-Pacific service to Manila started in May of 1939 and was soon extended to Japan and China. (The China Clipper was the best-known of these planes.)

But by 1953 the Clippers were ancient reminders of earlier days of glory. Without pressurized cabins, they could not fly above storms as the newer passenger planes could do. During the flight to Australia, the Mitchells' flight was overtaken by a severe thunderstorm, and the pilot had no choice but to ride it out. Turbulence was so great many of the passengers became ill. Some were injured when winds buffeted the plane about. Although he had charted many miles in the air, Mitchell felt he was in more danger during this flight than in any he had flown before.

But the plane arrived safely in Sydney, to the great relief of both the passengers and the friends and family members who were waiting for them. Radio reports had said the Clipper was lost in the storm, the Mitchells learned. Typical of remarks at the airport were "We were praying for you" and "We were afraid you were not going to make it through the storm."

Again in Australia, Mitchell was impressed with the efficient farming methods and with the friendliness and openness of the people. The Mitchells got a whirlwind tour of the land "Down Under": wheat research at Brisbane, Wuhin, Innisfail and Cairns; sheep at Mogumber; dairying at Mandurah; big timber south of Perth; cattle at Oodnadotta; big game fish at Naarooma; irrigation for fruit orchards at Mildura; wine-making at Adelaide; orchards, dairying and mining in the Melbourne area; iron, steel and shipping at Wynhalla. They even visited the aborigines at Hermansburg.

Mitchell noted that Australian farmers had to be particularly conservative with their use of water and that they had learned to irrigate crops using a great variety of methods. Wheat was the principal crop; he did not see corn or soybeans.

While in Sydney, Mitchell was one of three judges in the Junior Farmer All-Australian Leadership Competition. This event was similar to the National 4-H Club Congress held each fall in Chicago. He also attended the Royal Easter Fair at Sydney.

"I have seen many livestock shows all over the world, but none was as beautiful or as well laid out as the one in Sydney," Mitchell recalls. "There were 2,800 animals in the show ring at one time. And I have never seen anything like the artistic and beautiful way they arranged their vegetable displays."

The Mitchells found many similarities between Australia and American customs, but in 1953 they also found one big difference.

"The Australians at that time still felt most activities for men and women should be held separately. There were very few mixed events," Everett recalls. "The women in the host group entertained Clara very nicely while I was busy with the meetings."

After a nine-day stay in Australia, the Mitchell party left Darwin for Singapore and Malaya, with a brief stop in Jakarta, Java, first. In Malaya, Mitchell tried to interest rubber plantation owners in the International Farm Youth Exchange program, but he found himself very unwelcome. He had traveled one hundred and fifty miles into the jungle south of Singapore to talk to the plantation owners. The owners, who were European, employed mostly native Malayan workers. When Mitchell suggested they send eight young Malayans to the western countries for six months, he was greeted with contempt.

"If we get them educated, they will want more money. Then how do you expect us to get our rubber harvested for what it costs us now? Why don't you go home and mind your own business?" was the message they gave him.

Returning to Singapore, the Mitchells encountered an unpleasant and potentially dangerous situation. Someone had planted a false news story in the papers saying the group had three million dollars to give to the youth of Singapore. The news had drawn a huge crowd to the hotel where the party was staying.

"We were mobbed," Mitchell said. "And the next morning, when we were to leave, the mob outside the hotel was so great the authorities had to sneak us out a back door and take us on a roundabout route to the airport."

The Mitchells were afraid they were going to miss their plane because of the delay. In fact, they did miss their plane, but it was one of the most fortunate things that ever happened to them.

"The plane, a British Comet, a jet aircraft which went into service in 1952, crashed soon after takeoff and all aboard were killed. Three of the victims were men we had met at the rubber plantation the day before who had refused to let their workers join the youth exchange," Mitchell recalls.

The last major stops were India and Pakistan. In India, Mitchell spent four days in New Delhi, where he was able to have a private interview with Jawaharlal Nehru, long-time prime minister, son of the country's former leader and brother of the present prime minister, Indira Ghandi. The two men talked of global issues. Nehru advocated non-aggression and, surprisingly at that time, urged an end to hydrogen bomb tests then underway on Johnston Island atoll. Mitchell noted Nehru's strong disinclination to become involved in the power struggle between the western powers and Russia and his desire to keep his country neutral.

Mitchell saw strange contradictions in India, which had a bearing on the nation's agriculture and its ability to feed its people.

Although India enthusiastically welcomed the chance to exchange students with other nations, Mitchell saw that religious beliefs held back food production and utilization. The sacred cow (which could not be eaten because it was believed to house the soul of an ancestor) was merely one example. He also encountered the belief that it was sacrilegious to plow the soil deeply.

"Instead of plowing, they would just scratch the soil. Beneath the surface was a deep, hard shale. When seed was planted on top of that hardpan the roots couldn't penetrate and the plant would die. I saw a demonstration with an English-made plow in which soil was plowed to twenty-four inches. By this kind of plowing alone, their agricultural experts said, they could increase their crop yield by twenty-five percent," Mitchell says.

In 1953 India was far from being able to feed its own people, but its openness to learning new things about agriculture was also apparent. Mitchell was struck by the eagerness of the Indian families to send their young people abroad on the Farm Youth Exchange program. When the Mitchells left India, they were accompanying forty young men who were in the program, headed for American farms; this was the greatest number Mitchell had ever seen in a single exchange.

Choosing which boys could go, however, had been a problem. Many rich families wanted to send their sons, but so did many less affluent families. Local government officials finally compromised. For each "rich" student who was chosen, a "poor" boy was also allowed to take part. The Mitchells accompanied the youths to Rome, where because of transportation arrangements they had to part company, but they met the group again in Chicago before the youths dispersed to their separate assignments.

Pakistan, too, was quick to accept exchanges of students and information from the rest of the world and to put new methods to work. But poverty in both countries was rampant when Mitchell was there. In Pakistan, he learned, some households had a servant stay up all night and sit on the front steps to keep watch so that crops and belongings were not stolen.

The Mitchells left India April 14, and after several days in London flew back to the United States, where Mitchell immediately began to work on his live *National Farm and Home Hour* broadcast for April 18. In all, they had been away for thirty-three days and had traveled thirty thousand miles, twenty-five thousand by air and the other five thousand by automobile or jeep.

Mitchell made one more trip abroad in his study of international agriculture. His destination was a most unusual one for that time. He was host for a tour to the Union of Soviet Socialist Republics, and his group was only the second that had been permitted to visit Russia since the late Josef Stalin had closed his country to foreigners in the last years of the 1940s.

Mitchell and the Harvest Tour set out early in August of 1956. The eighteen members of his party represented various segments of American agriculture: there were seedsmen, dairy farmers, sheep farmers, grain farmers, and representatives of all kinds of industries working with agricultural products, such as packing, milling and refining industries. The only woman in the group, Mary Thompson of Chicago, represented a packing industry.

After stops at Copenhagen, Denmark, and Helsinki, Finland, the group flew to Moscow, where they were scheduled for four days of conferences, visits to collective and state farms and to state-operated industries, and some sightseeing.

Intourist, the Soviet government travel agency which schedules the tours for all visitors to Russia, had made arrangements for the Harvest Tour to stay in the Hotel Moscow, considered one of the country's luxury hotels. But there were some disadvantages in the arrangements. The tour members were separated by being put on different floors, possibly for easier surveillance, Mitchell thought.

Although the hotel was elegantly appointed, in many ways it was not convenient according to American standards, and there appeared to be problems with maintenance. The tour members soon learned, for example, that while it was permissible for them to use the elevators going up to their rooms they were expected to walk downstairs.

"I had a bathtub in my room but Paul Seabrook, the assistant tour guide, did not," Mitchell recalls. "He had to use either the public bath or the tub in my room. Just as he stepped from my tub one day, the plaster ceiling fell, showering plaster all over Paul and the tub. He had to clean himself off as best he could without using the tub again, which was full of plaster."

Although the hotel served meals, Intourist had arranged for the tour group to eat at other restaurants, an inconvenience which Mitchell still does not understand.

"It was obvious there was a shortage of meat when we were there," Mitchell reports. "Much of their meat was mixed with soybeans to add filler. In our country, we refine the soybeans to remove the bitter taste, but the Russians did not. We could not recognize any piece of meat with any certainty, even chicken. The mainstay of most meals was a sort of stew."

Mitchell also noticed that dairy products were scarce and not of good quality, according to American standards. Today, many years later, the Soviets are still suffering from shortages of meat and dairy products.

In contrast, produce was plentiful and of good quality. (Mitchell was later to learn why.) Cabbage and cucumbers were staples, with the cucumbers turning up in many different kinds of dishes. Fresh fish was plentiful and also good. Bread was a major item in the Russian diet, and tea was a more popular breakfast drink than coffee, Mitchell found.

Housing was also in short supply during Mitchell's visit, with as many as six people living in a two-room apartment. "The people worked around the clock, so one family member might just be getting out of bed to go to work when another was coming home," Mitchell reported.

Consumer goods were also scarce, and members of Mitchell's party had offers to buy their socks, shoes, shirts and personal items. These would be resold on the black market. "The quality of our products assured them a good price," Mitchell said.

Equality for women, at least in some areas, was already a fact of life in Russia, Mitchell observed. There appeared to be little job discrimination because of sex.

"Most of the construction work is done by women. They do carpentry, tuckpointing, sewer work, street repair and various construction jobs, as well as holding the kinds of jobs we Americans think of as women's work. There are many women doctors, scientists and college professors. One of the first directors of their equivalent of our Atomic Energy Commission was a woman. They also serve as guides and translators," he said.

However, there were some disadvantages to this "equality" for women, at least in the view of the American group. On Russian trains it is not uncommon for men and women to share a compartment. On the train trip the Harvest Tour made to Kiev Mrs. Thompson, the only woman in the group, found herself booked to share a compartment with three Russian men. In consternation she turned to Mitchell. He managed to persuade a Russian woman who was sharing a compartment with other Russian women to change places with Mrs. Thompson.

In Moscow, the tour group visited the tomb which held the bodies of Nikolai Lenin and Josef Stalin. Stalin had been dead for three years in 1956, but there were still many rumors being whispered about that he had been assassinated, shot with his own gun by a member of the Russian secret police. The guide at the tomb passed this rumor along to Mitchell. Such rumors still persist today.

"Stalin and Lenin looked so lifelike in their glass-enclosed tomb that I wondered if it was refrigerated to perserve them so well," Mitchell reports.

One of the visits scheduled on the Moscow itinerary was to the U.S.S.R. Agricultural Exhibition, one of the largest permanent exhibitions in the world. Here, the visitors were able to see Russian farm equipment.

"The Soviets wanted to make their machinery bigger and heavier than ours, but they were not always able to make it work. They copied nearly every kind of farm machinery we make. One of the pieces they had copied was the Allis-Chalmers round binder, but they could not make the twine operate properly. They had even tried to get the Allis-Chalmers dealer in Denmark to tell them how to work it, but he refused."

One of the major problems with the Soviet farming system, Mitchell believes, is that there are no farm equipment dealers who know how to service the machinery and will take the responsibility of keeping it in good repair. The government-owned factories which build the machinery do not assume that responsibility, he found.

"If it did not work when it came off the assembly line, and a lot of things didn't, no one did anything about it. Their attitude was 'Let the farmer worry about it.' You could not find people to repair machinery over there. On many of the farms I visited I saw equipment sitting in barns that could not be used," Mitchell says.

From Moscow the group went on to the Ukraine, Russia's richest agricultural region. Here they visited an agricultural research station, a school for farm laborers and one of the largest collective farms in the country. His visits to the collective farms left Mitchell with the conviction that the Soviets will never increase their agricultural production enough to be self-sufficient under their present political system.

"Instead of a free give and take of information, the Soviet farm overseers keep their knowledge to themselves," he reports. "The reason is that they do not want their quota raised. They know that if they exceed their quota this year, it will be raised next year. They have no incentive to work harder, and if they produce more than their quota they have a strong incentive to hide that fact. Any farm overseer who makes a record crop is not going to reveal it to anyone."

The difference private incentive makes was demonstrated in the production of the individual garden plots which are allotted to each rural family. These plots, usually two and one-half acres, are worked entirely by a family and are for that family's private use. They are cultivated intensively and they not only feed the families that care for them, they produce at least two-thirds of the garden produce on the market in Russia, Mitchell learned. Then he understood why produce in Russia was of good quality and in good supply.

In contrast, he believes, farmers on the collectives have no real incentive to work harder, since they see no direct benefit. They also struggle with machinery that is not properly maintained. Still another disadvantage is that in its desperate need to produce more food, Russia is using land for agriculture that is also marginal. For all of these reasons, Mitchell thinks the Russians will continue to be major importers of agricultural products.

While in the Ukraine, Mitchell came up against an incident in which he felt he must speak up for his country, no matter what the risk. This was not the first such incident during his travels, but it was no doubt one of the riskiest.

The overseer of the farm the Harvest Tour was visiting came back from a wedding "three-quarters in his cups," Mitchell reports. At a lunch with the members of the tour, the overseer swept the glasses off the table with one gesture, called for more wine, then drank a toast in which he insulted the United States.

"I thought, 'Here I am among all these people. This man has spoken out against my country. If I defend my country, I may go to Siberia. If I don't I will never have a clear conscience.'"

Today Mitchell does have a clear conscience. He stood up and said, "I would like to make a short statement."

"I believe my friend (and I said my friend) is misinformed. I would like to ask him a few questions." He turned to his host, the farm overseer.

"Do you recall all the American boys who lost their lives fighting for your country? Do you recall the shiploads of food given to your country? Do you recall the loans made to your country? Do you recall all the military aid that was given to your country, and all the warships and destroyers? Do you recall the agricultural supplies given to your country?

303

"With that, the overseer struck the table with his hand. For a moment I did not know what he was going to do. Then he called for more wine and drank a toast to the United States."

Later, when lunch was over, another farm worker came up to Mitchell rather quietly. "What you told us at lunch was a surprise to some of us. We didn't know that," the Russian said.

After the stop in Kiev, the tour took a train to Odessa, the Black Sea port which is the marketing-storage center for the Ukraine. After visiting more farms and a sheep ranch, the tour left Odessa by steamship and went to Yalta, site of the conference held by United States President Franklin D. Roosevelt, Britain's Prime Minister Winston Churchill and Stalin in February of 1945. Here the three great powers were to determine the fate of much of Europe after World War II was ended.

The group was able to tour the building where the conference had taken place and the bedroom which Roosevelt had occupied. Guides told them that during the conference, Roosevelt had been so ill that he was only able to go from his bedroom to the conference room, not far away. The President died only weeks after the Yalta Conference.

The tour group had to return to Moscow before being allowed to leave Russia. In their hotel the last evening of their stay, an incident occurred which revealed much about Russian attitudes toward their visitors.

When entering the country, the tourists were required to deposit enough American money to pay for the tour and exchange the rest for Russian rubles, with which they could buy what consumer goods they could find while in the Soviet Union. The rate of exchange was not favorable to the Americans, and they were promised extra rubles to make up for it. These rubles were never delivered until the last day the tourists were in Russia. Then, officials brought the money, about one thousand rubles, to the hotel and gave it to Mitchell.

By now it was after 5 p.m., all the stores were closed and there was no place the Americans could spend the money. They knew it would be confiscated when they left the country next day at Riga, formerly the capital of Latvia, which was by then a part of the Soviet Union.

The group members conferred, searching for a way to make some use of the money and beat the Russians at their game. One member, Claire Golden of Cordova, Illinois, a hybrid corn breeder, had attended a Baptist church in Moscow. The group decided to donate the money to the church, one of the few Christian churches permitted to continue holding services during a time of great religious repression in the U.S.S.R. Golden took the money to the minister of the church, who was delighted with the contribution. The story later appeared in American newspapers.

Another incident showed how closely the American tourists were watched while in Russia. Mitchell had taken a Bible and a picture of Christ with him on the trip. When he went through Russian customs in Moscow, customs officers were about to confiscate the Bible and the picture, but Mitchell persuaded them to let him keep his possessions. They insisted, however, that he must take his Bible out when he left the country.

When he went through customs again in Riga, Mitchell was not at all surprised to find the officials there knew about the incident. They insisted on seeing that he had the Bible and the picture of Christ before they would clear him to leave.

The aftermath of the Russian tour might have been disastrous for Mitchell if he had not had a firmly-established reputation as a loyal American. It was the time of the great "witch-hunts" in America, when Senator Joseph McCarthy of Wisconsin was conducting the sensational hearings into Communist activities. These probes to expose Communists and Communist sympathizers among, particularly, the intelligentsia and famous entertainers, ended by hurting many innocent people. Anyone in public life who could not clear himself of the charges immediately was blacklisted and shut out of the job market.

"When I came back from the tour, the Russians tried to 'use' me," Mitchell reports. "Nineteen pieces of Communist literature were sent to me in the mail. Whenever I was scheduled to speak in public about the Russian tour, the Communists would plant hecklers in the crowd to try to discredit me.

"But worst of all they tried to label me as a Communist. People from the Russian Council office went to Allis-Chalmers and told them I was secretly a Communist. They also spread those rumors at NBC. William A. Roberts, Allis-Chalmers president, just scoffed at those ridiculous charges. So did my old friend Niles Trammell, who was by that time president of NBC.

"But if I hadn't had a good reputation, my good friends and a complete security clearance from the FBI, I could have been in a great deal of trouble."

Chickens played a role in Everett Mitchell's childhood when at the age of five he was assigned the chore of feeding the family flock. On his Beautiful Day Farm, Wheaton, he experimented with advanced theories of raising poultry and egg production.

## Chapter 29
# Farewell Old Friend

Then came that day in July, 1960. The *Farm and Home Hour* began with "It's a beautiful day in Chicago. . ." as heartily as ever. Whitey Berquist and the Homesteaders orchestra played the music loved through the years by farm families across the nation. Layne Beaty, director of broadcasting services for the United States Department of Agriculture, presented the agricultural highlights of the past week and the week to come. The broadcast was carried by the entire NBC network of two hundred stations and heard by listeners on both the Atlantic and Pacific coasts. Everett Mitchell's closing words, "Goodbye and lots of good luck everybody," were full throat.

After more than than five thousand six hundred broadcasts, a record still unmatched to this day in either radio or television, the final *National Farm and Home Hour* had been presented.

The end was not a sudden matter. President William A. Roberts had died following a massive heart attack two years before, and a new leadership had taken over at Allis Chalmers. The new president, Theodore Stevens, was a close personal friend of Mitchell's but his management team wished to use new patterns of promotion. This called for greater use of print media for promoting Allis Chalmers, which Roberts had transformed during the *Farm and Home Hour* years from a small farm machinery manufacturer into one of the industry's leaders. In 1959 NBC was advised that when the Allis Chalmers sponsorship ended the next year, the contract would not be renewed.

It was a sobering moment for everyone who had been a part of the *National Farm and Home Hour* during its thirty-two years. Frank Mullen, who had originated the program when Calvin Coolidge was President, listened to the final broadcast at his home in California. The *Farm and Home Hour* had come into

307

being during the great prosperity of the 1920s and had spanned the Great Depression, the greatest of world wars and the years of growth and prosperity that followed.

No one felt the pain of the final broadcast more than Mitchell. In the preceding thirty years he had presided over more than forty-five hundred broadcasts and had planned more programs, conducted more interviews and produced more on-the-scene segments than anyone else ever connected with the program. Of the hundreds of people who had helped put the *Farm and Home Hour* on the air in the years before World War II, Mitchell was the only one who had stayed to the final broadcast.

It was Mitchell who had provided the continuity for all those programs, smoothing the switch from Chicago to Washington, D.C., and back again. It was Mitchell who faithfully preserved Mullen's original formula of sincerity, friendliness, good music, good entertainment and above all good sound information for farmers and homemakers.

Most important, despite the efforts of Mullen and others to claim credit, it was Mitchell who, when the six-day-a-week sustaining *Farm and Home Hour* ended in 1944, single-handedly brought about its continuation for another fifteen years as a weekly feature program. And when all other problems had been solved, it was Mitchell, and Mitchell alone, who secured Allis-Chalmers as a sponsor so the *National Farm and Home Hour* could go on.

There were many reasons for the demise of the program, but there was only one insurmountable problem. The other difficulties could have been resolved, but no one could change the fact that Everett Mitchell was now sixty-two years old. Even then, Mitchell had plans for developing another new *Farm and Home Hour*. He was sure there would be a large audience for a half hour program at noon on Monday, Wednesday and Saturday, which might be broadcast on both radio and television. He even had prospective sponsors in mind. But what he felt he could not do was pledge his personal commitment to a new program for the next five to ten years, and he knew sponsors would have to have such a pledge to be seriously interested. Reluctantly, Mitchell made the decision that this time he would not try to keep the *National Farm and Home Hour* alive.

The astronomic advance in American food production since the beginning of the century is the greatest breakthrough of its kind that man has ever seen. In the last decade alone the United

States has provided nearly sixty percent of the world-wide grain exports. The work that led to this revolution in grain production, and especially the production of hybrid corn, began before the turn of the century and reached its culmination in the record crops of the 1970s. Much of the information that contributed to producing the supercrops that continue to set and then break new records was brought together and presented to the nation's farmers for the first time on the *National Farm and Home Hour.*

Something of Everett Mitchell, Frank Mullen, Morse Salisbury, David Sarnoff, Merlin Aylesworth and countless others went into the setting of the new records. So did part of the National Broadcasting Company and its affiliated radio stations who spent millions to make the broadcasts possible, without any expectation of remuneration or even recognition other than knowing they helped farmers produce more and prosper.

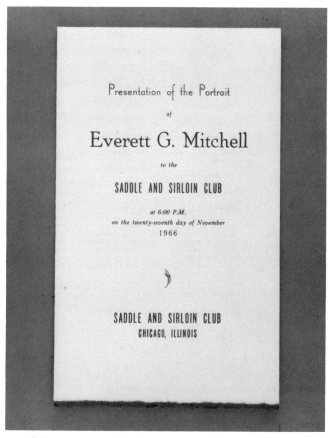

Presentation of the Portrait

*of*

# Everett G. Mitchell

*to the*

SADDLE AND SIRLOIN CLUB

*at 6:00 P.M.*
*on the twenty-seventh day of November*
1966

SADDLE AND SIRLOIN CLUB
CHICAGO, ILLINOIS

A copy of the program for the evening Everett Mitchell's portrait was hung in the Saddle and Sirloin Club in Chicago. While he received many tributes that evening, the one from his young son, Peter, was a tribute from a child to a busy father.

# Chapter 30
# Years of Gold

In 1960, Everett Mitchell was once again at a place where his broadcasting career might have ended. He had been before a microphone every year for thirty-seven years, often working long stretches of seven-day weeks. The end of the weekly *National Farm and Home Hour* might have seemed the logical time for him to consider retirement, but Mitchell had other plans. Instead, in 1960, he entered a period of golden years that brought him his greatest recognition and was the climax of his career—one which encompassed the first five decades of broadcasting.

Already a legend in his own time, at sixty-two Mitchell continued to work as hard as ever. He left his Beautiful Day Farm near Wheaton each morning at 3 a.m. to prepare for his early morning *Town and Farm* program. Now in its twenty-first year, the program was heard and seen every morning but Sunday over NBC's big midwest radio station, WMAQ, and televised over WNBQ-TV (now Channel 5).

In the fall of 1960, Mitchell inaugurated still another new program, the *National Farm Forum*, a weekend radio and television program heard and seen over many NBC network stations. The *Farm Forum* brought outstanding farmers and farm leaders together to exchange ideas on a wide range of subjects covering agricultural research, production, and marketing. With Mitchell presiding over the Forum in his role as NBC's Director of Agriculture, the program continued until his retirement in 1968.

Besides his demanding broadcasting responsibilities, there had never been a time when so many interests competed for his attention. Peter was now in grade school, and Mitchell reserved every possible hour to be with his son. He had major farming responsibilities, even to tending the livestock much of the time himself.[1] Without the heavy travel that had been required by the *Farm*

311

*and Home Hour*, he was devoting more time to his church.

In addition, there were always telephone calls and visitors, many of them agricultural leaders wanting to consult with Mitchell, who by now had personally observed farming in more states and foreign countries than any other American. Others were listeners who had followed his broadcasts for years and wanted to meet and talk to him.

The farm was imparting another dimension to Mitchell's life during his final years of broadcasting. The Mitchells, Everett, Clara and Peter, age one month, had come to the farm on Butterfield Road south of suburban Wheaton on Christmas Eve, 1954. Even with the excitement of a new baby the new all-electric home was a lonely place on that first Christmas Eve.

Suddenly from the front yard, they heard the familiar sounds of Christmas carolers led by Mitchell's friend at NBC, Dick Noble, who lived in Wheaton, his wife, Beri, and a group of their friends. When the caroling ended, the singers were invited into the new home for refreshments and a visit. The moment was prophetic. From this first day until the Mitchells left twenty-three years later, Beautiful Day Farm was a place of pleasant visits with neighbors, friends and callers, some of them from the other side of the world.

The farm was especially designed to complement Mitchell's work. Located only thirty miles from the NBC headquarters in the Merchandise Mart, it had a home studio that permitted direct broadcasts. There was also a library and a conference room large enough for fifty people.

Mitchell had two objectives in establishing Beautiful Day Farm. One was to give his son, Peter, a chance to grow up in rural surroundings, and the other was to conduct his own experiments with new farming practices in both crops and livestock. The NBC mail told him that listeners were keenly interested in what he was doing on his farm. From the first Mitchell was surprised and impressed by the intense interest in his personal research. Farm families especially were fascinated that the Voice of American Agriculture would purchase, equip (there were no buildings on the land) and himself operate a farm of his own. Listeners calling at their own expense from several states away would question Mitchell in great detail about his crops and his livestock.

The field experiments at Beautiful Day Farm focused on the three crops—corn, soybeans and alfalfa—best suited to its soil and climate. Dr. James Holbert's newest Funk corn hybrids, some of them not yet released to the public, were planted on field scale. Several times the then coveted hundred-bushel-an-acre barrier was broken at Beautiful Day Farm. One year a top field average of 154 bushels an acre was attained.

Mitchell was among the first to use nitrogen fertilizer at seeding time on soybeans to give the crop an early boost before the plants' own nitrogen fixation systems could begin working. The Certified Alfalfa Seed Council in California, where most of the nation's alfalfa seed is produced, provided Beautiful Day Farm with not-yet-released new varieties. One of them, Vernal, later was widely used across the northern United States from New England to the Dakotas.

Mitchell also experimented with livestock. He did significant work with Dorset Horned Sheep, a breed noted for its strong horns and fine-textured wool. During the sheep breeding project, Beautiful Day Farm was host to an event which occurs only once in every hundred million births—quintuplets. Mitchell assisted the ewe all through the night with the difficult births. All five of the lambs lived, a phenomenon which attracted the attention of sheep farmers near and far.

A poultry demonstration involved five thousand hens that laid eggs twenty-four hours a day. The flock, although not confined, was housed in an experimental aluminum poultry building developed and being tested by one of Mitchell's former sponsors, Sears Roebuck and Company. The constant laying was brought about by a system of automatic lighting and temperature controls.

Beautiful Day Farm participated in a far-reaching feeder cattle cross-breeding project whose goal was to produce more quality beef from animals better able to withstand summer heat and drought. This was done in cooperation with the famous Norris Farms, whose operations centered in Illinois but extended to other states. Norris provided Beautiful Day Farm a Brahman sire, a huge humped-back animal descended from an ancient breed of cattle in India where high temperatures and insect problems are critical. The Brahman bull, named Junior, was brought to Wheaton from the Norris farms in Florida.

Mitchell had small herds of both Angus and Hereford cattle. He produced crossbreds from the Brahman bull and the Angus and Hereford cows. Interestingly, the large hump of the Brahman disappeared completely in the first generation of crossbreeding with both the Angus and Herefords. At two years of age, the crossbred animals were slaughtered and the meat-waste ratio

313

studied. Both Brahman crosses produced more meat of equal or better quality per feeding unit than purebred cattle from the same Angus and Hereford parents. This confirmed findings on the Norris Farms. Later the crosses were recognized as new breeds known as Brangus and Brerefords.

Junior, the Brahman bull, proved to be an amazing animal in other ways. He became Mrs. Mitchell's pet. In August of 1956, while her husband was conducting an agricultural tour in Russia, Junior became involved in a near-tragic incident. One morning after Clara Mitchell and Peter had finished breakfast, she received a telephone call from the St. James Farm, home of Brooks McCormick, board chairman of the International Harvester Company. McCormick's farm was a mile west on Butterfield Road. The caller advised Mrs. Mitchell that her prize bull had escaped during the night and had wandered to the other farm. He said a posse had been formed and the men were ready with rifles in hand to shoot the fearsome-looking animal.

"Please don't shoot Junior," she begged. "I'll bring his leash down to your farm and lead him back home."

After a promise from the caller that they would give her time to retrieve the wayward animal, Clara went to the barn for Junior's leash, which was actually the leash for the family's large German Shepherd dog. She drove to the McCormick farm, parked her car and quickly walked to the area where Junior was holding the posse at bay. Calling him by name, she waited quietly as the large animal came lumbering meekly down the path, lowering his head for the leash as he approached her.

Clara Mitchell attached the leash to Junior's collar and began leading him back to Beautiful Day Farm. The amazed posse members, guns still in hand, stood and gazed at the once hostile creature, who responded so willingly and quickly to the tiny woman when she called his name. As Clara and the bull neared Beautiful Day Farm, Junior tugged at his leash, ran ahead and jumped back over the fence. Then he waited until she caught up to him for a display of affection from his rescuer.

On less exciting days, Junior would wait for Clara to come and pet him. He had learned to expect some little bit of food as a reward for his admiration. He would lower his head and shoulders until she put her arm around his neck and ever so gently he would lift her off the ground and then back down.

Some of the Beautiful Day Farm demonstration projects led to 4-H activities for Peter. His sheep projects not only yielded funds for college but provided excellent exhibits for county fairs.

The receipt of honors was not unknown to Mitchell, but considering his long service in broadcasting there had not been many, and most were from colleges and universities. Before World War II he had been made a life member of the Future Farmers of America. Also before the war Mitchell was asked to come to the campus of the University of Kentucky in Lexington to receive an "Honorary-at-large" membership in the nation's most prestigious agricultural fraternity, Alpha Zeta. In 1948 Iowa State University invited Mitchell to its campus where president Charles E. Friley presented him a life membership in Sigma Delta Chi.

The next year Mitchell received an honorary Doctor of Letters Degree from Carthage College in Illinois for his "unique role in promoting better understanding between people in town and on the farm."

Amid all the broadcasting, family and farm activities, the closing years of Mitchell's career were spiced with awards recognizing his role as the leader in the nation's radio and television farm programming. These honors began as he completed forty years of broadcasting.

Except for the Chicago Association of Commerce honor which had come to Mitchell thirty years earlier, Chicago had not recognized his unusual service to the city and to broadcasting. In the fall of 1963 Mayor Richard J. Daley corrected this oversight. Exactly forty years to the day after Mitchell's first broadcast, Mayor Daley and the Chicago City Council proclaimed November 4 to be "It's a Beautiful Day in Chicago Day."

While none of the honors were expected, there was one which was most surprising to Mitchell and his friends. In the fall of 1966, as a part of the opening ceremonies for Chicago's famous International Livestock Show, Mitchell became the first person in communications to be given hall-of-fame honors by the Saddle and Sirloin Club of Chicago, the premiere livestock society in America's largest meat processing center.

The Saddle and Sirloin Club, with its massive banquet hall, was located in the Chicago Union Stockyards. On the twenty-foot walls of this great hall hung life-sized full-length portraits of the great leaders of the livestock industry in the United States from the post-Civil War era forward. Looking down from those walls were the early giants, including Gustavus Swift and Philip D. Armour. One of the recent portraits honored Mitchell's longtime friend, former Scretary of Agriculture Claude Wickard of Indiana. So life-like were the portraits that those who entered the great hall had the feeling that these famous persons were looking down and reviewing each decision made and each honor conferred in their presence.

Mitchell's portrait was hung November 25, 1966.

Six hundred of the nation's agricultural and agribusiness leaders assembled to pay their respects. Jerry Satola, Armour and Company executive, was master-of-ceremonies. Dr. Earl Butz, Dean of Agriculture at Purdue University, later to become Secretary of Agriculture, thanked Mitchell for all that he had done to make the work of the nation's Land Grant Colleges more effective. Kenneth Anderson of the National 4-H Service Committee lauded Mitchell for his efforts in behalf of 4-H clubs and his role as a founder of the International Farm Youth Exchange. Robert Lemon, NBC vice-president in Chicago, saluted his associate.

Although Mitchell was aware in advance of most of the plans for the evening, there was one item on the agenda of which he knew nothing until he was seated at the speakers' table and opened his program. The third speaker of the evening was his ten-year-old son, paying a special tribute to his father. When the time came for Peter's remarks, an usher placed a box in front of the podium so the boy could speak into the microphone.

Although Peter had rehearsed with his mother, he had arranged his own remarks. The boy spoke flawlessly from his own notes. He said that in spite of a crowded schedule of broadcasting and travel, his father found time to do a great many things with him both at Beautiful Day Farm and on trips.

"I am grateful that my father and mother made it possible for me to grow up on a farm where I could have my dog and my pony and where there are ducks and geese and chickens and sheep. But I am especially grateful that I have a father with whom it is so much fun doing things together."

In his response Mitchell disclaimed having any special gift. He spoke of his parents and how their Christian training had prepared him for his work. He closed by giving his creed for farm broadcasting.

> We were blessed by earning the confidence of the American farmers and ranchers and their families. We reported only facts that had been carefully checked. At no time ever did we attempt to dictate to our listeners—tell them what to do. I have always thought of our broadcasts as being like

an encyclopedia. Our farmers and ranchers could listen if they wanted to and then decide how they would deal with their own problems. I think this is the best way to serve the farm audience.

In the summer of 1967, Secretary of Agriculture, Orville Freeman, invited Mitchell to Washington to receive a Great Service to America award. He was honored as a part of a special occasion held by the United States Department of Agriculture for the outstanding agricultural scientists of the nation.

The awards continued up to and even after Mitchell's retirement in 1968. On all of these occasions there were tributes and appraisals of his impact on agriculture and broadcasting. No one described Mitchell's achievements in nearly half a century before the microphone better than Dean Louis B. Howard of the College of Agriculture at the University of Illinois. He spoke before hundreds of Chicago civic leaders attending the dinner at the Conrad Hilton Hotel given in Mitchell's honor by the Chicago Junior Chamber of Commerce and Industry.

I take great pleasure this evening in recognizing you both as the Chicago Man of the Year in Agriculture and for your completion of forty years of service in broadcasting — a rare achievement indeed. We honor you for your contribution to communications in American and world agriculture.

Our award recognizes your unfaltering efforts to provide more opportunity for farm young people. Your help with nearly twenty annual National 4-H Club Congress banquets is evidence. The historic work you did in developing the International Farm Youth Exchange is another instance.

Finally, Everett, we honor you for your creation of the Beautiful Day Spirit which has enriched the lives of so many. An entire generations of Americans set their watch and their heart by your "It's a beautiful day in Chicago, it's a great day to be alive and I hope it is even more beautiful wherever you are."

### FOOTNOTE

(1) Mitchell refused the role of "gentleman farmer," but he did have the help of several individuals, including Edward Kuefler and his brother-in-law, John Kupjack, who doubled as assistant farm manager and back-up for him. Mitchell worked closely with the livestock, handling all the nighttime chores. As Peter grew older, he took an increasingly larger role in the farm work.

The Beautiful Day Farm at Wheaton, Illinois, was home to the Mitchell family from the time Peter was a newborn baby until 1977. Clara, Everett and Peter are shown in the front yard of the 160-acre experimental farm which was one of the few all-electric homes and farm buildings of the period. The home included a studio.

# Epilogue
# "As Close to Heaven"

From early childhood, Everett Mitchell has been a deeply religious person blessed with a capacity to find his God in everyday experiences. His extraordinary intuition (which Mitchell calls his "hunches") has constantly enabled him to find what are to him God's solutions to the most complex problems.

At home or on the other side of the world, he has had many experiences which convinced him that for brief moments he has been in a close communion with his Lord. He has met with presidents, kings, dictators, leaders of the world's great religions, the man next door, a neighbor's child or the farmer down the road. Each in his or her own way has confirmed Mitchell's faith and strong commitment to the Christian way of living.

Many of these special moments have been included in this book. A few of the many others are presented in this epilogue.

\*\*\*

**Speak his name:** Shortly after World War II, the president of Tuskegee Institute, the distinguished private educational and research center in Alabama for black students made hallowed by the work of Booker T. Washington and George Washington Carver, wrote to the Secretary of Agriculture with a petition. Would he arrange for Everett Mitchell of the *National Farm and Home Hour* to come to Tuskegee and address a meeting of the nation's Negro county agents?

The event would be held on a late summer day. Unless it was raining, the address would be held at noon outdoors and there would be a picnic. The plans called for Mitchell to take the early morning flight from Chicago to Montgomery. He would be met at the airport and driven the fifty miles east to Tuskegee Institute. There would be ample time.

Unfortunately, Mitchell's flight was delayed, and he was more than an hour late arriving in Montgomery. The delay did not seem serious. Mitchell asked the Tuskegee hosts who met him to call and report that he could not be present for the picnic but that he would arrive in time to speak as scheduled.

But when Mitchell arrived, he found that the nearly one thousand county agents had not begun the picnic, having decided by popular vote to wait until their guest of honor arrived.

Mitchell spoke for nearly an hour. When he finished there was no ovation. Instead the great throng arose and became a mighty chorus to sing, "Jesus Speak His Name."

\*\*\*

**Work, play and pray:** In December, 1950, Everett Mitchell went to Funk Farms in Illinois to visit Mother Funk. Mrs. Eugene Funk, one of the remarkable American women of her generation, was an inspiration to a wide circle of friends in Illinois and across the nation. The new year was but a few days away. There was great apprehension across America. The Korean War had begun, and there was fear that the Chinese and Russians, closely allied at this time, might jointly intervene and set the stage for World War III.

As Mitchell got up to leave, he turned to Mrs. Funk and said, "Mother Funk, you have lived through a lot of changes. You have seen war and peace, hard times and good times, and I wonder what suggestions you have for all of us as we move toward this critical new year?"

"Everett," Mother Funk replied without a moment's hesitation, "in 1917 during the First World War, Herbert Hoover sent a New Year's message to my children urging them in the New Year to 'Work hard, play hard and pray hard.' I think his advice will be just as good for this year as it was then."

\*\*\*

**But you have to have a ticket:** The question of the relative merits of the churches has often been put to Everett Mitchell. He has always side-stepped controversy by recalling something that his Quaker father told him on the day that he was fourteen. His father referred to the often intense animosity that existed between members of various churches and faiths.

"Do not ever let these matters bother you," his father said. "If you are confronted with such questions just say that there are as many ways to get to Heaven as there are trains going to New York, but you have to have a ticket."

\*\*\*

**If you have faith, we will make it:** Early in the

320

afternoon of November 2, 1951, Everett Mitchell boarded a Northwest Airlines plane at Chicago's Midway Airport for the most difficult of his assignments overseas. At the invitation of the U.S. Army, he was on a special mission that would take him to Korea and the war zones.

In Minneapolis darkness gathered as Mitchell changed to an Army Transport command plane for the long flight over Canada and on to Anchorage, Alaska. He arrived there the next afternoon in the semi-darkness of Alaska's long winter night. Although it had by now been three days and three nights since he had had the opportunity to go to bed, he was advised that his two-day flight over the Arctic Ocean with a refueling stop at the island of Shimya would soon be ready to leave.

An hour later, Mitchell boarded a propeller-driven DC-6 for the overnight trip to Shimya, a small island at the western end of the Aleutians about four miles long and two miles wide. The winds are so high on this tiny dot in the Pacific that the military installations are built underground.

The weather was unsettled and Mitchell wondered if the flight might be delayed, but the Transport Command personnel treated the preparations as routine. Mitchell had to admit that he was concerned about finding the little island two thousand miles away on a dark and turbulent Arctic night, knowing that no alternate landing site existed for more miles than a DC-6 could fly.

Adding to this concern an hour or so out of Anchorage was the unusual flying pattern. First, the pilot climbed up, then he came back down, often swiftly. He kept the lights on the wings, and soon Mitchell saw that icing on the wings was the cause of the erratic flying pattern. Mitchell's concern was so great that, tired as he was, he sat upright in his seat unable to relax. Then, as he recalls, he received a lesson in faith.

"The co-pilot came over to me and said he had noticed that I was not sleeping. He advised me to do my best to go to sleep, since it was a long trip. I told him that I had been watching the icing conditions and that they were the worst I had seen in many flights. Then I asked him if he thought we would make it."

"He said, 'If you have faith, we will make it. There's a Man with His hand on the prow of this ship who guides us. If you have faith, you will go to sleep and I will see you in the morning in Shimya,'" Mitchell remembers.

Mitchell did sleep for a time, but despite the darkness that enveloped everything, he was awake when the co-pilot came back to him. "I see you had faith," the co-pilot said. "It is 7 a.m. and we are in Shimya. We made it about on time. Thanks for having faith."

***

**The greatest of these is love:** In his first trip to Germany after World War II, Mitchell interviewed Walter Kolb, a former Nazi tank commander. Fighting on the Western Front as the Americans advanced into Germany, Kolb's tank was pen-etrated by an American artillery shell and so completely destroyed that Kolb was thrown from it and buried in the shell hole. Only the Nazi's head and face remained above the ground. Un-able to move his body, arms and legs and scarcely able to breath, he soon lost consciousness.

"I found myself with my Lutheran mother, and I promised her that if the Lord allowed me to live, I would return to her religion and devote years of my life teaching others, especially young people, the futility and the horror of war," Kolb reported.

"I was buried for an hour or more before one of my men discovered me, at first thinking me dead. He dug me out, and when I regained consciousness I was in the U.S. Army hospital.

"I was terrified. Our officers had told us that if we were captured by Americans we would be tortured, hung up by our thumbs. Soon an Army nurse, an understanding young woman, came, asked how I felt, gave me some medication and said I should try to eat. An orderly came with food, and I saw it was the same food being given to wounded Americans. The next Sunday I was invited to attend church services in the hospital chapel.

"Soon after I was selected to take part in the U.S. Army's German de-Nazification program. I was sent to the United States for six months to learn about the way things are done in your country so that I could come back home and report on what America and Americans are like.

"In the five years since returning, I have devoted much of my time to speaking before church and community groups, most of them young people, telling them about the horror of war and how I was treated after being captured by the Americans; how instead of being tortured, they treated my wounds, gave me food and invited me to attend church services. I have traveled so much speaking about this I have worn out two motorcycles."

Mitchell asked the former Nazi lieutenant if he had a message for the young people of America?

322

"Not only for the young people of America but for the young people of the whole world. My people have sinned, but the American people reached down, lifted us up, bound our wounds and fed us. If I could speak good English, I would quote First Corinthians, chapter thirteen—'...faith, hope and love and the greatest of these is love.' "

\*\*\*

**"Bang! Bang! You go dead!":** When Mitchell was in Jerusalem, just three years after the nation of Israel had been founded, he encountered a chilling experience which could have ended in quick disaster. He had gone by himself to seen and photograph Jerusalem's famed ancient wall, which now separates the Jews and Arabs in the Holy City.

He was generally aware of the situation. The Arabs maintained a constant guard on the wall as a protection for the shrines held sacred by Moslems, Jews and Christians alike. Mitchell also noticed there was a continuous and dense barbed wire fortification a distance in front of the wall. On the walk in front of the barbed wire, there was a group of small Jewish children playing.

Mitchell was following the walk, stopping from place to place to take pictures. At a point of special interest to him, he stepped off the walk and moved up to the barbed wire for a better picture taking position. In the process he thrust his camera lens between strands of the barbed wire.

Instantly he felt a child pulling on the back of his shirt and a frantic shout, "No! No! Bang! Bang! You go dead."

Almost as reflex, Mitchell stepped back and looked up toward the top of the wall. There stood the Arab guard less than fifty feet away, his rifle in firing position and pointed squarely at the American broadcaster.

Mitchell suddenly felt weak. His brow was wet. Then he turned to find the children from whom his warning came. All of them except one little boy had faded away. Later he learned the little boy had been following him at a short distance and rushed in when he saw the Arab rifleman raise his gun. The urgency in the child's voice left no doubt but that he had earlier witnessed tragic situations in front of the Jerusalem wall.

Mitchell gathererd the little Jewish boy up in his arms and held him close for a long moment. After thanking him and slipping a gift of American money into his little shirt pocket, he asked the boy how he had learned to speak English. The boy attended a school in the Israeli section of Jerusalem maintained by the Lutheran Church in America. Mitchell had for years contributed to this mission work.

"I had supported our Lutheran mission work and had in some small way helped support this very school in Jerusalem, but I never expected to reap such a personal dividend," he later told his NBC audience in a report to the American people on his trip into Israel.

***

**As close to heaven as I can take you:** Everett Mitchell had a flight on a Northwest Airlines flight into Minneapolis one fall evening that he will always remember as one of the most beautiful moments of his life. Seated on the west side of the northbound plane, Mitchell suddenly became aware that a miracle was unfolding in the western sky. The drama of color continued to build until the entire sky, all that could be seen from the window of the plane, presented one mass of giant shafts of solid colors ranging from bright yellow to red to crimson.

As the splendor reached its zenith, the plane's captain, who had learned that "Beautiful Day" was among his passengers, stopped for a visit.

"Good to have you with us this evening. How is the flight?" the captain asked.

"Captain, I have been flying since the days of the two-seater and all around the world, and this is the most beautiful and overpowering sunset I have ever seen," Mitchell said. "This is almost heavenly."

Together they marveled at the glorious sunset that the pilot, too, acknowledged was as remarkable as any he had seen. When the captain got up to return to the cockpit, he turned and said, "Mr. Mitchell, this is as close to heaven as I can take you. You will have to go the rest of the way on your own."

Grand marshal for the 1982 Fourth of July parade in Wheaton
was Everett Mitchell, a member of the DuPage Heritage Gallery
Hall of Fame. He is shown with his wife, Clara.

Father and son sport look-alike smiles as they observed a recent family gathering. Peter is an advertising account executive living in Dallas, Texas, while his parents continue to make their home in Wheaton.

# Index

330

332

While Junior, the Brahman bull, strikes a show stance here for Everett Mitchell, he was Clara Mitchell's pet. A sheriff's posse once held the animal at bay but he responded on command to Mrs. Mitchell's order to "Go Home!".